process of knowing- both awareness
and judgement

W9-AAF-713

A
THEOLOGY OF
CHRISTIAN
EDUCATION

BOOKS BY LAWRENCE O. RICHARDS

A New Face for the Church
Creative Bible Study
How I Can Be Real
How Far I Can Go
How I Can Experience God
How I Can Make Decisions
How I Can Fit In
69 Ways to Start a Study Group
Three Churches in Renewal
Reshaping Evangelical Higher Education
     (with Marvin K. Mayers)
A Theology of Christian Education
A Theology of Church Leadership
     (with Clyde Hoeldtke)
A Theology of Personal Ministry
     (with Gib Martin)
A Theology of Children's Ministry
Discipling Resources Series
     (with Norman Wakefield)
Believer's Promise Book
The Believer's Guidebook

A THEOLOGY OF CHRISTIAN EDUCATION

LAWRENCE O. RICHARDS

Ministry Resources Library

Zondervan Publishing House • Grand Rapids, MI

MINISTRY RESOURCES LIBRARY is an imprint of Zondervan Publishing House,
1415 Lake Drive, S.E., Grand Rapids, Michigan 49506

A THEOLOGY OF CHRISTIAN EDUCATION
© 1975 by The Zondervan Corporation, Grand Rapids, Michigan

Library of Congress Catalog Card Number 74-25353
ISBN 0-310-31940-4

Unless otherwise indicated, the New Testament references are taken
from *The New International Version.*

Appreciation is expressed to the following Bible publishers for permission
to quote from their copyrighted translations:

MACMILLAN COMPANY for texts from *The New Testament in Modern
English* by J. B. Phillips. Copyright 1958, 1959, 1960, 1972 by J. B. Phillips.

NATIONAL COUNCIL OF CHURCHES for texts from the *Revised Standard Version.*
Copyright 1952 and 1972 by the Division of Christian Education,
National Council of Churches of Christ in the United States of America.

ZONDERVAN CORPORATION for texts from *The New International Version,
New Testament.* Copyright 1973 by the New York Bible Society International.

Printed in the United States of America

84 85 86 87 88 — 20 19 18 17 16 15 14 13 12

contents

introduction

"Christian education" is breaking out of the mold of the school. Fresh questions are being asked about the nature of teaching and learning, and we've caught a glimpse of Christian nurture as something involving *all* the activities and transactions that take place within the Body of Christ. The classroom, which once was our whole vision of Christian education, is now recognized to be only a part — and not even the most important part.

That's why this book begins with an examination of the Church. What is said throughout is rooted in the conviction that ecclesiology must be the source of our educational understanding and that Christian education is truly a theological discipline. I am convinced that such an approach to Christian education will lead us not only to challenge many old assumptions but also to gain exciting new insights that open up the future to possibilities we've been blind to far too long.

This book is written as *a* theology of Christian education, not *the* theology of Christian education. It is exploratory. It often gives mere glances at themes that deserve book-length treatment in themselves. It is meant to be a seed bed — a source from which richer and fuller understandings can be developed by others.

This book is written also as a text. Suggested activities are included with each chapter to encourage thinking, probing, and interaction with the concepts explored. It is not a text for those eager for a closed system — a system that presents "the answer." But for those who, like myself, are eager to work out in the life of the local church principles being rediscovered today in the Word. I trust it will be a help along the way and that the concepts it explores will increasingly become a part of our common experience as, under God's Spirit, we move to ever fuller realization of all that growth in Christ implies.

LARRY RICHARDS

PART I: theological considerations

A. understandings of the church
    1. life: what the church is
    2. life's goal: what the church does
    3. life's communication: how the church edifies
    4. life's dynamic: the fellowship relationship
    5. life's transmission: evangelism

B. implications for Christian education
    6. a whole-person focus
    7. a discipling purpose
    8. a modeling method
    9. an interpersonal dimension
    10. an overflowing outcome

1

life: what the church is

THE CHURCH	IMPLICATIONS
LIFE	A WHOLE-PERSON FOCUS
LIFE'S GOAL	A DISCIPLING PURPOSE
LIFE'S COM-MUNICATION	A MODELING METHOD
LIFE'S DYNAMIC	AN INTER-PERSONAL DIMENSION
LIFE'S TRANS-MISSION	AN OVER-FLOWING OUTCOME

Where do we begin in our thinking about Christian education? The critical place is with our assumptions. What do we view being "Christian" to mean? That we hold a certain set of beliefs? That we have certain moral values? That we behave in certain ways? Or is there something beyond these, something essential, that defines who we are?

For me the starting point is found in these words of Jesus: "I have come that they may have life, and have it to the full" (John 10:10)

Life and death are basic Bible themes. From God's early warning to Adam, "the day that you eat of it, you shall die" (Gen. 2:17, RSV), on through the final invitation to "take the free gift of the water of life" (Rev. 22:17), death and life are portrayed vividly as realities to be experienced here and now, and as ultimate realities stretching beyond time. It's instructive, then, to survey these concepts and their development in Scripture.

Life. The most common Hebrew root (חיה) appears in verb, adjective, and noun forms. The range of verbal meanings, which includes to live, to have life, to remain alive, to sustain life, and, in the Piel, to preserve or give life, gives little insight into usage.

11

Nor does the adjectival, which essentially means "alive," or "living," and is applied to God as the ever-living One, to man, and to animals. The noun form means simply "living thing."

The usage of these terms in the Old Testament, however, clearly indicates that more than physical vitality is meant. Moses speaks to God's people of life and death as set before them, and invites them to choose life (Deut. 30:15-20). David speaks of a path of life which God shows men (Ps. 16:11), and views God as the fountain of life and the source of all life (Ps. 36:9). While most of the Old Testament usages of "life" focus on experience in this world, it's clear that there is also a "forever" dimension in the Hebrew concept. From the early Genesis reference to the possibility that men might live forever (3:22) to the psalmist's confident assertion, "seek him: your heart shall live forever" (22:26, KJV. See also Pss. 49:9; 69:32), the Bible indicates that life's meaning cannot be summed up in the brief span of years between a man's birth and his burial.

The New Testament expands and provides sharper insights into the meaning of "life." While one word ($\beta \acute{\iota} o \varsigma$) speaks only of earthly life and its functions (cf. Luke 8:14; 2 Tim. 2:4; 1 Peter 4:2, 3), another ($\zeta \omega \acute{\eta}$, Rom. 7:3) has a rich and varied set of meanings.

On the one hand $\zeta \omega \acute{\eta}$ speaks of life in the physical sense (cf. Rom. 8:38; 1 Cor. 3:22; 15:19; Phil. 1:20; Jas. 4:14, etc.). On the other it speaks of a supernatural life that is essentially God's (cf. John 5:21, 26), but which God shares with men through Christ. This supernatural life is provided through the gospel and is viewed as new, not based in man's space/time experience (cf. John 6:63, 68; Acts 5:20; Rom. 6:4; 2 Cor. 4:12; Eph. 4:18; Phil. 2:16; 2 Tim. 1:10, etc.). John commonly designates this life "life eternal," and usually states expressly that not only is it a result of faith in Christ, but also that Jesus' followers possess it now (John 3:15f., 36; 5:24, 40; 6:40, 47; 10:10; 20:31; 1 John 3:15; 5:12, 13, etc.). To say, then, that Christ gives "eternal life" (an affirmation found in Matt., Mark, Luke, Acts, Rom., Gal., 1 Tim., 2 Tim., Titus, and Jude as well as John) is in fact to speak of that life's quality and nature as much as of its duration.

The life with which the Bible is concerned and with which the gospel deals is not simply an outgrowth of the natural processes of birth and growth. The Bible insists that we see God as the One who makes men alive (1 Tim. 6:13), a task that no moral ideal, no matter how exalted, can accomplish (Gal. 3:21).

Human beings who have been born into this world, have grown and developed according to the natural laws governing the physical universe, are presented in Scripture as dead to the supernatural life, and in need of being made alive (ζωοποιέω) by God's personal act of intervention through the gospel.

Death. The adversary of life is death. The New Testament word (θάνατος) is used in its literal sense of the natural death of the body. But a figurative sense receives primary attention. Somehow a spiritual death that stands in stark contrast to eternal life has come to cast its dark shadow over all mankind. Unless called to life by God, men are viewed as frozen in a state of death (John 5:24; 8:51; Rom. 7:10; 8:6; 1 John 3:14, etc.). This death not only has a close relationship to sin (Rom. 7:13), but also merges into an eternal death from which every quality of eternal life is cut off forever (Rom. 1:32; 6:16, 21, 23; 7:5; 2 Cor. 7:10; 2 Tim. 1:10; Heb. 2:14, etc.).

Nowhere is the adversary relationship between death and life, and the need of men as spiritually dead, more clearly shown than in Ephesians 2.

> As for you, you were dead in your transgressions and sins, in which you used to live when you followed the ways of this world and of the ruler of the kingdom of the air, the spirit who is now at work in those who are disobedient. All of us lived among them at one time, gratifying the cravings of our sinful nature and following its desires and thoughts. Like the rest, we were by nature objects of wrath. But because of his great love for us, God who is rich in mercy made us alive with Christ even when we were dead in transgressions — it is by grace you have been saved. And God raised us up with Christ and seated us with him in the heavenly realms in Christ Jesus, in order that in the coming ages he might show the incomparable riches of his grace, expressed in his kindness to us in Christ Jesus. For it is by grace you have been saved, through faith — and this is not from yourselves, it is the gift of God — not by works, so that no one can boast. For we are God's workmanship, created in Christ Jesus to do good works, which God prepared in advance for us to do (vv. 1-10).

How clearly the contrast is drawn here. The gospel is a proclamation of life, an affirmation that by a work of God Himself personalities which are dead in sin are made alive in Christ. *It is life and death that define Christ's Church and His people. It is the possession of life that distinguishes a Christian from all other men: it is as a community of men who share the divine life that the Church is set apart from every human institution. And it is understanding our faith as life that gives us the clue to the development of a distinctive and theologically sound Christian education.*

an understanding of man

Marking off the issue of life versus death is not unusual in conservative theology. Historically Christians have understood sin as a reality, and have accepted the fall not as a myth but as something real in space and time, with tragic outcomes which have in turn been worked out in space/time history.

The early chapters of Genesis are a rich source of self-understanding, and define in a unique way who human beings are. They also help us guard against some of the oversimplifications of our conservative theology which have led to distortions in educational practice. In brief, these chapters insist that we see humanity both as dead in sin, and as bearing the mark of the eternal!

the mark. The creation of man stands in Scripture as a unique act. Only of man did God say, "Let us make man in our image, after our likeness; and let them have dominion" (Gen. 1:26, 27, KJV). Even after the Fall, the specialness of man is affirmed in the demand for capital punishment recorded in Genesis 9:6. "Whoever sheds the blood of man, by man shall his blood be shed" is not the archaic expression of a primitive vengeance ethic, but an affirmation of the unique value and worth of human life. The reason Genesis 9:6 ascribes for this command, "for God made man in his own image," brings home the fact that even frozen in spiritual death each person has intrinsic worth in God's eyes — a worth so great that only the extreme penalty for murder can adequately affirm it. In the New Testament too (James 3:9) man's dignity and worth as bearer of the divine image is reaffirmed.

the Fall. While fallen man has worth and dignity, Adam's act of sin brought mankind into a state of spiritual death; a condition which, with the *imago Dei,* has been transmitted to all (cf. Rom. 5:12-21). The Fall did not destroy men as persons, for we all share with God all the attributes of personality. Mind, emotion, will, individuality, all are retained. Genesis 4 demonstrates the ability of men to live successfully in the world. Human culture developed: a culture marked by agricultural, aesthetic, and industrial attainments (Gen. 4:19-22). Yet the impact of spiritual death also is clearly seen. Revelation is unable to restrain Cain's rebellion against God and the murder of his brother (4:5-7). Moral philosophy becomes a tool by which to justify ungodly acts (4:23, 24). While the Fall did not destroy the essential humanness of mankind, it did introduce alienation and conflict. It did impose selfishness and fear.

So the Fall has not destroyed the capacity of men to live and to learn and to create within the framework of the natural universe. The Fall has not destroyed the capacity of men to dream dreams, or to imagine utopias. What the Fall has destroyed is man's capacity to grasp the *super*natural, and to experience envisioned relationships that demand submersion of the selfish in God's kind of love.

life restored. The gospel message of life speaks particularly to the fallen state of man. The promise of eternal life speaks of a restoration of the lost capacities. With life comes a new ability to perceive reality (Heb. 11:3). With life comes a capacity to experience and express genuine love (1 Tim. 1:5; 1 Peter 1:22). With life comes the option of living life responsively with God (cf. Heb. 2:12-15).

But the promise of life does *not* speak of restoration to "humanity." Spiritually dead and spiritually alive persons share a common humanity, for man's essence is rooted in the *imago Dei* and not in the fallen state. Thus new life will not make a person more of a human being. New life will not make a person more valuable, or give him a greater dignity. New life will not necessarily change a person's intellectual powers, make him a better scientist, or a better carpenter. *Neither will the gift of God's life change the essential way that human beings learn and grow.* The commonness of our humanity is vital to grasp.

What then does change as Christ gives us new life? The capacity to understand and to enter into the meaning of life as God designed it is new. The ability to experience all that other faiths hold up as distant ideals is new. In every area where the Fall brought death, Christ brings life, and with that life He brings energizing power, freeing us to grow and be transformed. *Seeing in life the distinctive of the Christian faith, Christian education is given a clearer focus. Valuing all men as persons, respecting all men as having worth and dignity, Christian education seeks to communicate and to nurture faith-as-life.*

individual and corporate

This is another thing that is important to grasp about the life Scripture speaks of. Spiritual life has both individual and corporate dimensions.

On the one hand we read that "whoever (singular) believes

in [the Son] shall not perish but have everlasting life" (John 3:16), and on the other hand we read that individuals who have life are united in a Body. And, says 1 Corinthians 12:12, "The body is a unit, though it is made up of many parts; and though all its parts are many, they form one body. So it is with Christ." So too the Bible speaks of a maturing of the new life within the individual believer (Heb. 5:11-14), and of a maturing of the Body together (Eph. 4:12, 13). It is clear, in fact, that the growth of the new life given by God to the individual is interrelated with the growth of Body life. Paul in Ephesians puts it this way: "speaking the truth in love, we will in all things grow up into him who is the Head, that is, Christ. From him the whole body, joined and held together by every supporting ligament, grows and builds itself up in love, as each part does its work" (4:15, 16).

Christian education then can never deal with individual life alone. Christian education has to <u>concern itself with the processes within the Body which nurture corporate and individual growth</u> in Christ. Any Christian educational approach which focuses on either the individual or the group in exclusion of the other is bound to fall short.

In Christian education the central issue is life. While all men are valued and affirmed, the biblical distinction between death and life is maintained. The Christian is a person who has, in Jesus Christ, been raised by God's action from spiritual death to spiritual life. The Christian is a person in whom new capacities and possibilities have been created which are to be nurtured until they are experienced as realities. What's more, the Christian is a person who, while he shares a common humanity with all mankind, shares the divine life only with other believers. Between believers the shared life of God exists as an unbreakable link, binding all together into Christ's Body. Thus the Church of Christ is a living organism, not merely an organization. And principles for its growth and nurture must be sought in its nature as an organism, not in its organizational expressions.

It is life that sets the Christian apart.

It is life that sets the Church apart.

And it must be a concern for life — for its transmission and its nurture — that sets Christian education apart.

PROBE
  case histories
  discussion questions

thought-provokers
resources

1. Roy A. Edenfelt, discussing "The Reform of Education and Teacher Education: A Complex Task" in the Summer 1972 *Journal of Teacher Education* (p. 123), illustrates three possible models of a school. Look over the following chart (p. 18), and determine:

    a. which model most closely parallels Christian education approaches you have experienced

    b. which model is most appropriate if *life* is understood to be the focus of Christian education

2. From the Edenfelt charts (p. 18), attempt to write three one-page "philosophy of Christian education" papers, expressing principles and concepts which would find appropriate expression through Model A, Model B, and Model C schools. That is, what would have to be true about the nature of faith, the nature of teaching/learning, the needs and capacities of human beings, and the goals of Christian education, for the kinds of school approaches described to be appropriate in religious education?

3. The following excerpt is taken from an article in *Psychology Today* by Dwight D. Allen (March, 1971, p. 71). In "How They Mangle the Young" Allen attacks some assumptions that seem to underlie secular educational systems. Read the excerpt about the Myth of Isolated Learning and react in writing to the questions which follow.

    We seem to assume that learning takes place in school and nowhere else. Nothing could be further from the truth than this myth of Isolated Learning. For example, linguists tell us that a child has learned the grammar of his native tongue by the time he reaches the age of five — just when we send him to school to learn grammar. At school he must learn the language all over again in a way far less congenial to his nature.

    No importance is placed on the child's activities outside the classroom, except, of course, insofar as they may detract from his school work, which on its face is assumed to be of primary importance to any decent child.

    Because we are so unquestioningly convinced of the value of what schools will do for them, we rob our children of their natural interests. Quite simply, we expect schools to prepare children for life in our competitive society, to be perfect status-holders in a hierarchical social system. Beyond these goals, which have a degree of social validity, there is the mythic goal of perfection itself. We reverse the natural learning process by trying to stuff our children full of truth rather than allowing them to gain truths through insight and experience.

    Children have a faculty for learning and they take it with them to school; we do not provide it when they arrive. I sometimes think

ILLUSTRATIONS OF POSSIBLE MODELS OF SCHOOL

	Model A	Model B	Model C
Primary emphasis	Subject matter and skill development primary; academic subjects have priority	Intellectual, emotional, social, physical, aesthetic development	A productive life experience for students during years spent in school
Learning decided by	Learning developed sequentially by experts and professionals	Learning developed along individual and personal lines depending on the student's ability and interest	Learning determined by students, with consultation of teachers, parents, and community contact people
Content determined by	Curriculum content dispensed by teachers and texts and workbooks	Content drawn from all sources of knowledge, depending on problems a student or students are attacking	Content incidental to learning, emphasis on learning how to learn and make decisions, encounters are with experience as it occurs
Curriculum organization	Curriculum organized around subjects, courses, or disciplines	Curriculum organized around the individual development of each student	Curriculum organized around the experience students have, the problems they face
Teacher's main function	Teaching involves directing student learning along prescribed lines	Teaching includes any form of interaction with students which is designed to assist learning	Teacher mainly a sounding board, a constructive critic, a resource person
Criteria for learning	Evaluation of learning largely by paper-and-pencil, teacher-made, or standardized tests	Evaluation of learning employs multiple devices for assessment, with emphasis on behavioral change and self-appraisal	Evaluation of learning based primarily on student-developed goals — assessed by students as well as faculty and community-involved people
Schedule for school learning	School day 5-5½ hours, five days a week, 175-190 days a year	"School" extended to any hours devoted to learning — in or out of school under the auspices of school	School serves as the base from which work-study program extends — calendar is developed for the individual
Organization of students	Students organized into classes, taught in classes, and grouped by age and academic ability within age	Students organized, in groups or individually, in terms of purpose determined by students, teachers, and parents	Students organized sociometrically, this balanced with teacher having some options to organize for new exposures
Organization of teachers	Teachers organized in faculties by grade level in elementary and subject at high school level.	Teachers organized into teams, including a variety of types or personnel, professional, paraprofessional, and ancillary people	Teachers reorganized periodically for students' benefit and challenge. Central guideline is bringing together a vital, stimulating team

that school need not do much positive good to succeed if it will just refrain from doing much positive harm.

We accomplish little of value, and much positive harm, when we attempt to force-fit students into preset curriculums and then blithely flunk them when they don't fit. The Greeks had a name for this mythic foolishness, the Procrustean bed.[1]

    a. Which elements of his argument do you feel validly challenge traditional Christian education? Why?

    b. Which elements of his argument do you feel are irrelevant to Christian education? Why?

    c. If you were to construct an educational system based on an understanding of faith as life, what would you do to avoid the assumptions about learning that Allen challenges?

4. It's always fruitful to explore the biblical concepts underlying any theology of Christian education. Here are some possible approaches to further exploration of the idea of *life* as developed in Scripture.

    a. The words *nephesh* (נפש) and *psuche* ($\psi v\chi\acute\eta$) also are sometimes translated "life" in Old and New Testaments. How do they differ from *chayah* (חיה) and *zoe* ($\zeta\omega\acute\eta$)?

    b. Using a concordance, attempt to distinguish different usages of "life," and particularly to discover what it is about life that sets believers apart from those who do not know God.

    c. Select key passages (such as Deut. 30:15-20, Gal. 2:19, 20, or study the usage of "life" in John's Gospel, etc.) and write a brief commentary.

    d. Explain, by comparison with other Scripture, affirmations like that in Ephesians 4:18, that men are "separated from the life of God because of the ignorance that is in them due to the hardening of their hearts."

    e. Study and do reports on any of the following theological questions:

        (1) What happened to human personality in the fall?

        (2) What does restoration to life in Christ promise in terms of man's intellect? his emotions? his will? other capacities?

        (3) What is the relationship between the individual and the Church? Is it accurate to say that one exists for the other?

        (4) What are the evidences of new life in the individual? in the Body?

5. From your present understanding, write a brief paragraph stating what you feel taking *life* as the essence of Christian faith might imply for Christian education.

[1]Reprinted from *Psychology Today*, March 1971. Copyright © 1971 Ziff-Davis Publishing Company. All rights reserved.

life's goal: what the church does

THE CHURCH	IMPLICATIONS
LIFE	A WHOLE-PERSON FOCUS
LIFE'S GOAL	A DISCIPLING PURPOSE
LIFE'S COMMUNI-CATION	A MODELING METHOD
LIFE'S DYNAMIC	AN INTER-PERSONAL DIMENSION
LIFE'S TRANS-MISSION	AN OVER-FLOWING OUTCOME

It's not difficult to see why we each, individually, need new life from God. But why form us into a living Body?

The purposes and meaning of the Body are far ranging. But educationally it's clear that the Body is designed to support a purpose inherent in the nature of the new life God gives us in Christ. A purpose the Bible hints at in these words of Paul: God has chosen us "to be conformed to the likeness of his Son, that he might be the firstborn among many brothers" (Rom. 8:29).

All life has a character and nature of its own. Hold a grain of corn in your hand. Holding it you know the kind of plant that will spring from it when it germinates and grows.

The single cell first formed by sperm and ovum looks like any other cell under a microscope. But let that cell grow, and the nature of its life will be revealed. The germ cell of rabbits will produce rabbits; of the horse will surely come a colt; of the human, an infant.

It's important to realize that the life God gives us in Christ has its own nature and character too. Simply put, the life we are given in Christ is God's own life. As that life grows in us, we become more and more like Him. The apostle Peter puts it boldly: "For you are not just mortals now but sons of God; the live, permanent Word of the living God has given you his own indestructible heredity" (1 Peter 1:23, Phillips). Because we have been given His life, it is our destiny to be like Him.

The concept of likeness is a common one in Scripture. Jesus, in teaching His disciples to love even their enemies, points out that they are to be "sons of your Father in heaven. He causes his sun to rise on the evil and the good, and sends rain on the righteous and the unrighteous." Jesus' conclusion? "Be perfect, therefore, as your heavenly Father is perfect" (Matt. 5:45-47). Paul, in Romans, points out that believers have been called "according to his purpose," and then goes on to explain that, "For those God foreknew he also predistined to be conformed to the likeness of his Son" (Rom. 8:28, 29).

Because God has planted His own life in our personalities, it is our destiny to be like Him.

perfect likeness. In one respect, the Bible's teaching about our likeness to God is eschatological. John writes, "Dear friends, now we are children of God, and what we will be has not yet been made known. But we know that when he appears, we shall be like him, for we shall see him as he is" (1 John 3:2). Paul, sure that as sons we are to share Christ's glory, waits with the creation in "eager expectation for the sons of God to be revealed" (Rom. 8:16-19). And in speaking of the coming resurrection he teaches that "just as we have borne the likeness of the earthly man, so we shall bear the likeness of the man from heaven" (1 Cor. 15:49). So the Bible speaks with confidence about the destiny of those who have been given a share in God's life. As His sons now, it is our destiny to be like Him.

present likeness. At the same time the Bible speaks of a present impact of eternal life. Because we have eternal life *now*, we are to be becoming more and more like Him as we live in our present space and time! Jesus speaks of Himself as the Light of the world . . . and calls us lights. Jesus speaks of Himself as our Teacher . . . and says that "it is enough for . . . the [disciple] like his master" (Matt. 10:25). 1 John 4:16, 17 speaks of living "in God," and adds, "in this world we are like him."

Strikingly, many moral exhortations of Scripture are based on the fact of likeness-through-life. "Forgive one another," Ephesians says, "just as in Christ God forgave you" (Eph. 4:32). Because we live in Him, John says we do not "continue in sin" (1 John 3:4-10). According to Colossians it is because we have "put on the new self, which is being renewed in knowledge in the image of its Creator," that we are free to rid ourselves of the selfishness and sins which mar the experience of men (Col. 3:1-11).

Life has come to us in Jesus. Because we presently possess the life of God Himself, we are to become like Him more and more.

transformation

There are many indications in Scripture that the experience and expression of our new life is to be progressive. Simply possessing new life does not bring automatic or immediate change. God's life, as all other life, must *grow* within us. Thus Ephesians 4:15 encourages us to "in all things grow up into him who is the Head, that is, Christ."

The element of process is stressed in many ways. The Colossians passage just referred to points out that the new self "*is being* renewed" (Col. 3:10). Phillips captures the progressive implications of "transformation" as he paraphrases Romans 12:2, "Let God re-make you so that your whole attitude of mind is changed." Paul expresses the reality of transformation beautifully in 2 Corinthians 3:18, where he says that "we . . . are being transformed into his likeness with ever-increasing glory, which comes from the Lord, who is the Spirit."

It's important to grasp the implications of the fact that this is a *process. Christian education is not to be designed to produce a product. It is to be designed to supply what is needed for the process of growth to proceed normally and healthily.*

It is not difficult to design an educational system to produce a product of content knowledge. But knowledge of content, even of biblical content, is *not* the goal on which Christian education is to focus.

It is not difficult to design an educational system to produce behavioral conformity! B. F. Skinner's followers have shown *how* operant conditioning and selective reinforcement can be used to modify behavior. But behavior, even moral behavior, is not the goal on which Christian education is to focus.

Christian education is concerned with (life) and with the growth of eternal life within the human personality, toward likeness to the God who gives it. Christian education is concerned with the progressive transformation of the believer toward the character, values, motives, attitudes, and understandings of God Himself. "As he is, so are we in the world" focuses our attention on the development of the total personality as one which reflects ever more accurately the personality of Jesus

Christ. "Christ living in me" (Gal. 2:20) is the only adequate expression of Christian education's concern that we can formulate if we take seriously the idea that the essence of our faith is life!

to edify. When we take growth and the support of growth to be the main concern of Christian education, we see a fresh significance in Bible terms like edify (build up), strengthen, encourage, minister, instruct, etc. When we see the support of growth as the main concern of Christian education, we also see the purpose of the Body in a fresh way.

It is the calling of believers to be involved in edifying one another (1 Thess. 5:11). Two of the four basic passages on the Body in the New Testament emphasize and reemphasize its building-up purpose (cf. Eph. 4:12, 16, 19, 29 and 1 Cor. 14:4, 5, 12, 17). In Romans 12, following the exhortation to believers to open themselves up to transformation, Paul goes on to explore some of the spiritual gifts through which believers can minister to one another (vv. 3-8) and the relationships within the fellowship which makes such ministry possible (vv. 9-18). In 1 Corinthians 12-14 the apostle develops at length the fact that each believer is gifted by the Holy Spirit to enable him to minister to others "for the common good" (12:7). By distributing abilities to minister throughout the Body, God has "harmonized the whole" and provided all that is "essential to life" (12:24). The primary focus of these gifts is their use in edifying: "for the building up of the faith of one man, the encouragement of another or the consolation of another" (14:3, Phillips). Within the Body all are to contribute; all are to participate to make the Body and the individual strong in the faith (14:26).

This same emphasis is found in Ephesians 4. Here again the unity of the Body is affirmed, the importance of each member explained, and the service of members focused on building up the whole until individuals and the community arrive at "real maturity — that measure of development which is meant by 'the fullness of Christ" (4:13, Phillips). So again we see stressed the function of the community as an educational, or "building up" entity (cf. also 4:14-16). A final mention of the Body in conjunction with spiritual gifts is found in 1 Peter 4. Here too we see gifts designed to "serve the Church" (4:11), and support the believer's growth toward Christ's likeness.

spiritual gifts. In each of the "Body" passages we've glanced at, spiritual gifts have been in peculiar focus. The Body has been seen as united, in intimate and warm relationship (a theme to be developed in chap. 4), and is involved in ministry to its members to support and stimulate growth.

Seen in this context, the idea of "spiritual gift" is not difficult to grasp. It is, most simply, a Holy Spirit-given and -energized ability to contribute to the development of others in faith's life. It is through the functioning of each believer as he uses his gift for upbuilding that growth toward maturity of the Body and the individual takes place (Eph. 4:16).

An understanding of edifying and of spiritual gifts, then, forces us to realize that to adequately support the progressive development of Christ's life in believers, Christian education must deal with the Body as a whole! Isolating the "educational ministry of the church" from the congregation's total life is a deadly error. Christian education must deal with the bringing of all members *of the Body into ministering relationship with each other.*

When we recognize life as the distinctive of our faith, and when we go on to see the supporting of the growth of eternal life in the believer as the concern of Christian education, we gain a new appreciation for the reason why ecclesiology is the starting point for a theology of Christian education. The Bible makes it clear that the Body was formed to support the believer. One of the primary purposes of God in linking us to one another as the Church is that the Body might minister to the individual, and support the individual's growth in Christ. To make this ministry possible, each individual is equipped to minister to others. Thus the Christian community becomes a dynamic, transforming, supporting, and mutually *educating* whole.

other elements in transformation. In pointing up the importance of the community of believers in supporting progress toward Christlikeness, I have not meant to imply that this is the only means God uses. For instance, Jesus asks the Father to "sanctify them by the truth; your word is truth" (John 17:17). Certainly for growth it is necessary for the believer to hold to Jesus' teachings (John 8:31), and to be obedient rather than disobedient when God speaks to him (cf. Heb. 3:7-19). One also can speak of the role of prayer in the Christian life. But even these elements are found in Scripture in a context.

It is not simply the Word as a belief-system that is to be taught. According to Deuteronomy the process of teaching the Word involves first personal experience of the Word by the teacher, then speaking of God's words to the learner in the context of a shared life, where the lived meaning of the Word can be demonstrated as well as verbalized (cf. Deut. 6:6, 7)! *It is not simply the teaching of the Word that is important in Christian education. It is how the Word is taught!*

As we move on in our exploration of Christian education, we will see more and more clearly that teaching for transformation — teaching designed to support the process of growth in Christlikeness — is a unique kind of teaching. It involves bringing the Word into the ongoing life of believers as an integral part of their ministry to each other in the Body. A growing understanding of how the Body is related to nurture will not rule out the Bible, but will instead teach us *how* to communicate the Bible God's way! But this theme too is one we will examine in greater detail later on.

What, then, have we said so far?

First, that <u>the secret of our faith is life.</u> God's life, given to us in Christ, is what sets the believer from other men, and the Church apart from human institutions.

Second, that <u>God's own life,</u> the eternal life which is ours through faith, <u>has a distinctive character and goal.</u> That goal is *Christlikeness.* Thus Christian education's focus is on the support of the believer's growth in Christlikeness. Christian education is concerned about a process of personality and character transformation!

Third, <u>support for the believer's growth is provided by the Body.</u> It is in the ministry of believers to each other that each finds himself being built toward the "fullness of Christ," and finds the community itself maturing in godliness. Christian education, then, does not deal with learning *in isolation,* but with learning that takes place in the interaction of men and women who share together in that divine life offered to all through the gospel of our Lord Jesus Christ.

PROBE
   case histories
   discussion questions
   thought-provokers
   resources

It is not difficult to measure educational product as long as that product is simple and discreet. For instance, we can give a test over a series of lessons on John's Gospel, and determine with reasonable accuracy what an individual *knows.* But if our education focuses on a *process of growth* and on *character,* measurement is not so easy!

Writing in *Educational Technology* (January, 1970), Mary B. Harbeck comments on "Instructional Objectives in the Affective Domain."

   If the truly educated person can be described as one who has a well-defined value system (character) that he lives by and is willing to defend, an appreciation of the arts, a concern for the future of mankind, and the ability to live in harmony with his fellows, then educational objectives must certainly be formulated in the affective domain, as described by Krathwohl, as well as in the higher levels of the cognitive domain.

Educational goals at these levels have been in existence for a long time, but they are usually stated once in some obscure document such as a school philosophy, and then are largely forgotten when the actual instructional sequences are planned. Teachers do not often consciously teach or test for objectives in the affective domain. More or less on faith, we assume that people will develop a value complex as they continue to learn. If we are to guarantee quality in education, we can no longer afford to make assumptions and then fail to measure the actual outcome.

The problem this poses is a challenging one for Christian education. *How do we measure learning outcomes in terms of growth of the believer and the Body toward Christlikeness?* Here are some possible avenues of approach to exploring this significant issue in Christian education.

1. You have been invited by the board of a local church to evaluate their ministry and help them plan goals for the next five years. They have given you data from their records on Sunday school size and growth over the past ten years, on the number of baptisms, and the size of local and missions budgets.

   a. How meaningful will these criteria be in measuring the ministry of the church if your concern is life and the growth of believers toward maturity in Christ?

   b. What kinds of things would you want to measure to evaluate progress toward a "Christlikeness" goal? Can you develop from Scripture a description of the "mature believer" and the "mature church" which will help you plan your evaluation approaches?

   c. From your study, can you list a number of goals which you feel might be helpful in guiding the ministry of a local congregation?

2. Emphasis currently is being placed on *operationalizing* objectives. T. A. Ryan (ET, June, 1969) describes an operational system as "one which is synthesized to progress in orderly fashion toward a goal. This means that a system is created for a purpose; that basic to any attempt at understanding, modifying, or controlling systems is an explication of the system purpose, that is, the mission goal. This is a task which calls for studying the situation, determining the need which will be or is being satisfied, defining objectives which contribute to satisfying the needs, and selecting criteria to measure how well objectives are being met. At the outset abstractly stated aims must be translated to *measurable* terms. This process

of operationalizing objectives with precision is crucial to system effectiveness."

If we conceive of Christian education as a system designed to reach a unique goal, it may be helpful to translate "abstractly stated" terms like "Christlikeness" into "measurable" terms. Activity 1.b, above, initiated that process. But probably the terminology in which goals were stated is still relatively abstract.

How do we break down terms with abstract meaning (like "love"!) into operational definitions? This extract from Statts' *Complex Human Behavior* will help explain a task you may want to undertake now.

> An operational definition, in its simplest form, specifies the observational operations used to identify phenomenon. . . . As an example, let us look at a concept that is frequently used, the concept of "emotional maturity." Can this term be appropriately used? As long as the term means only certain observations, the answer might be affirmative. It might be said, for instance, that a child is emotionally mature if he studies by himself without being coerced, if he is not overly demanding, if he has good relationships with other children, etc. On the other hand, a child who does not study well by himself, who is disruptive in his demands, who does not get along with other children, who has temper tantrums, and so on, might be termed "emotionally immature."
>
> When the definition of a concept consists of the observations that are made and labeled by the concept, the concept is said to be operationally defined (pp. 12, 13).[1]

With this in mind, you might approach operationalizing the goals of Christian education in a number of ways.

    a. Look over David R. Krathwohl, *Taxonomy of Educational Objectives: Handbook II, The Affective Domain* (David McKay Company, Inc., New York, 1956), to determine which measures might be appropriate in Christian education.

    b. Do more intensive research in measurement techniques to determine what tools are available to help us operationally define biblical concepts, and to recognize operational definitions which do appear in Scripture. Some significant sources:

> Don E. Byrne, *An Introduction to Personality: A Research Approach* (Prentice-Hall, Inc., Englewood Cliffs, N.J., 1969).
>
> Dorothy H. Cohen and Virginia Stern, *Observing and Recording the Behavior of Young Children* (Teacher's College Press, Columbia University, New York, 1958).
>
> Robert R. Holt, *Assessing Personality* (Harcourt Brace Javanovich, Inc., New York, 1971).

[1]From *Complex Human Behavior* by Staats and Staats. Copyright 1973 by Holt, Rinehart and Winston. Used by permission.

Douglas Jackson and Samuel Messick, *Problems in Human Assessment* (McGraw Hill, New York, 1967).

Joseph B. Sidowski, *Experimental Methods and Instrumentation in Psychology* (McGraw Hill, New York, 1966).

Gene F. Summers (ed.), *Attitude Measurement* (Rand McNally and Company, Chicago, 1970).

E. J. Webb, D. T. Campbell, R. D. Schwartz, and L. Sechrest, *Unobtrusive Measures: Nonreactive Research in the Social Sciences* (Rand McNally, Chicago, 1966).

c. *Education 200: The Individual and the School, is a book pro-duced by the College of Education, Michigan State University, and copyrighted by Judith E. Henderson, 1972. Pages 193-214 contain fine examples of breaking a concept down to behavioral indicators. Modeled on this breakdown, how might one goal for growth in Christ be operationalized?*

d. The Bible contains its own operationalized, or behavioral, state-ments of abstract terms. For example, Jesus' command that we "love one another" is operationally defined, and indicators of the love relationship stated, wherever the phrase "one another" occurs in the New Testament. Using a concordance, locate these passages, and develop an operationalized description of "love" as it is to exist and be expressed between members of the Body.

3. Operational definitions of constructs associated with growth in Christ are helpful to force us away from abstractions and to remind us that growth in Christ does involve expressing, in practical ways, the life of God in our everyday world. Having available a set of behavioral indicators of growth also helps us in evaluating our edu-cational ministry. *If changes are not being observed in these indi-cators,* then we want to reevaluate the way in which we are going about "Christian education" — even if progress in other areas (such as in communicating knowledge) is being made.

Yet there are problems in relying too heavily on behavioral in-dicators. React, for instance, to each of the following statements which may or may not be generally true.

a. The same criteria should be used for measuring children's growth as for measuring the growth of adults.

b. There is a specific time within which progress should be dem-onstrated in change along specified behavioral indicators.

c. Growth should not be expected to take place in every dimen-sion of a person's character at the same rate.

d. Change along biblically defined indicators of growth can be applied only to the group, not to individuals.

e. Since Christian growth is a *process* with fulfillment found in a product only achieved in the resurrection, a statement of indicators of maturity in Christ or Christlikeness can never be validly applied.

f. It would make no difference in the practice of Christian education in the local church if we had no idea at all of the goal of Christian nurture . . . or of the indicators of progress toward that goal.

4. One last project may be instructive. In *Foundations for a Philosophy of Christian Education,* Lawrence C. Little suggests that those engaged in various Christian education ministries seldom "understand the real nature of their work and the full significance of what they are attempting to do" (p. 15).

This suggestion should be relatively easy to test. Why not develop a simple questionnaire, and ask various teachers and educational leaders in the Church to fill it out. Design your questionnaire to avoid giving away your own biases. For instance, open-ended sentences are helpful tools:

"Each Sunday I try to . . ."

"I use the Bible in my ministry because . . ."

"I'll be satisfied that God has used me if . . ."

And so on.

Then analyze the results. Look, for instance, at how often static "knowledge" words show up. How often do active, personal growth and change words show up? How often are attitudes and values and behaviors, as well as cognitive operations, mentioned? From the results . . .

a. Deduce the operating philosophy of Christian education of those surveyed.

b. State how you would expect the expressed philosophy to affect educational *practice*.

c. Finally, if the persons surveyed should develop an understanding of Christian education as supporting growth toward Christlikeness, how might the *practice* change?

3

life's communication: how the church edifies

THE CHURCH	IMPLICATIONS
LIFE	A WHOLE-PERSON FOCUS
LIFE'S GOAL	A DISCIPLING PURPOSE
LIFE'S COMMUNI-CATION	A MODELING METHOD
LIFE'S DYNAMIC	AN INTER-PERSONAL DIMENSION
LIFE'S TRANS-MISSION	AN OVER-FLOWING OUTCOME

I can teach you to know. But how do I teach you to live? We have solid insights into how to teach for understanding. But how do we build persons up in Christ's life? How do we reach, and free, and support growth of the total personality?

Jesus gives us a starting point as we observe with Mark that He chose twelve men "that they might be with him" (3:14). Our understanding is fulfilled in Jesus' own words, "everyone who is fully trained will be like his teacher" (Luke 6:40).

Much of education is concerned with helping people know what their teachers know. Christian education is concerned with helping people become what their teachers are.

The focus on life, which gives us our starting point in thinking about Christian education, helps us keep this issue clear. We're concerned about transformation. We "teach" to communicate and to build up the life of God which faith in Christ plants firmly in the believer. Christian education seeks to support a process of growth; the gradual growing up of the believer into Christ and into ever more adequate representation of His character.

This unique task of building up men and women toward Christ's likeness is the task of making disciples.

the making of a disciple

It's instructive to look at Jesus' relationship with His disciples, both to discover what His goal was, and how He ministered to reach it.

In the first place, the Luke 6:40 phrase "fully trained" is somewhat deceptive. It makes us think of a mechanic, who when fully trained has learned the techniques and skills needed to tear down and repair an engine. The word in the original, *katartidzo* (here in the participle form κατηρτισμένος), means first restore, or put to rights, and then in its New Testament usages means "put into proper condition," or "made complete." Thus 1 Thessalonians 3:10 speaks of making complete what is lacking in one's faith; Hebrews 13:21 of "equip you with everything good"; 1 Corinthians 1:10 of a local body being "perfectly united in mind and thought."

The "training" of a disciple focuses on making the disciple a complete person, a mature believer. As Jesus lived with and taught the Twelve, He was concerned about transformation: His goal was the nurture of life.

It is instructive then (in view of the command that *we* are to "make disciples," cf. Matt. 28:19; Acts 14:21) to look at the contexts in which the word "disciple" appears and see what is happening as Jesus and the Twelve live together through three significant years.

A cursory and non-exhaustive examination of the passage shows that a range of transactions was involved. This was no typical "school" where those being trained appeared to listen to the teacher for an hour, then went back out into life without him. Jesus and the disciples lived together; they shared the experiences and traumas of life. They were constantly interacting; constantly initiating and reacting to each other.

Often we see the disciples listening as Jesus taught and in-

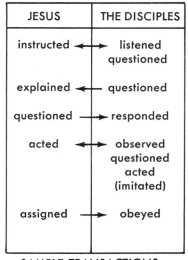

JESUS	THE DISCIPLES
instructed ←→	listened
	questioned
explained ←—	questioned
questioned —→	responded
acted ←→	observed
	questioned
	acted
	(imitated)
assigned —→	obeyed

SAMPLE TRANSACTIONS
BETWEEN JESUS AND
THE DISCIPLES

31

structed (cf. Matt. 10:23; 16:24; 20:26; Mark 3:9; 4:34; 9:31; 11:14; Luke 9:1, 14, 43; 12:1, 22; 14:26, 27; 20:34). Often we have the disciples observing Jesus' responses in situations, and His handling of people and events (cf. Matt. 14:26; 16:21; 21:20; 26:8; Mark 9:28; John 18:5, 22, etc.). More than once what the disciples saw and heard stimulated them to question Jesus, asking for explanation and interpretation (Matt. 14:23; 24:1, 3; Mark 6:35; 7:17; 13:1; 14:12; Luke 8:9; 11:1; John 4:31; etc.). Not only that, the disciples themselves were at times questioned by Jesus (Matt. 16:13; 17:20; Mark 8:1, 4, 27; etc.). We also see the discipling relationship as one involving the learner being under authority. Jesus was free to command; the disciples obeyed (Mark 6:45; 10:23; 14:24; 16:20; etc.). Often, too, the disciples became involved in the kind of activities that Jesus Himself was involved in. They participated in His ministry (Matt. 11:1, 2; 14:36; Mark 11:1; Luke 19:29; etc.).

Just these few illustrations help us see that the making of disciples is an interpersonal and transactional process, involving teacher and learner in a wide range of real life experiences. The support and nurture of God's life within (and thus Christian education itself) seems to require a life-context, a model from whom those being discipled can learn, and a transactional relationship between persons.

to teach and learn

The impression that Christian education involves more than cognition and the processing of Bible information is strengthened when we look at the concepts of teaching and learning in the Old and New Testaments.

For instance, the Hebrew ידע , "come to know," includes the idea that experience teaches (cf. Job 32:7). The Hebrew ירה , "to show, direct, teach," has definite practical import, as in Psalm 86:11, "teach me thy way, O LORD, that I may walk in thy truth" (cf. also Pss. 25:8, 12; 119:102; etc.). While the Hebrew למד seems to focus more on understanding (cf. Deut. 4:5, 10; 11:19; 20:18; 31:19; Ezra 7:10; Jer. 32:33, etc.), still the same word expresses the development of warrior skills (cf. 2 Sam. 22:35; Pss. 18:3, 4; 114:1).

The Greek διδάσκω is used most often of verbal instruction. But here too a concept like "show us how to pray" (Luke 11:1) is not foreign to its import (cf. Matt. 4:23; 5:2; 9:35; 13:54; 26:55; Mark 1:21; 4:1, 2; 6:34; 8:31; Luke 4:15; 5:3, 17; 19:47; 20:1; John 6:59; 7:14; 8:20, 28; Acts 4:18; 5:25; 11:26;

18:11). Often "do and teach" are combined (as in Matt. 5:19; Acts 1:1), and it is not unusual to see the church worship as the "teaching" of one another in "psalms, hymns and spiritual songs" (Col. 3:16).

Yet another word, παιδεύω , speaks of bringing up or educating as a child (cf. Acts 7:22; 22:3), and this word also implies discipline and correction (cf. 1 Cor. 11:32; 2 Cor. 6:9; 1 Tim. 1:20; 2 Tim. 2:25; Titus 2:12).

The point of all this is, of course, simple. While "to teach" *can* bring to mind the teacher and the formal classroom, far more is involved in the concept than this! To limit Christian education to the formal setting, as we traditionally have, is to tragically limit our idea of teaching and learning.

The same point is made if we skim the range of meanings of the Bible words for "know." One who has learned, and thus come to know, certainly will have information. But having information in no way exhausts the meaning of having knowledge.

The Hebrew ידע has wide usage. Even in its simplest meaning, "to know, or learn to know," it speaks of the recognition and experience of good and evil (Gen. 3:22; 39:6; 1 Sam. 28:9); of perception (Gen. 19:33, 35; 1 Sam. 12:17); of ability to distinguish or discriminate (Jonah 4:11); and of a knowledge gained through experience (Josh. 23:14; Ps. 51:5; Isa. 59:12).

Additional usages include acquaintance with a person (Gen. 29:5; Exod. 1:8; Job 42:11) and even knowledge of how to do a thing (Isa. 29:11, 12; Jer. 1:6; 6:15; Amos 3:10).

The same range is found in various Greek terms. One, γινώσκω , involves knowing or coming to know about (truth, John 8:32; God's will, Luke 12:47; a tree by its fruit, Matt. 12:33). It also is used of finding out (Mark 5:43; Luke 24:18), comprehending (Luke 18:34; Heb. 3:10) or realizing (Luke 8:46), and recognizing or acknowledging (Matt. 7:23). Another basic Greek word, οἶδα, includes knowing a person or about him (Mark 1:34; John 1:26, 31, 33; 6:42; 7:28; Acts 3:16; 7:18; Gal. 4:8; 1 Thess. 4:5; Heb. 10:30), being intimately acquainted (Matt. 26:72, 74; Mark 14:71; Luke 22:57; 2 Cor. 5:16), and of knowing how, or being able (Matt. 7:11; Luke 11:13; cf. 1 Thess. 4:4; 1 Tim. 3:5; James 4:17). In addition it is used of knowing God in a relational, not theoretical, way (Matt. 25:12; John 7:28; 8:19; 2 Thess. 1:8; Titus 1:16). A third ἐπιγινώσκω , emphasizes the completeness of knowledge, but can have the same range of usages as the other two.

Just as the biblical terms for teaching and learning place no special premium on the ability to process information, so the terms for knowing fail to exalt the intellectual as an end in itself. Once again we're driven back to Jesus' words to capture the central meaning of teaching and learning as they are to be understood in Christian education: "everyone who is fully trained, will be like his teacher" (Luke 6:40). He will be like him in what he knows, yes. But knowing what the teacher knows is not the goal. <u>The goal is likeness to his *person*</u>. In understanding of life, in attitude, in values, in emotion, in commitment, the communication of life demands sharing of all that a person is with another that through such sharing growth toward Christlikeness might take place.

to follow and imitate

It seems to be important in the communication of life for an example or model to be present. Jesus, in washing the disciples' feet (John 13:15), said, "I have given you an example." The word he used, ὑπόδειγμα, means example, model, or pattern. It's used in the New Testament in a good sense: as something that should motivate or encourage others to imitate, to act, or to avoid (cf. Heb. 4:11; 2 James 5:10; 2 Peter 2:6).

The same idea is found in the familiar exhortation of Jesus to "follow me" (Matt. 9:9; 19:21; Mark 1:18; 2:14; 8:34; Luke 5:11; cf. also John 1:40, 43). "Follow me," Jesus said, "and I will make you fishers of men" (Matt. 4:19). In effect, I will make you like Me.

The idea of imitating or emulating a model occurs in other ways in the New Testament. The verb μιμέομαι (imitate) is translated accurately by Phillips in Ephesians 5:1, "So then you should try to become like God, for you are his children and he loves you." In other places it is rendered "follow." "You yourselves know how you ought to follow our example. . . . We did this . . . in order to make ourseves a model for you to follow" (2 Thess. 3:7, 9; cf. also Heb. 13:7; 3 John 11). The noun form of the same word, μιμητής , speaks of believers as followers, or imitators, or reproducers of a model. And, strikingly, this imitation moves beyond imitation of behavior! Attitudes and values of the model are to become part of the personality of the one being discipled (cf. 1 Cor. 4:16; 11:1; Eph. 5:1; 1 Thess. 1:6; Heb. 6:12), and even concepts ("that which is good") can become a model for us (cf. 1 Peter 3:13).

Jesus called His disciples to *be with* Him because they needed to see enfleshed the concepts which He taught. They needed to see the Word incarnated if they were to truly understand and be moved to respond, and thus *become like* their teacher!

The twin concepts of "being with" and "modeling" are of vital significance to Christian education. We must be ready to abandon our dependence on precedents established in a secular educational system which is not concerned with *likeness* but with information, and to design a unique educational process rooted in Scripture's concern for the nurture of life. In that new design, the roles of teacher and of learner must be harmonized with need for a model who, through shared learning experience, can "make disciples."

a critical passage

The themes explored in this chapter help bring into focus the importance of an Old Testament passage of central concern to Christian education. The instruction, given in Deuteronomy 6, comes at a critical historical juncture. Here communication of the reality of God ceased to be by direct divine intervention (e.g., the events of the Exodus, Jericho, etc.), and from this time was to be through the written revelation given by Moses.

Then, as now, God's people were faced with the task of communicating the written Word in such a way as to transform life. It is at this point in time that Scripture gives a pattern for the communication of written revelation which still provides the basic guidelines for a theologically sound Christian education.

After summarizing the importance of the commands God gives, and revealing the motive of love which moved Him to speak, the passage outlines the pattern for communication.

> Hear, O Israel: The LORD our God is one LORD; and you shall love the LORD your God with all your heart, and with all your soul, and with all your might. And these words which I command you this day shall be upon your heart; and you shall teach them diligently to your children, and shall talk of them when you sit in your house, and when you walk by the way, and when you lie down, and when you rise.

Examining this short passage we see reflected the critical elements already observed in Jesus' discipling ministry.

a prerequisite model. Verses 4, 5, and 6 concentrate our attention on the person of the teacher. He or she is to be a person who has a personal love relationship with the Lord. What's more, that love is to be demonstrated and fulfilled by the internalization of the words of Scripture. Revealed truth is to be incarnated truth as well.

a transactional relationship. With the focus of Moses' instruction placed on the succeeding generations, parents are viewed as the primary communicators of faith's life to their children. The unique relationship between parents and children — are extended, stable, loving, varied, and transactional relationship — provides the ideal context in which the communication of revealed truth and its life impact can take place. That relationship not only enhances the impact of the parents' modeling; it also facilitates the understanding of motives, feelings, and attitudes as well as imitation of behavior.

While all Christian education is not to take place in the home, a "family relationship" or "family feeling" *is* to be of concern in every teaching/learning setting. Rather than abandoning the home as the nurture center for children in favor of an imitation of school, we are to reaffirm the centrality of the home, and take seriously our task of devising educational systems which will support parents in that task.

a life context. It is clear from the passage that God's words are to be taught and talked about. The written word is a necessary element in Christian education. What is significant here is not that affirmation, which conservatives have always accepted, but insight into the critical context in which the Word is to be introduced. We do not have here a classroom portrait of teaching! Instead we have a foreshadowing of Jesus' discipling method. Teacher and learner share life's experiences together. Here, in life itself, the Word is taught and talked about!

It is these elements, if we are truly concerned about life, that Christian education must reaffirm. And it is with these dimensions of teaching and learning — the prerequisite model, the transactional relationship, and the life context — that we must be ready to approach the reconstruction of Christian education in the Church.

PROBE
    case histories
    discussion questions
    thought-provokers
    resources

1. The first two chapters in this book concluded with a series of affirmations about the nature of our faith, the goal and focus of Christian education, and the support of growth within the Christian community (cf. pp. 16, 25). This chapter lacks a similar summary.
   Reread chapter 3, and try your hand at writing the kind of summation you believe the author might want to include here.

2. The material discussed in this chapter opens many doors for depth

study of biblical terms and concepts. Here are just a few of the possible studies that might be attempted:

a. Look at the context of every passage where the word "disciple" is found, and analyze the transactions between disciple, teacher, and environment.

b. Study in depth several critical passages concerning discipleship, such as Matthew 10:32-39 or Luke 14:26f.

c. Do an in-depth study of each appearance of one or more of the following words:

ידע— know, learn, cause to know
γινώσκω— know, come to know
οἶδα— know
σοφία— wisdom
ירה— show, direct, teach
למד— teach
διδάσκω— instruct
μανθάνω— learn

d. Examine commentaries on Deuteronomy 6, and summarize your findings.

e. Read the available literature on discipling and discipleship, and do a critical evaluation.

3. In *Change, Conflict, and Self Determination: Next Steps in Religious Education,* Iris V. Cully (Westminster Press; Philadelphia, 1972) writes:

> The "model" for religious education has long been the school, rather narrowly conceived as a classroom experience, age-graded, with a teacher as authority figure who has knowledge, skill, and understanding. But this model is breaking down. With the criticism being leveled at general education, the church's educational security has vanished. Its educational outlook faces drastic change with resultant conflict (p. 161).

Each of the following three excerpts reflect one or more kind of criticism being ranged against the school model of education. Select one, and evaluate it in writing in view of the concepts discussed in this third chapter.

a. Schooling (that part of education conducted in a formalized setting by specialists) began in the context of authority and of the passing on by rote methods of universal truths that could not be questioned by young learners. The teacher knew, and that was why he was the teacher; the learner did not know, and that was why he was the learner. Communication between teacher and learners was one way at a time with the odds heavily weighted on the side of the teacher. First, the teacher would teach by lecturing and demonstrating; then, the learner would recite orally or on paper so that the teacher could determine whether understanding had taken place. Thus the now well-defined roles of teacher and student were developed. The teacher planned, introduced, developed, explained, illustrated, and summarized usually by oral means, though he might use drawings or models from time to time. The listening learner took notes, did individual thinking, and then demonstrated his success or failure to understand, or at least to recite, what he had been taught.

Alfred H. Gorman, *Teachers and Learners: The Interactive Process of Education* (Allyn and Bacon, Inc., Boston, 1969).[1]

b. Peter F. Drucker, writing about "School Around the Bend" in *Psychology Today* (June, 1972, p. 84), lists the following as assumptions which underlie schooling in every country.

1) learning is a separate and distinct "intellectual" activity;
2) learning goes on in a separate organ, the mind, divorced from the body or emotions;
3) learning is divorced from doing — indeed, opposed to it; at best it is preparation for doing; and
4) learning, because it is preparation, is for the young.

c. The following brief chapter appears in Rolf E. Aaseng's little book, *Anyone Can Teach (They Said).*[2]

> "You shouldn't always use the same method in teaching."
> "Amen!" I said with conviction — silently, of course.
>
> The speaker droned on. "How can you expect to hold the interest of a group of youngsters, much less have them really learn anything, if you just stand up in front of them and drone away?"
>
> Half-heartedly I tried to muffle a yawn as I looked around at the group of teachers who had braved the nice weather to attend our monthly teachers' meeting. Several full-length eyelids were in view.
>
> Now we'll at least get a chance to stretch, I thought, when I heard the statement, "Even adults get tired of the same thing all the time. Use variety in your presentations."
>
> He went right on. "Visual aids should not be overlooked." Then he proceeded to lecture on these means of teaching.
>
> Finally the hour was over. The leader came over to me. "I really appreciate your coming so faithfully to these teachers' meetings. It's a shame so few attend. I wish I knew what to do about it."
>
> Should I tell him?
>
> He went on. "It's the same way at Bible study. Just a few come."

[1]From *Teachers and Learners: The Interactive Process of Education.* Copyright 1969 by Allyn and Bacon Inc., Boston. Used by permission.

[2]From *Anyone Can Teach (They Said)* by Rolf E. Aaseng. Copyright 1965, Augsburg Publishing House, Minneapolis, Minnesota. Used by permission.

Oh, yes, the Bible study class. I had attended a few times. The instructor used to keep saying something like this: "You must get into the Word yourself before it can really benefit you as it should." Then he would use the rest of the period to lecture us on what we would learn if we would read the Bible.

Suddenly my own class came to mind. I could hear myself saying, "You must memorize this." But my book was open in front of me so I could tell whether or not they had done it.

Or I have growled, "A Christian should be happy."

Again I have demanded, "Why don't you kids bring your Bibles to Sunday school?" — while finding the place for myself in a copy from the supply shelf.

"Bring your friends to Sunday school," I've told them. But have I ever invited anyone? I impress on them the need for daily prayer and Bible study; but frankly I hope they are more faithful than I.

Though I emphasize the importance of love and forgiveness, it seems to be less important after they have played a prank on me.

Sometimes I have scolded them for not worshiping during the opening service. I knew they weren't because I was standing guard at the back of the room.

"Don't do as I do; do as I say," a rather unambitious teacher once told his class. But we never followed that advice.

Students never do.

life's dynamic: the church's "family" relationship

As soon as we begin to think of Christian education as transactional — as the interplay between teachers and learners in life — we raise the question of relationships. What marks that learning relationship? What facilitates the modeling process in which the growing disciple becomes like his teacher?

Jesus brings the relationship into potent focus: "As I have loved you, so you must love one another" (John 13:34).

THE CHURCH	IMPLICATIONS
LIFE	A WHOLE-PERSON FOCUS
LIFE'S GOAL	A DISCIPLING PURPOSE
LIFE'S COMMUNI-CATION	A MODELING METHOD
LIFE'S DYNAMIC	AN INTER-PERSONAL DIMENSION
LIFE'S TRANS-MISSION	AN OVER-FLOWING OUTCOME

It's hard to miss the emphasis on love in the New Testament. Jesus speaks of love as the "new commandment" (John 13:34, 35), a command often referred to by Paul and other New Testament writers. To James, this need for love within the Body becomes "the Law of Christ" (and he points to practical expressions of that royal demand in his chap. 2). Peter insists that the gospel's purification cleanses us so that we can "have sincere love for your brothers" and insists, "so love one another deeply, with all your hearts" (1 Peter 1:22). John sees love of those in the family of God as evidence of relationship with God and of the reality of our new life: "We know that we have passed from death to life, because we love our brothers" (1 John 3:14). Paul affirms that our total obligation to others is to love them, for the one loving automatically fulfills all that law expresses (cf. Rom. 13:8-10). He repeats this thought in Galatians, urging us to "serve one another in love" (5:13-18). In fact, Paul is bold enough to write to Timothy that the goal of teaching truth and sound doctrine is "love, which comes from a pure heart, a good conscience and a sincere faith" (1 Tim. 1:5).

Love, within the Body as a special mark of family relationship, and love expressed to those yet without life as evidence of God's concern, is a theme with which we are all familiar. *The peculiar thing is that we have missed its significance for Christian education! Accepting the "schooling" concept of teaching faith, we have lost sight of the communication of faith-as-life. Without a clear understanding of the fact that it is life we are concerned with, we have missed the utter necessity of the love relationship for growth in Christ.*

the body ministers

As soon as we begin to think about Christian education as growth toward Christlikeness, we're struck by passages in the New Testament that speak of the Body and its ministry. As I noted in chapter 2, growth of the individual and the community through edifying (building up) seems clearly to involve the Body, and to involve the exercise of spiritual gifts by each member of the Body for one another. Ephesians 4 makes this thought clear: the whole body "grows and builds itself up in love, as each part does its work" (v. 16). Clearly this is the reason why the writer to the Hebrews insists that we "consider how we may spur one another on toward love and good deeds." And he goes on, "Let us not give up meeting together, as some are in the habit of doing, but let us encourage one another — and all the more as you see the Day approaching" (10:24, 25). The Body has been formed for ministry. It is as we minister to one another that we grow in Christ's life, individually and corporately.

How significant then that in every Body passage, close attention is paid to the relational context in which this kind of mutual nurture and ministry take place! In Romans 12 Paul encourages believers to open their hearts and minds to transformation, moves on to the role of the Body and spiritual gifts, and *immediately* focuses attention on interpersonal relationships by insisting "Love must be sincere" (12:9). He then goes on to describe relationships within the Body and with those outside, touching on attitudes and motives as well as behaviors.

> Be devoted to one another in brotherly love. Honor one another above yourselves. Never be lacking in zeal, but keep your spiritual fervor, serving the Lord. Be joyful in hope, patient in

> affliction, faithful in prayer. Share with God's people who are in need. Practice hospitality.
>
> Bless those who persecute you; bless and do not curse. Rejoice with those who rejoice; mourn with those who mourn. Live in harmony with one another. Don't be proud but be willing to associate with people of low position. Don't be conceited. Do not repay anyone evil for evil. Be careful to do what is right in the sight of everybody. If it is possible, as far as it depends on you, live at peace with everyone.

Paul's careful attention to interpersonal relationships here is not nagging. It is a concerned affirmation of the fact that for transformation to take place, and for conformity to be rejected (12:2), the quality of relationships which exist within the church is of vital importance.

This same thought is given even more stress in 1 Corinthians. Speaking to a local church that had dashed like children after the more spectacular gifts of the Spirit, Paul focuses on the need in the Body for every manifestation of the Spirit's work (12:14-26), and encourages the church members not to think of themselves as individuals but as parts of the Body; as a community. Keeping this orientation, they are to recognize the priority of edifying or building up gifts (12:27-31), and as a Body to be eager to see the greater gifts at work among them (12:31). But immediately Paul says, "And now I will show you the most excellent way," and launches into an exposition of love and its impact on the individual, its expression in the community, and its centrality in the church's experience.

Without love, Paul affirms, whatever a man may do for God or others *cannot benefit him* (13:1-3). Others may be helped by his gifts to the poor: but there is no profit or growth for the giver. But what *is* love; how is it expressed in interpersonal relationships?

> Love is patient, love is kind. It does not envy, it does not boast, it is not proud. It is not rude, it is not self-seeking, it is not easily angered, it keeps no record of wrongs. Love does not delight in evil but rejoices in the truth. It always protects, always trusts, always hopes, always perseveres.

It is this quality of relationships within the Body that give love its advantage over prophecy, tongues, and even knowledge. These may fail in contributing to the transformation of the human personality toward Christ's likeness. But "love never fails" (v. 8).

The priority of love over knowledge is something that bothers conservatives, who tend to place the highest value on Truth. Yet it is a priority which Paul does not shrink back from affirming.

Looking at the same issue in 1 Corinthians 8, and analyzing a "Truth" dispute in the church between those who "knew" it was wrong to eat meat sold at pagan temple meat markets, and those who "knew" it was all right because the idols were only wood and stone and metal anyway, Paul writes,

> It is easy to think that we "know" over problems like this, but we should remember that while this "knowing" may make a man look big, it is only love that can make him grow to his full stature. For if a man thinks he "knows," he may still be quite ignorant of what he ought to know. But if he loves God he is the man who is known to God (1 Cor. 8:1, 2, Phillips).

So Paul goes on to encourage the believers to handle this dispute on the basis of love, willing to give up "rights" and even "the right" out of consideration for the conscience of others who have not yet found the freedom there is in Christ.

Now be careful. It is easy for a dichotomistic thinker (one who must organize all things into opposing pairs) to misunderstand the point I am making, and what Paul is saying. *I am not saying we must choose love or truth.* Nor is Paul. What I am pointing out is that Scripture says *truth without love* may bring a *knowledge that does not transform, but "puffs up!" For Truth to have its transforming impact on the human personality, love is utterly essential! It is Truth that is communicated in the context of a close and loving relationship that will be used by God to remold and renew the believer's personality toward Christ!*

No wonder in the other passages that speak of the Body we see the same concern for interpersonal relationships. Explaining the working of the Body in building up in Ephesians 4, Paul immediately writes, beginning with verse 17:

> So I tell you this, and insist on it in the Lord, that you must no longer live as the Gentiles do, in the futility of their thinking. . . . You were taught, with regard to your former way of life, to put off your old self, which is being corrupted by its deceitful desires: to be made new in the attitudes of your minds; and to put on the new self, created to be like God in true righteousness and holiness.
> Therefore, each of you must put off falsehood and speak truthfully to his neighbor, for we are all members of one body. In your anger do not sin: Do not let the sun go down while you are still angry, and do not give the devil a foothold. . . . Do not let any unwholesome talk come out of your mouths, but only what is helpful for building others up according to their needs, that it may benefit those who listen. And do not grieve the Holy Spirit of God, with whom you were sealed for the day of redemption. Get rid of all bitterness, rage and anger, brawling and slander, along with every form of malice. Be kind and

compassionate to one another, forgiving each other, just as in Christ God forgave you.

As a transforming community, the Body of Christ is to express in every way the personality of God. *And it is as a community of "imitators of God ... as dearly loved children," who "live a life of love, just as Christ loved us and gave himself up for us" (Eph. 5:1), that the Church itself becomes the most powerful force possible in Christian education.*

truth in life

Earlier I noted that in insisting on the importance of relationships (and particularly of the love relationship) in Christian education, I am in no way abandoning or lessening commitment to Truth. Scripture clearly speaks of itself as propositional truth to which man (limited as he is to discovery through experience within space/time) has no access. This information about the very "thoughts of God" has been revealed to us by the Holy Spirit through men who were specially inspired and given words not "taught us by human wisdom but in words taught by the Spirit" (cf. 1 Cor. 3:8-16). So confident are we of this that we can say with the apostle that because of revelation "we have the mind of Christ."

At the same time, God has not contented Himself with merely giving us Truth as information. He also has given us truth *in life.* This is, of course, one of the powerful reasons behind the incarnation. Beside redemption stands the purpose of revelation: "in these last days (God) has spoken to us by his Son" (Heb. 1:2). Concepts *about* God were given living expression when the Word became flesh "and lived for a while among us" (John 1:14). This thought is one John seems constantly aware of: "That which was from the beginning, which we have heard, which we have seen with our eyes, which we have looked at and our hands have touched — this we proclaim concerning the Word of life" (1 John 1:1-3). Information communicated in words had been believed by the godly: that same truth revealed in the personality of a human being was not only believed — it was perceived as a *jolting reality.*

This is part of the genius and the uniqueness of the task of Christian education. God's truth must be revealed as reality, so that increasingly the believer will trust himself to God to experience the realities the Word portrays. Truth and example are always to go together. Word and incarnation are to be inseparable. Concept and human model are twin essentials, never to be torn apart. *This is why Christian education is an inter-personal ministry.* This is why when we design Christian educa-tion systems we *must* provide for exploration of the Word in a relational context, in which the liveable reality of God's words can be seen and experienced through others. This too is why we need an intimate relational context, where love and trust free us to truly know and reveal ourselves to one another.

No wonder Paul writes to young Timothy, "Watch your *life* and doctrine closely" (1 Tim. 4:16), and encourages him to "set an example for the believers in speech, in life, in love, in faith and in purity" (4:12). Just as Timothy knew "all about" Paul's "teaching, my way of life, my purpose, faith, patience, love, en-durance, persecutions, sufferings" (2 Tim. 3:10), so other be-lievers were to know all about Timothy. In Timothy's person truth and life were to harmonize. In Timothy, the *reality* of con-cepts God's Word expressed was to be visibly expressed.

process, not product. The intimacy of relationship implied by the incarnation of reality which is to accompany the teaching of revealed truth is something many people find threatening. One of the reasons for this threat is their awareness of their own imperfection. Yet it is clear that the relationships which the Bible describes as appropriate between Christians are extremely self-revealing. We are to share and bear each other's burdens (Gal. 6:1). We are at times going to become angry ... and the anger is not to be buried but dealt with before the sun goes down (Eph. 4:26). Both depressed and joyful states are to be shared (1 Cor. 12:26). We are going to hurt each other, and sin against each other ... and will constantly need to have strained relationships restored by giving and receiving forgive-ness (Eph. 4:32; Col. 3:13). Apparently we are even to be so close that it is possible for us to admit our sins to each other and join in prayer for wholeness (James 5:16).

It is clear from indications like these that intimate relation-ships in the Church will reveal a lack of perfection! We will not be able to model perfectly, as Jesus did, the character that is to become ours. What then do believers model as they come to know one another in the Body's love relationship? We *model for one another the process of transformation.* We can afford to let ourselves be known as imperfect persons, for in revealing our imperfection we also reveal the ministry which the Holy Spirit is performing in working His progressive change!

Second Corinthians 3 is very instructive here. Paul reminds us of Moses, whose face shown with glory after his time with God on Sinai. The transformed face stunned Israel with its radiance ... and Moses was glad! But soon Moses noticed that the radiance was fading. He was beginning to look human again. And so Moses put on a veil "to keep the Israelites from gazing at [his face] while the radiance was fading away" (3:13). A process of *deterioration* was taking place, and Moses had to hide it. Now Paul applies to us the freedom that the Spirit's ministry in us brings. In us no *deterioration* is taking place, but rather *transformation*. The process does not involve progressive *loss* of glory, but a progressive *gaining* of glory. *And because we are sure that God is working in us, we remove the veils that hide us from others!* How exciting! "Where the Spirit of the Lord is, there is freedom," Paul says. "And we, who with unveiled faces all reflect the Lord's glory, are being transformed into his likeness with ever-increasing glory, which comes from the Lord, who is the Spirit" (3:17, 18).

freedom to grow. Understanding God's work in us as a process, and finding in the love and acceptance of other believers freedom to be ourselves and to accept ourselves, we also find the freedom to grow. In the Body love moves us to "Accept him whose faith is weak, without passing judgment on disputable matters" (Rom. 14:1). Rather than "passing judgment on one another," we are to "make up [our] mind not to put any stumbling block or obstacle in [our] brother's way" and "act in love" (Rom. 14:13, 15). Concentration in the community is on "every effort to do what leads to peace and mutual edification" (Rom. 14:19). Given this kind of freedom to be ourselves, supported by the love of others who not only reflect Christ's love for us but also reveal in their personalities the reality of Scripture's transforming promise, believers experience the freedom to grow.

multiple models. It is important in thinking of Christian education theologically to realize that this portrait of the community points up the need for multiple models of faith's life. For children, parents surely are primary models. For the church, leaders are to provide powerful models and examples. (No wonder the emphasis on character in the 1 Timothy and Titus description of spiritual leaders for the church!) But the doctrine of the priesthood of all believers, and the parallel teaching that each person in the Body has spiritual gifts to be used in edifying others, highlights the fact that God has provided multiple models of faith's life. *The "school" model of education, with its single teacher whose concern is with content, is totally inadequate for Christian education. Whatever educational approaches the Chris-*

tian develops to express the unique educational ministry of nurturing the development of Christ's life, those approaches must reflect the Bible's teaching that the communication of life is a mutual ministry of and for all.

Christian education *is* different.

In Christian education, our focus is on life.

In Christian education, our goal is transformation.

In Christian education, the total community is involved.

In Christian education, modeling and interpersonal relationships are critical concerns.

PROBE
  case histories
  discussion questions
  thought-provokers
  resources

1. There are many thoughts in this chapter that might well be explored in rather intensive Bible study. Here are a few possible study projects:

   a. Examine 1 Thessalonians 2:4-14, a rather penetrating portrait of Paul's approach to reaching a new community. Possible study questions are: How did the Thessalonians know God loved them? Describe the relationship between Paul and the Thessalonians. How large was the group when Paul ministered there? What was Paul's ministry goal? How could one tell if he reached it? What is the significance of "you know" (v. 5), "share . . . our lives" (v. 8), and "each of you" (v. 11)?

   b. Examine the qualifications for leaders in the church (1 Tim. 3 and Titus 2) and relate each "requirement" to an underlying purpose or a role in facilitating transformation.

   c. Survey the epistles, and pinpoint all that is said in them concerning interpersonal relationships in the Body. From what you find, develop a detailed analysis of the kind of relationships we need to be concerned about in educational settings.

2. Writing in *Educational Technology*, David B. Crispin ("The Technology of Interaction Analysis," 1970, pp. 13-17) summarizes one approach to evaluating relational and behavioral patterns in the classroom. As this article illustrates, educators have been concerned with classroom relationships . . . increasingly so in the past decade. So look over the following quote and explanation of the Flanders system (cf. *The Role of the Teacher in the Classroom*, by Edmund Amidon and Ned Flanders, Association for Productive Teaching, Inc., Minneapolis, 1967). Then (a) describe the kinds of relationships which seem to be implied by the various criteria, and (b) develop your own analysis criterion for observation of a Sunday school or other Christian education teaching/learning situation.

If you have opportunity, visit a classroom and attempt to fill out an evaluation form. What would you expect to find? What do you find? Here's the quote:

Flanders classifies all teacher statements as either *direct* or *indirect. Direct statements minimize student freedom to respond. Indirect teacher statements maximize student response freedom.* There are four categories of teacher behavior subsumed within the *indirect* class:

1. *Accepts feeling: accepts and clarifies the feeling tone of the student in a non-threatening manner. Feelings may be positive or negative. Also, predicting or recalling feelings.*
2. *Praises or encourages student behavior. Jokes that release tension, not at the expense of another.*
3. *Accepts or uses ideas of student: clarifying, building, developing ideas, suggestions, by a student.*
4. *Asks questions, about content or procedure, with the intent that a student should answer.*

Flanders' direct class includes three categories:

5. *Lectures: gives facts, or opinions, about content or procedure; expressing his own idea; asking rhetorical questions.*
6. *Gives directions: commands, orders, with which a student is expected to comply.*
7. *Criticizes or justifies authority; statements intended to change student behavior from nonacceptable to acceptable pattern; bawling out someone; extreme self-reference.*

There are two categories of student behavior:

8. *Student talk — response: the teacher initiates the contact or solicits student statement. The student answers a question asked by the teacher, or he responds to a direction the teacher has given. His response is predictable.*
9. *Student talk — initiation: the student initiated the statement. The student wanted to talk. His statement is unpredictable.*

And the last category is other behavior. It includes anything else not included in the other nine:

10. *Silence or confusion: pauses, short periods of silence; periods of confusion in which communication cannot be understood by the observer.*

The Flanders categories are most briefly set forth as follows:

	1 *Accepts feeling*
Indirect	2 *Praises or encourages*
Influence	3 *Accepts, uses, student's ideas*
	4 *Asks questions*
Teacher Talk	5 *Lectures*
Direct	6 *Gives directions*
Influence	7 *Criticizes, justifies authority*

Student Talk	8 Student response to teacher
	9 Student self-initiated response

10 Silence or confusion

3. While educators have been concerned with relational and inter-
actional dimensions of the classroom, many have been discouraged
about the possibility of anything other than cognitive operations
taking place in the school setting. For instance, Richard E. Farson
writes like this in a *Psychology Today* article, "Emotional Barriers to
Education." See if you would agree that his complaint is appropriate as an evaluation of our traditional Christian education
approaches as well.

*At present noncognitive and nonverbal skills just aren't con-
sidered academically respectable. They have not yet been formulated into a conceptual structure; and they seem imprecise, fuzzy,
vague, and even threatening. We feel we must keep the lid on
tightly on Pandora's box, for we fear that it contains the irra-
tional, the potentially explosive elements of human nature.*

*When emotionality or interpersonal relationships escape from
the box, we flinch and take refuge in the dictum that only the
qualified professional is capable of dealing with the layers of
humanness below the rational. Old-fashioned psychiatry is largely
responsible for the prevailing attitude that teachers should avoid
tampering with children's psyches. This nonsense has so fright-
ened teachers that they shun almost any engagement with the
student as a person.*

*We treat each other as if we were very fragile, as if any hurt
or penetration of our defenses would lead to a crumbling of the
entire person; or we regard each other as a tenuously contrived
set of social roles which serves to cover what might be the
frightening reality — a vicious beast, or at best man's "animal
nature."*

*There is no doubt that educating for humanness will call upon
teachers and students to encounter each other in their totality as
human beings, with all of the problems and possibilities, the
hopes and fears, the angers and joys, that make up a person.
To relate to each other in this way, we will have to learn to be
less afraid of what people are like and to recognize that they
are not likely to shatter the moment anyone engages them on an
emotional level.*

*This fear of emotionality is in part, I think, responsible for
our widespread fear of intimacy. We dare not reveal ourselves,
share our feelings. We have developed an elaborate set of social
devices which allows us to put distance between ourselves and
others, which lubricates our relationships, and which gives us
privacy in a crowded and complex society. Even to use such
terms as "intimate" and "loving" disturbs most people. Popular*

belief and much professional opinion holds that the machinery of any social organization, and certainly of a school, will become clogged if people are concerned with each other instead of tending to business. Nevertheless, we have a deep need for moments of shared feeling, for they give us a sense of community, and remind us of our membership in the human race.

What Farson says here might well stimulate us to ask some personal questions about our relationships with others as Christians.

* *What's my reaction to such terms as "intimate" and "loving"?
* *Do I feel comfortable about encountering other believers on an emotional level?
* *Do I dare reveal myself and my emotions?
* *Do I feel somehow that the Bible-teaching business of the church and C.E. would somehow become clogged if we teachers and learners became concerned about each other?
* *Am I eager to "encounter others in their totality as human beings" as a basic part of my Christian experience?

These are questions which will disturb many believers. But these are questions which must be faced. *These are issues in which we must be willing to let the Word of God guide and shape our attitudes and understandings.* How strange if, while aggressively insisting on standing for the Truth of God's Word, we were unwilling to submit to it.

By the way, based on concepts explored in this chapter, and all that can be found in Scripture on this subject, what do you believe is an appropriate response to each of the starred (*) questions above?

life's transmission: the church evangelizing

THE CHURCH	IMPLICATIONS
LIFE	A WHOLE-PERSON FOCUS
LIFE'S GOAL	A DISCIPLING PURPOSE
LIFE'S COMMUNI-CATION	A MODELING METHOD
LIFE'S DYNAMIC	AN INTER-PERSONAL DIMENSION
LIFE'S TRANS-MISSION	AN OVER-FLOWING OUTCOME

A dimension of all life is re-production. To see the Church as growing and building itself up in love (Eph. 4:16) and as commissioned to make disciples (Matt. 28:19) implies not only the nurture of its members, but also evangelism.

And how shall we approach evangelism? Again Jesus provides the key: "Love one another," He begins. And concludes that by this "all men will know that you are my disciples" (John 13:35).

It is important to recognize parallels between the educational and evangelization ministries of the Church. Both, of course, are concerned with the divine life. Both are essentially supernatural ministries, yet are carried on within the context of the natural world.

Paul, writing to the Romans, speaks of his eagerness to preach the gospel at Rome. "I am not ashamed of the gospel," he goes on to say, "because it is the power of God for the salvation of everyone who believes; first for the Jew, then for the Gentile. For in the gospel a righteousness from God is revealed, a righteousness that is by faith from first to last, just as it is written: 'The righteous will live by faith'" (Rom. 1:15-17).

How striking! To communicate a message that is "the power of God for salvation" the great apostle wants to come to Rome . . . and *talk*.

It almost seems inappropriate. Surely the transmission of God's life ought to involve something less common than preaching or conversation. Surely such common, such *natural* means, can hardly do for communicating or nurturing *life*.

And yet, constantly in Scripture, we find that the supernatural is not in conflict with the natural. Channels of communication which any culture uses to transmit beliefs, values, and understandings of life *are just those channels* which the Holy Spirit adapts to the communication and nurture of the divine life! There are words. There are living models to give visible expression to abstract concepts. There are interpersonal relationships which encourage (or discourage) internalization. There is acceptance, and the kind of personal transparency that motivates and moves. There is persuasion, explanation, teaching. There is an active doing to learn new skills and ways of living. There is questioning, dialogue, authority, and obedience. *The Word of God which brings us God's life is processed in human experience in exactly the same way that any words about life to be expressed as culture are processed.*

evangelism as education

The affirmation that God uses natural means to communicate the Word of life is something we have not given sufficient attention to in Christian education or in evangelism. If we do accept this premise, we see interesting parallels between the Church's evangelism and its educational approaches.

For instance,
*In each case, the Word of God is involved.
*In each case, a faith-response is desired.
*In each case, this response is viewed as involving a work of the Holy Spirit.
*In each case, this response is viewed also as actively involving the person.
*In each case, <u>response is facilitated by relationships!</u>

Probably only this last assertion might raise questions. We have been conditioned to see evangelism as a mass meeting in a football stadium, or as knocking on dormitory doors to give a college student a simple four-step prescription. Certainly God does use these means. I am not speaking *against* them. I am suggesting, however, that these represent only *part* of what evangelism can mean . . . and that a relational evangelism, just as a relational Christian education, is in fact to be the emphasis of God's people. We see this when we explore both community evangelism (the way the Body itself communicates new life) and individual evangelism (the ministry of the individual believer to his world).

the witnessing community: The words of Jesus with which we opened the chapter actually are jolting words. Teaching us that His disciples are marked off by love for one another, the Lord goes on to add, "by this shall all men know that you are my disciples."

The emphasis here is not on the fact that we are disciples, but on the fact that we are *His.* The visible, totally convincing reality of Christ's love expressed within the Body of Christ is the most compelling evidence of the gospel's truth we can present. This, along with our communication of the Word, brings the exclamation, "God is really among you" (1 Cor. 14:25)! Such an awareness, of course, need not always stimulate conversion. Paul speaks of it as a testimony of judgment to those who oppose the gospel. And he exhorts the Church to worthy behavior and to unity as such a corporate testimony (Phil. 1:26-30). Still, the nature and character of the Christian community serves as "a model to all the believers in Macedonia and Achaia," and specifically, in the case of the Thessalonians, to the way in which "the Lord's message rang out from you ... everywhere" (cf. 1 Thess. 1:4-10).

We are not to see evangelism as an individual ministry alone, but as a corporate ministry of the Body. The love relationship existing in the Body is the key to the gospel's communication to "all men."

the witnessing individual. While we do have cases of "stranger evangelism" (such as Jesus at the well and Philip with the Ethiopian eunuch), it still is clear that relationships are vital in the individual's witness. Paul warns believers against withdrawing from pagan contacts (1 Cor. 5:9-13). He speaks of believers as testimonials, "written in our hearts and yet open for anyone to inspect and read. You are," he says, "an open letter about Christ, delivered by us and written, not with pen and ink but with the Spirit of the living God, engraved not on stone, but on human hearts" (2 Cor. 3:1-3, Phillips).

Whatever the initial reaction of the spiritually dead to the new attitudes and behaviors growing within those who have been given life, the believers' "conduct among the surrounding peoples in your different countries should always be good and right." There may be opposition and even slander as "evil-doers." Yet, when troubles come, and the commitment of the believer to love is revealed, "they will glorify God when they see how well you conduct yourselves" (cf. 1 Peter 2:12, Phillips).

The contact which the believer has in the world with the not yet saved provides a channel for two kinds of witness: the reflective witness, and the initiative witness. By *reflective witness* I mean the opportunity to see the character transformation which God the Spirit is working. The fruit He produces, the love and joy and peace and patience spoken of in Galatians 5:22, 23, are compelling proof of Christ's reality. *To incarnate the Spirit's work before men, we need to be close enough to them for them to see Jesus in us.* The withdrawal of Christians from involvement in society, and from close relationships with acquaintances, is hardly supportive of God's purposes in evangelism.

But the Bible speaks also of an *initiative witness.* Strikingly, this is not portrayed in Scripture so much as an initiative in speaking the Word, though we are to be always "prepared to give an answer to everyone who asks you to give the reason for the hope that you have" and then to do so "as one speaking the very words of God," (1 Peter 3:15; 4:11). Instead we are to be *aggressive lovers of men,* obeying Jesus' command to "Love your enemies" (Luke 6:27).

This entire Luke 6 passage (vv. 27-42) is significant. Jesus begins with the command to love enemies . . . even those who curse, strike, or steal from you (vv. 27-31). He notes that there is a kind of love in human society based on reciprocity: men normally love those who love them (vv. 32-34). But the Christian has now taken a stand with God: God's own life has been given to him. In taking a share in the divine nature, the believer also finds himself unwillingly at odds with men who lack the divine life. The non-Christian, spiritually dead and an enemy of God (Rom. 5:6-10), may take the adversary role with us as well!

How are we to respond? *As God does.* Christ "died for the ungodly" (Rom. 5:6). It was when we were enemies that the great sacrifice was made. It is here, the Bible says, that we discover the meaning of love. "God loved us, and gave his son for us" (1 John 4:10). The atoning sacrifice of Jesus for us is the ultimate revelation of the love we are invited now to receive by faith in Christ. Now Jesus' words come to us with the invitation to participate in this same kind of relationship with the men and women around us. "Love your enemies," He says, "do good to them, and lend to them without expecting to get anything back. Then your reward will be great, and you will be sons of the

Most High, because he is kind to the ungrateful and wicked. Be merciful, just as your Father is merciful" (Luke 6:35, 36).

Living as Jesus lived in our world means taking the initiative, and reaching out in love. Even to our enemies. As sons of the Father, bearers of His heredity, we are to enter the society of our world and live out His life of love.

But the Luke passage continues. What will happen if we take love's initiative? People will respond! "The measure you use, it will be measured to you" (v. 38).

And then Jesus gave the parable of the blind man leading the blind. The point? To lead, you must see. To love, you must experience love and grow in your capacity to express it. At this point Jesus introduces that pungent statement about discipleship. When fully equipped the disciple will "be like" his teacher (vv. 39, 40). How clear the message is. We are called to live God's love in a lost world. *But to live love, we must bear God's likeness. To reflect His character, we must have His character. The discipling of the believer is essential in initiative evangelism.* It is this distinctive aspect of the relationship between Christian education and evangelism we have tended to overlook. Rather than focus in our churches on building believers whose increasing maturity will equip them for evangelism, we have tended to take the Church and reshape it as an evangelistic tool. Forsaking and ignoring the Bible's clear emphasis on the Church as a community whose primary ministry is a nurturing one, we have attempted to give *words* to persons whose lives do not incarnate them, and to hurl them against the world. And we have for the most part come to experience failure, frustration, and defeat.

Is there no awareness of the impact of Jesus' next words in Luke? "First pay attention to the plank in your own eye," He insists. Then work on the speck in your brother's eye (6:41, 42). We must see clearly before we hurry to heal others. The distortions that mark our own understandings and attitudes need to be dealt with. Ultimately the goodness of a tree is recognized by its fruit (Luke 6:43-45). The "overflow the heart" *will be* expressed in what the mouth speaks. The tree *will be* "recognized by its fruit."

Christian education and evangelism

Christian education, theologically conceived, has a complex and intimate relationship with evangelism.

The two are related, for both are concerned with life and life's communication. Thus there is no intrinsic difference between how one educates and how one evangelizes! The specific content of the message may differ, but the medium through which the transmission of the message is facilitated is the same.

The two are related, again, because one is an outgrowth of the other. Effective evangelism hinges on discipleship . . . on likeness to Christ. It is for this task of nurturing the development of God's life within believers that the Body is designed. The fruit of transformation will enable the non-Christian to recognize the tree from which it grows. Love, incarnated in the community and in the individual, is the divinely ordained, confirming witness to the gospel's Word.

The two, then, are related also in priority. As the first concern of the Church we *must* retain the nurture of the Body. For this is God's order, God's design, God's strategy. This is no retreat from evangelism. Instead it is an affirmation of the evangelistic mission of the people of God. As we grow into His likeness, His love will motivate us, His concern energize us, and the evidence of His presence enable us to witness in power.

PROBE
case histories
discussion questions
thought-provokers
resources

1. Recently an evaluative study of the high-school use of films was conducted for Youth Films, Inc. In the final report, Dr. John S. Stewart, project coordinator and Co-Director of Michigan State University's Values Development Education Program, provides the following summary. He is speaking, of course, of the *evangelistic* process which young people in the Christian community go through in coming to personal commitment.

   How much of what he says do you agree with? In what ways do you feel he is describing education *rather than* evangelism? What kind of distinctions do you want to make between education and evangelism . . . or do you want to make distinctions? Keeping questions like these in mind, probe what Dr. Stewart concludes.

   The job, then, of the religious and moral educator is very simple to describe: it is the job of helping a youth to become a full human being. It is obvious from our developmental conceptual framework that there is a danger in asking a young person to declare himself on this, or that, or the other before he is prepared to answer the question, "Who am I?" Perhaps adults, including dedicated and devout Christians, are demanding that their children be Christians before they are even ready to be people. Christianity is a very demanding religion, requiring enor-

mous faith and dedication. It is a religion that one must grow and develop into, not accept like a package. Perhaps if religious educators stopped worrying about whether or not they were "making Christians out of their students" and worried more about helping them to become people, the students might learn that a good way to be a human being is to become a Christian.

Young people are intensely sensitive to commitment long before they are prepared to give it. If these sensitive young people have a maximum number of opportunities to witness committed Christians truly living their faith then their own sensitivity could eventually develop into the same kind of commitment. Youth must actually see and transact with people who show with their words, their actions, their love, and their lives that they really mean it when they say: "Christ is! Christ lives now! and Christ is the Son of God!" This requires educators who speak from their hearts, and not from their chalkboards; from their lives, not from their books. A true religious educator is not one who merely speaks about Christianity — he is one who is Christianity!

Young people are justifiably tired of adults who do nothing but condemn and warn. They are tired of being told that their clothes are not right, that they are sloppy and lazy, that their music is too loud or too vulgar, and on and on. The way of Jesus Christ is not condemnation, but affirmation! Young people need to see adults who are willing to try to understand them and accept them, adults who express faith and joy, adults who can help them in their sometimes misguided, but always striving, efforts to discover the mystery of life. And so the Christian educator must be able to see the birth of Christ in the life of youth and help the youth to see the mystery for himself. Christ cannot be packaged and sold like a commodity, nor can he be prescribed like a drug or a cure for all that troubles youth. Only witness and faith in the inner developmental processes of the youth can encourage the natural growth of that spirit and light (pp. IX-13, 14).

2. In an article in *Action* magazine ("American Church Growth: Update 1974," Spring, 1974, p. 14) C. Peter Wagner reports four kinds or types of "Church growth" distinguished by the Fuller Seminary Institute of Church Growth. The classification system involves four types of growth, and three kinds of evangelism. Look the typology over, and then respond to the questions following it.

Type 1, *Internal Growth*. This is what happens within the body. It includes organic growth, church renewal, body life, prayer, tithing, social service, koinonia, theologizing, ministerial training, etc. It also includes E(1) evangelism which means leading unconverted church members to Christ wherever necessary.

Type 2, *Expansion Growth*. This is the local church adding membership to its rolls; it is what happens for example when the

Coral Ridge Presbyterian Church grows from 17 to 2,500 members in ten years.

Type 3, Extension Growth. This is also called "church planting." The local church or denomination grows by planting churches which in turn grow to become independent congregations. Extension growth is not stressed enough as an evangelistic tool in America.

Type 4, Bridging Growth. Bridging growth is the most complex, since it involves church planting in a different culture. The missionary task of the church is most deeply involved here, although crosscultural church planting opportunities are plentiful in the United States and Canada as well.

As for evangelism, the typology includes:

E(1) reaching people of the same cultural background
E(2) reaching people of slightly different cultural background
E(3) reaching people of vastly different cultural background

Looking at this typology, it is clear that Dr. Stewart (see 1, above) seems to be talking about Type 1 growth and E(1) evangelism.

(a) Can you define ways that gospel communication *would* differ in other Type and E(2), E(3) settings?
(b) Can you define ways that gospel communication *should* differ?
(c) Can you define ways that gospel communication should be the same?
(d) Do you see any advantages or any dangers in equating evangelism and "church growth"? (For instance, are the two the same? What kind of "programs" are likely to result if they are equated which may not be implied if they are not equated?)

3. The concept of the overflow of Christ's life through the believer cannot be summed up in evangelism alone. There is the question of the believer's total contact and influence on the society in which he lives.

In an earlier book (*A New Face for the Church,* Zondervan, Grand Rapids, 1970), I wrote about the Church as existing primarily for itself; that is, with the purpose of the Body designed by God essentially for nurture. There too I wrote of an "Overflow of Life." Here is a paragraph beginning that section. You might find it interesting to use this paragraph as a "lead," and go on to "complete" the rest of that chapter . . . either as you think I might have, or as you think it should have been completed. If you want to check what you write against what I wrote, you can find my discussion on pages 136-139 of that book.

So here's that lead paragraph. Take off from here . . . and have fun!

My understanding of the church, bound as it is by Scripture, is that it must be different. The church described in the Word, and realized at various times in history, does exist for itself. The church, the community of those who believe, ministers as a community only to believers. It is no "church" which organizes itself to minister to the broader society beyond itself.

At the same time, I insist that this view of the church is not a selfish one. It does not constitute withdrawal from or abandonment of the world. In fact, letting the church be herself, a transforming community, is the only way we can effectively communicate God's love to the men around us. The Christian called to live Christ's life in the world (John 17) must be involved!

What does involvement mean?

6

a whole-person focus

THE CHURCH	IMPLICATIONS
LIFE	A WHOLE-PERSON FOCUS
LIFE'S GOAL	A DISCIPLING PURPOSE
LIFE'S COMMUNI-CATION	A MODELING METHOD
LIFE'S DYNAMIC	AN INTER-PERSONAL DIMENSION
LIFE'S TRANS-MISSION	AN OVER-FLOWING OUTCOME

To affirm that Life sets the Church apart, and that Life is the central concern of Christian education, challenges our traditional approach to C.E. We have (rightly) been concerned with transmitting truth about God: with belief. We have (rightly) been concerned with behavior. But we have failed in one significant respect. We have not maintained a balanced, whole-person focus in our educational ministries. We have not designed our educational ministry to link in a holistic way all that Christian faith means to the learner.

We are all used to thinking of the personality as composed of more than one's beliefs. We speak of attitudes. Of emotions (affect). Of perception ... the particular way an individual understands and relates to people and situations. Of behavior. Of values.

All these, usually not too well-defined in our thinking, are recognized as playing significant parts in personality. And we can add others. Self-concept. Motives. Faith. And so on. What is interesting is that in our culture we have picked out one element and given it a peculiar priority. That element is *belief*. Somehow all of our educational efforts seem to hinge on the idea that if we change belief, we change the personality in every respect. We also assume that to change belief we need only to provide new information.

This is not a new notion. It's a pre-Christian concept, rooted deeply in Western thought. It was expressed many centuries ago by Plato who insisted that if a man only knew the Good, he would surely choose it. Thus "knowing" was given the highest priority, for through knowing, beliefs, attitudes, values, and behaviors were to be reshaped.

At first glance this may seem to be a Christian idea as well. We read in Scripture things like "you will know the truth, and the truth will set you free" (John 8:32). Even the famous transformation verse, "be transformed through the renewing of your mind," seems to give priority to information and to belief. But it is only at first glance. Jesus' statement about "knowing the truth" was preceded by an exhortation to continue in His words. When you respond to My teaching, He was saying, you will *know by experience* the Truth which revelation reveals. As for Romans 12:2, the transformation is said to be by the "renewing of your *voũs* (nous)." In Greek this speaks not of belief, but of the "*mind, attitude, way of thinking,* as the sum total of the whole mental and moral state of being" (Arndt and Gingrich, *Greek-English Lexicon,* p. 547). Our word "perception" may be closer here to the meaning of *voũs* . The apostle is pointing out that our whole understanding of life must be restructured if we are to "be able to test and approve what God's will is" (Rom. 12:2b).

Behavioral scientists who have struggled with concepts like attitude have moved toward the holistic as well. For instance, some tended to take "attitude" as a unidimensional concept, referring only to one's positive, negative, or neutral "feelings" about an object (cf. Thurstone). Later theorists distinguished between beliefs about an object and attitude toward an object, suggesting that "belief about" is a predictor of attitude. (See M. A. Fishbein's investigation of the interrelationship between beliefs about an object and the attitude toward that object. Unpublished doctoral dissertation, U.C.L.A., 1961.) Rosenberg ("Cognitive Structure and Attitudinal Affect," *Journal of Abnormal and Social Psychology,* 1956) noted that the use of a concept was more significant in the development of an attitude than a formally learned idea. That is, when an idea about an object has been informally learned through situations in which the concept has been applied, that idea has a more direct impact on attitude.

Later still Rosenberg and others explored the relationships between affective, behavioral, and cognitive components of attitude. It was noted that changes could occur in any direction — from behavior to affect and cognition, from affect to behavior and cognition, as well as from cognition to affect and behavior. And many have noted that supposedly appropriate changes induced in one dimension (particularly the cognitive) *need not* be reflected in changes in the others. For instance, information may be provided and accepted that Blacks are *not* intellectually inferior . . . but the prejudiced person who has argued a supposed inferiority to justify his prejudice is unlikely to change his affective orientation or his behavior.

linked systems

The concept that all the dimensions of personality are linked is one that we would of course want to accept. The idea that we can change the equilibrium of the system, and cause change (growth, learning, or whatever one might want to term it), is, on the face of it, both reasonable and certain.

Dissonance (the feeling of being out of harmony) is something that does seem to exist in us and something that is a cause for change.

But the assumption that attack on a *single* system element will produce desired change is *not* reasonable, nor certain! There are too many intervening variables. There are too many ways to isolate or modify the impact of isolated changes.

For instance, let's suppose we are trying to touch the whole person through his beliefs. It would seem, because

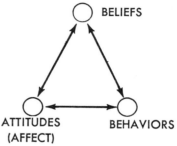

These elements and others of the personality are linked in a generally harmonious way. Normally there will be a balanced relationship between how a person believes, feels, and acts, toward an object.

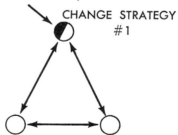

Our educational or change strategy relies on intervening at one point in the system: here in the cognitive.

the systems are linked, that we would change the whole person by changing his beliefs. But this is not necessarily so! There are a number of ways the person can handle new information to isolate it from the system.

→ *He may deny it.* "I believe the Bible, but that can't be true."

→ *He may relativize it.* "This is true only for certain people at certain times."

→ *He may redefine it.* "There are two possible meanings, and this is the one I accept for this word."

→ *He may compartmentalize it.* "This is a spiritual concept, for my Sunday but not my Monday life."

→ *He may reintegrate it.* "This speaks of a goal; when I have more faith it may be possible for me, but it's not now."

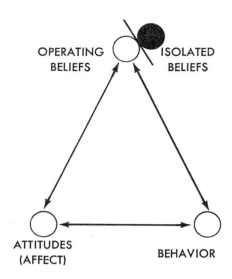

Intervention at a single point is more likely to lead to isolation of taught beliefs from the operating beliefs which actually function with other system elements in daily life.

In these and *many other ways* a person can reduce dissonance or disequilibrium within his personality. When Christians use such mechanisms it is not at all unusual for them to attend church, hold conservative beliefs, and fail completely to develop attitudes, values, and behaviors which are in harmony with the gospel!

Current criticism of schooling often focuses on just this tendency of formal learning to develop isolated rather than operating beliefs. Recall Drucker's description of assumptions underlying schooling "in every country" (p. 38):

1) learning is a separate and distinct "intellectual" activity;
2) learning goes on in a separate organ, the mind, divorced from the body or emotions;
3) learning is divorced from doing — indeed, opposed to it; at best it is preparation for doing; and
4) learning, because it is preparation, is for the young.

Given the general validity of this description, *why should we be surprised if such teaching and learning seems to have little impact on the total personality!*

Cole S. Brembeck, writing of "The Strategic Uses of Formal and Nonformal Education" in *New Strategies for Educational Development* points out that

> separation of learning from action has a deep psychological impact upon the learner. He begins his formal education knowing that what he will learn is removed from the everyday reality of adult society. It is academic. This awareness is revealed in many ways. For example, the common urge of students to "get out" of school expresses a great deal about the meaning they attach to being "in." We speak of education as being "preparation" for the "real" world, thus denying it a reality of its own. Constant calls that school be "relevant" implies that by nature it is not.
>
> All this is not to say that we do not value school learning. We obviously do. I am speaking about the *way* we value it, how that way illuminates the detached nature of schools, and how it subtly discounts the learning in the mind of the learner. Thus this structural characteristic of schooling modifies and shapes its capacity to perform educational tasks (p. 58).[1]

Brembeck is not arguing that school has *no* function or valid place in education. He is instead pointing out that while schools may be suited to *some purposes,* there are others for which they are *not* suited! Formal education may be effective in dealing with symbols and concepts abstracted from life. But when change and development in the total personality are desired, non-formal education has all the advantages.

Mayer Fortes' "Social and Psychological Aspects of Education in Taleland" (in Middleton [ed]; *From Child to Adult: Studies in the Anthropology of Education*) describes how the Tallensi

> teach through real situations which children are drawn to participate in because it is expected that they are capable and desirous of mastering the necessary skills.
>
> A training situation demands atomic modes of response; the real situation requires organic modes of response. In constructing a training situation we envisage a skill or observance as an end-product at the perfection of which we aim and therefore arrange it so as to evoke only motor or perceptual practice. Affective or motivational factors are eliminated or ignored. In the real situation behavior is compounded of affect, interest and motive, as well as perceptual and motor functions. Learning becomes purposive. Every advance in knowledge or skill is prag-

[1]From *New Strategies for Educational Development* by Cole S. Brembeck and Timothy J. Thompson (Lexington, Mass.: Lexington Books, D.C. Heath and Co., 1973). Used by permission.

matic, directed to achieve a result there and then, as well as adding to a previous level of adequacy (p. 38).[2]

✳ The point which both are making is this. *If we are dealing with life style issues, we must concern ourselves with the person as a whole! Rather than seeking to induce change and growth by contacting the personality at a single point (his knowledge or beliefs), we need to contact persons at every point of their personalities ... at the same time!*

✳ A second affirmation is involved in this first commitment. If we are to touch that total personality, *the primary context in which teaching/learning must take place is "real situations,"* not *the formal school where we have communicated to even the youngest that what is learned here is not really related to life.*

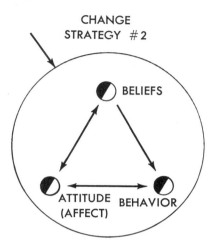

CHANGE STRATEGY #2

Our educational or change strategy relies on intervening at *all* points in the system at the same time.

belief vs. beliefs

It should, I hope, be clear that nothing in this chapter in any way challenges the idea that there is revealed Truth which we are to come to know. What instead is being challenged is the assumption that to have an *isolated belief* in what the Bible teaches is either sufficient or desirable!

John's use of the concept "believe" is an instructive one. His emphasis is not on the noun but on the verb! It is to him the *act of believing* which is important. This is vital for us to grasp. At heart, faith is a response to God; a readiness for wholehearted involvement in His will as He makes it known to us. Such faith integrates the totality of the human personality around what is known to be true. Grasping the truth conceptually, coming to perceive situations in view of truth, coming to desire what we

[2]From *From Child to Adult*. Copyright © 1970 by John Middleton. Used by permission of Doubleday & Co., Inc.

see to be God's will, choosing to respond in obedience to Him ... all these elements are essential to what Christian faith intrinsically is. It is *life* that makes the difference in our faith. And it is as a whole, a living personality, that we must learn and express Christian faith.

Because the critical issue in Christian faith is life, it follows that Christian education always must be concerned with life. Christian education must be designed for the whole person, not for a single dimension of his personality. For this reason we *must* begin to challenge what we have done and are doing in Christian education. We must begin to raise the question of whether we are communicating life ... or isolated beliefs. We must ask whether or not our acceptance of secular school structures as the context for the communication of faith may not actually hinder Christian growth. By attempting to teach faith in "school" settings we perhaps have inadvertently given learners the impression that biblical truth is for the mind only, divorced from doing, and that learning God's Word is a separate and distinct intellectual activity for the young!

Certainly we must at least recognize that formal and informal education are both options for the Church, and that each is best suited for certain specific tasks. We can hardly ask our educational agencies to do the *entire* task of nurturing faith as life. We need to ask ourselves, What specifically is the role of formal learning in Christianity? What specifically is the role of informal learning? How do we design educational ministries which enable each kind of learning to take place?

We will explore these questions and look further at the implications of our theology as we move on in this section. But for now, this summary highlights what is important:

*We are concerned with the whole person.

*Change strategy 1 (the formal schooling approach) is not adequate to effect changes across the total personality, tending instead to produce *isolated* rather than *operating* beliefs.

*Change strategy 2 (a nonformal learning approach) does a better job of producing whole-person growth and change, for it deals with all personality elements (affect, behaviors, values, perceptions, etc.) at the same time that it deals with belief (e.g., content).

Somehow it seems appropriate then to be ready to move in our Christian education toward greater dependence on the nonformal and away from dependence on the formal learning models for ministry.

PROBE
case histories
discussion questions
thought-provokers
resources

1. The distinction between formal and nonformal learning is an important one that will play a significant role in the position this book takes. If the terminology is unfamiliar, it may be helpful to take a look at the Brembeck and Thompson book quoted on page 64.

In the meantime, here are two quotes from that book which may be helpful. They also lead to several possible "stretching" assignments.

A. Brembeck describes a shepherd boy who at the age of ten has become skilled at his task. He uses this boy's "education" to illustrate something of the structure of nonformal education.

First, the shepherd boy's education took place within the context of immediate and meaningful action, work. Second, there was no gap between learning and the use of it. Indeed, learning grew out of the need for it. Learning and doing were so mixed up that it would have been hard to sort them out. Third, learning took place as a part of normal living; there was nothing of the apparatus of formal schools, no lessons or classes, no artificial rewards and punishments. Learning was so natural that the shepherd boy was hardly aware that it was taking place. Fourth, the learner saw a connection between one aspect of the task and the whole task. He could easily see what caring for a new lamb meant to the family's welfare, because he had observed the life cycle of a sheep and its relationship to what he wore and ate. The boy did not need to be told that caring for sheep was important; this was one of the accepted values by which his whole family survived. Fifth, the shepherd boy's "teacher" was associated with his "student" in carrying on meaningful action. In a sense the boy's father was a co-worker, superior only in knowledge and skill. The role of teacher and student balanced harmoniously. Sixth, the shepherd boy's education incorporated within itself some important factors that stimulate learning. There was no arbitrary decision about what the boy should be capable of doing at a certain stage of his development. As he demonstrated his readiness he simply assumed new responsibilities. He needed no external rewards, such as grades and certificates. His satisfaction came from assuming an adult role early in life. His learning provided a kind of security which comes from taking one's accepted place in the family among one's peers.[3]

  1) Looking at this report, to what extent can the structural characteristics of nonformal education be adapted to modern society? to the modern Christian world?

  2) Compare this passage from Brembeck with Deuteronomy 6:1-8. What parallels do you see? How does this help you to understand Deuteronomy better?

  3) Describe in detail how the doctrine of sovereignty might be taught/learned in (a) the formal teaching setting, (b) the nonformal setting.

  4) If we were to work toward the development of nonformal Christian education ministries, what might be involved? Can you develop several functional equivalents of each of the several structural characteristics Brembeck distinguishes?

There is no doubt that forcing ourselves to think along unfamiliar pathways is difficult. As Brembeck says, it seems ironical that we are both familiar with such modes of learning, and in ignorance about them! But it is important that we learn to think of learning and education in ways which do not equate them with formal instruction.

B. In the same chapter Brembeck states ten working hypotheses about education. Which of them seem to you particularly valid for Christian education? Write a brief paragraph spelling out implications of each for C.E. as you see them.

  1. The unique characteristics of formal and nonformal education may be discovered in the structures of their respective learning environments.

  2. These unique structural characteristics equip each to perform certain tasks better than others.

  3. We have overloaded the formal system beyond its capacity with tasks it is not well suited to handle.

  4. We underutilize the nonformal system in terms of certain of its unique capacities.

  5. Prescriptions of reform of the formal system which ignore its structural capacity are exercises in futility.

  6. One of the critical differences between the structural environments of education is their proximity to work, immediate action, and the opportunity to put to use what is learned. This difference is basic, for nonformal education is characteristically carried on within a context of action, work, and use. Formal educa-

[3]Brembeck and Thompson, *New Strategies.*

tion, on the other hand, takes place outside this context, just by dint of taking place in a school.

7. For this reason nonformal education is a better mode where the object is to change immediate action or to create new action, and formal education is superior where immediate action is subordinated to abstract learning or concept building, looking toward longer range change.

8. Future education policy must become total in the sense that it employs *all* the available means of education to meet increasingly diverse types of demands. The time when formal education could cope with all the learning demands of a complex society is past. We should realize it and adjust education policy accordingly.

9. Future education policy must reckon with life spans rather than school years. The education process must be viewed in the context of a developmental sequence that begins early in life and ends, if it ever does, with adults participating in responsible citizenship.

10. Considering the changes that take place in an individual's educational needs over the life span and the variety of available modes of education, it becomes possible to sketch out a model for future educational policy and practice.

2. For a challenging exercise, select at random one Junior age Sunday school lesson. Examine what is being taught. Then attempt to specify (a) how that same content might be taught in a nonformal setting, and (b) what, if any, might you expect differences in outcome to be?

7

a discipling purpose

THE CHURCH	IMPLICATIONS
LIFE	A WHOLE-PERSON FOCUS
LIFE'S GOAL	A DISCIPLING PURPOSE
LIFE'S COMMUNI-CATION	A MODELING METHOD
LIFE'S DYNAMIC	AN INTER-PERSONAL DIMENSION
LIFE'S TRANS-MISSION	AN OVER-FLOWING OUTCOME

God's life within us has its own character—and goal. God is at work, shaping persons toward His likeness. This must be seen as a whole-person concern. We are to come to see life and its meaning through His eyes. We are to love as He loves. We are to choose His will as our will. We are to value what He holds important. Likeness is the goal of discipling ... and the task of Christian education.

To fasten on a discipling purpose for Christian education (a purpose defined by our theology and thus one to which we must give fullest commitment) means that we must seek educational strategies which facilitate growth in likeness. We cannot be satisfied to retrench; to insist that because in our present educational programs we do "teach the Bible," the programs themselves are beyond criticism.

This a common reaction. Somehow because what we are attempting to do ("teach the Bible") has validity, we tend to feel that our programs and methods are valid. And we tend to view criticism of methodology as an attack on "Bible teaching"! No matter how obviously different the two considerations (what is being communicated, and how it is being communicated), there is an emotional reaction that clouds the distinction, and permits

70

us to resist recognition of the weaknesses in what we have been doing.

So let's make a distinction here. Scripture as God's Word, as His revelation of Truth, must be taught — and learned. We need not and cannot retreat from a high view of Scripture's inspiration and its authority.

But Scripture need not be taught *as it has been taught!* In fact our "school" approach to Bible teaching has all the weaknesses of the first change strategy described in the last chapter. We have attempted to change persons by contact at one point of the personality (the cognitive), and by the simple expedient of providing new (revealed) information. The result far too often has been the development of a distorted faith: a faith that takes the form of beliefs isolated from the total personality. To a great extent, the reason individuals process faith's content as they do is that the Bible has been taught in that school setting which learners have taken to imply a content which is to be intellectualized, divorced from body and emotion, and divorced from doing.

The suggestion this book makes is that we rethink our approach to teaching, and reshape it for discipling; that we find a better match between how we communicate Scripture and what the Word is designed by God to do.

Such reshaping demands that we give serious attention to the nonformal learning setting ... and that we think more deeply about learning itself.

learning theory

There is today no coherent, generally agreed-on theory of human learning which guides educational efforts. Summing up the general situation, Walter B. Kolesnik in *Educational Psychology* writes:

> Several theories of learning, however, have been advanced, which may be classified into main schools: *associative* and *field* theories. Both association and field theories are based on monistic concepts of human nature. But even within the framework of monism, there is a difference of opinion as to what man is. To an associationist man is little more than a complex machine. His behavior is largely if not entirely determined by his environment. His purposes or goals are often irrelevant. Cognition is either denied or minimized. To a field theorist man is an energy system, an adaptive, purposeful creature whose behavior is determined by the manner in which he perceives his environment. Both these schools have their factions or splinter groups, so that not even all who are classed as associationists,

for example, are in complete agreement with one another on all relevant points.

Association theories of learning have been criticized on the grounds that they are mechanistic and deterministic. Man's conduct is made to depend on external factors over which he may have little or no control. Like a machine, man is "hooked up" so that, given a particular stimulus, a particular response may be expected almost automatically. Association theories, moreover, do not seem to offer adequate explanations of reasoning, creative thinking, or the operation of other higher mental processes. These theories, however, are simple, straightforward, and clear cut. They not only explain but help defend some of the practices in the more traditional or teacher-centered type of classroom. Field theories, on the other hand, have been attacked as vague and indefinite, and as little more than attempts to say some very commonplace things in esoteric language. These theories do not tell a teacher what to do or how to do it specifically as the associationist theories do, but they assign a larger role to man's cognitive powers and attempt to explain higher-level forms of learning. Educational practices which flow from field theories are more likely to be found in the progressively oriented, child-centered type of school.

Neither association nor field theories explain or attempt to explain learning in its ultimate, philosophical causes. Both theories, however, have some truth in them. Though each explains certain forms of learning, neither one explains all forms satisfactorily (p. 218).[1]

As Kolesnik's summary points up, no family of learning theories adequately explains *how* a person learns. What is more significant, however, learning theories do contain assumptions about man and his interactions with environment. It is far more fruitful to look at the assumptions than to attempt, as theorists do, to describe what goes inside a person when he "learns."

What typologies help us think about learning if we do look, not at learning mechanisms, but at assumptions about man and his transactions? Here are four typologies which may help us isolate issues:

➤ *Type one:* single-factor theory

Behaviorism provides a contemporary example of a single-factor theory. It is single-factored because it sees man as essentially undifferentiated from his environment. Both are products of a common evolution, both are determined in the sense of being controlled by antecedent causes. It is also single-factored because the behaviorist sees conditioning, a single cause, as key to teaching and learning. To behaviorists like B. F. Skinner, man (indi-

[1]From *Educational Psychology* by Walter B. Kolesnik. Copyright 1970 by McGraw Hill Book Company, New York. Used by permission.

vidually and socially) should now be scientifically conditioned and manipulated. Old concepts of human freedom and dignity have no meaning.

DETERMINISM

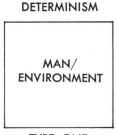

TYPE ONE:
SINGLE-FACTOR THEORY

→ *Type two:* two-factor theory

Field theories tend to be two-factor theories. They view man as active, as dynamically involved with his environment. This relationship between man and environment is transactional: persons organize the external world by their perceptions, shaping themselves and their culture and even natural environment. (For instance, Western music is based on an eight-tone system; much Eastern music on a twelve-tone system. Obviously a wide range of sounds exists in "nature." But it is man's selection of sounds, his organization and perception of them as "music," which gives them that status. There are no eight "ideal" tones *existing in nature* which man "discovers." Thus the relationship between man and environment is transactional: in the interaction of man and nature something new is created, affecting both!)

TRANSACTIONALISM

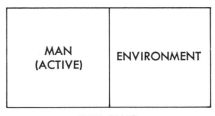

TYPE TWO:
TWO-FACTOR THEORY

→ *Type three:* three-factor theory

Recently the work of Piaget has added a sophistication to the general approach of field theorists. Piaget (who will be discussed later on) has stressed in his work with children and across cultures the fact that human beings must be better defined than as just an "active" organism. Piaget explored the cognitive structure of developing persons, and noted that the *way* man organizes his environment is controlled by cognitive capacities all men have, and which develop sequentially!

The impact of his work is to point up the fact that an infinite number of possibilities do not exist, but that man's "nature" limits and defines the ways in which he can interact with and organize his environment. While man is still seen as having a transactional relationship with the world, the structure of his mind plays a critical role in the transactions which can take place.

Thus Piaget adds a third factor to those we must be concerned with in thinking about learning ... a factor which has been of great concern recently in childhood education, but which also is of great philosophical significance to our thinking about man plus the nature of learning.

TRANSACTIONAL/STRUCTURAL

MAN (ACTIVE)	
	ENVIRONMENT
MAN (STRUCTURAL)	

TYPE THREE:
THREE-FACTOR THEORY

→ *Type four:* four-factor theory

The secular philosopher tends to stop at a three-factor level. He also tends, while today recognizing the structure of man's "nature" as something real, to deny a similar reality to the environment. That is, the *objective nature* of the environment as something differentiated from man and man's perceptions is denied. This denial is purposive: it is designed to eliminate an unhealthy dualism. Yet it cuts us off from a significant affirmation about the nature of creation itself: the affirmation that the material world as well as the human being has a "nature"! It also eliminates the possibility that absolute truth might exist apart from man. If "reality" is viewed solely as a function of man-in-transaction-with-his-environment, then clearly "reality" cannot exist apart from human perceptions. Moreover, all human constructs, and the world-views of all human cultures, have the same validity. There is nothing external to man, nothing objectively true, against which to measure the constructs of individuals and cultures. "Right" and "wrong" become either relative, or something which can be measured only by their place within a sequence of moral cognitions, à la Kohlberg.

What then does the Christian want to affirm? First that the natural environment of man itself permits only a finite number of reality-constructs, limited and determined by the structure of the physical universe. For instance, man cannot create by interaction with the environment a culture in which a person steps out a window and falls *up*. Or one in which there are three sexes. The structure of the physical universe imposes limitations on that kind of creation. But man can (and has!) constructed cultures in which power is equated with right, where war is valued over peace, where conquest of others is valued over service to others, and in which "food" is the mixed blood and milk of cattle rather than the meat. A great variety of possibilities do exist.

Second, the Christian also wants to affirm that there *is* an absolute standard by which constructs of reality can be judged. If you will, the Christian believes in a supernatural environment as well as a natural one: an environment which encompasses the natural and gives it shape and meaning, but which extends beyond it. The Christian believes in a God who Himself is a person, and whose own perceptions are determinative of what is true and false, good and bad, right and wrong, healthy and harmful, meaningful and meaningless, righteous and sinful. It is God's perception which determines these things, not man's.

Note that this affirmation makes *revelation* an absolute necessity. We might discover data about the natural world. We might gather data about world-views and life styles that individuals and cultures have constructed. *But only if God reveals His percep-tions of the universe will we be able to sort out that data and make judgments between competing systems. Only by committing ourselves to God's revelation and through keeping His words will we experience Truth, and will we find the freedom to be who we are.*

It is utterly essential in a four-factor theory of learning that revelation play a critical role.

A sketch of a four-factor theory still leaves us unable to describe the mechanisms' operating within the person which explains learning. But we can describe certain important dimensions of learning if we are concerned with discipling (over against, for instance, memorizing the multiplication tables).

TRANSACTIONAL/STRUCTURAL

MAN (ACTIVE)	ENVIRONMENT (NATURAL/STRUCTURAL)
MAN (STRUCTURAL)	ENVIRONMENT (SUPERNATURAL/REVELATIONAL)

TYPE FOUR:
FOUR-FACTOR THEORY

man is active. Persons always will interact with their environments, and this interaction will be *transactional*. That is, persons will take all kinds of data and attempt to integrate them in ways which make sense to them and which provide guidance for further interactions.

man is structured. There is a "human nature" which limits the number of possible ways which an individual will perceive and process environmental data.

environment is structured. There is a "nature" to the universe as well, which limits the number of possible ways in which an individual can manipulate its data, and thus the number of possible world-views men and cultures can develop.

reality is revealed. God in His grace has spoken to reveal the nature and structure of reality as *He* perceives it. Revelation gives us, through faith's response to God's words, the possibility of experiencing Truth and Reality and of living as free men; free to know the fullest harmony with our own natures, with God, and with the natural and supernatural universes within which we have been placed.

learning life

When conservatives have in the past insisted that there are absolutes, that Truth exists, and that God has revealed them to a mankind which, apart from revelation, could never have discovered or known them, images of indoctrination and "authoritarian" teaching have arisen. Thus John Stewart, in his outstanding work on values education (unpublished doctoral dissertation, Michigan State University, 1974), has characterized an absolutist approach to values as generally stressing the urgency of "early indoctrination, exposure, and training," with "exposure to other systems before the indoctrination process is complete" restricted (p. 29).

Now certainly Christianity is an absolutist faith: we own "one body and one Spirit . . . one Lord, one faith, one baptism; one God and Father of all, who is over all and through all and in all" (Eph. 4:4, 5). And we insist that there is truth, nobility, right, purity, loveliness, the admirable, and the praiseworthy (Phil. 4:4). The Christian, confident that revelation is reliable, trusts Scripture to distinguish also that which is false, base, wrong, impure, ugly, and which is to be rejected. *Yet this commitment in no way means that we must rely on indoctrination to communicate a reality which believers need to learn as a way of life!* In fact, because what God has revealed *is* a reality to be experienced, we can insist that *God's Truth must be learned in exactly the same ways that any "experienced reality" is to be learned!* That is, <u>*we are to be discipled into faith's life in the same way any person is discipled into his or her culture!*</u>

How does this take place? Stewart (p. 132) describes the process of development:

> Development is a transactional process that involves (1) the determining and limiting factors of genetic and maturational aspects of the organism's biological base, (2) the nature, quantity and quality of the organism's direct experience with the environment, (3) the nature and orientation of the socialization process, including parental influences, educational influences, languages, mores, sanctions, etc., and (4) the internal, self-regulating, self-generative process that modulates, mediates, and cybernetically regulates both the organism and its interpretation of the environment.

The third point here is of particular concern. Type three theorists (p. 73) do not overlook the social dimensions of learning, but they still tend to speak as if each person born into the world did in fact create (through process elements 1, 2, and 4 above) his own *unique* world. *But this is not true. His social environment exists as a culture into which he is discipled. The culture, the very language, communicates an existing world-view, an existing complex of attitudes, values, beliefs, and behaviors.* <u>A person learns his likeness through socialization within a culture!</u>

How does a Christian learn *his* likeness? How does he grow and change, learning the divine perceptions, attitudes, emotions, values, and behaviors? If likeness is our concern — if discipling is our goal — then we need to focus our educational efforts not on isolated verbalizations of Truth, but on <u>shaping a community in</u>

which Truth is lived as reality. We need to focus our educational efforts on understanding and using the Church, the Body of Christ, as a culture within which persons who receive the gift of God's life are to be involved, and through this involvement be *socialized* into all that it means to become like Him.

PROBE
    case histories
    discussion questions
    thought-provokers
    resources

1. Romans 12:2 speaks of the believer breaking out of *conformity* to the world and of being *transformed* by a renewing of his mind (cf. p. 61). Can you relate aspects of the type four theory (p. 74) to these two processes? What, for instance, does "conform" imply about man's nature? What does "transform" imply? Is it fair to say "transform" implies an *inner change to match reality?*

2. Colossians 3 speaks of the Christian as one who has put on a "new self" which is in a process of "being renewed in knowledge in the image of its Creator." Look carefully at the *context* of this statement. What evidence or indications do you find in this chapter that such renewal does involve socialization, and does involve the context of a culture?

3. Kolesnik suggests that *field* learning theories are hard to translate into specific do's and don'ts as far as the practice of education is concerned.

    Try to think of "education" in the sense of nonformal education or socialization, and develop a list of at least twenty *do's and don'ts* which, at this point, you feel might guide the practice of a distinctive Christian education.

4. Learning theory is a complex, fascinating, and frustrating field. If you want to sample it, you might glance at the following:

    Frances J. Kelly and John J. Cody, *Educational Psychology: a Behavioral Approach,* Merrill, Chicago (1969).

    Gale Edw. Jensen, *Educational Sociology,* Center for Applied Research in Education, New York (1965).

    Robert F. Boehlke, *Theories of Learning in Christian Education,* The Westminster Press, Philadelphia (1962).

    Morris L. Bigge, *Learning Theories for Teachers,* Harper and Row, New York (1964).

    Paul E. Johnson, *Learning: Theory and Practice,* Thomas Y. Crowell Co., New York (1971).

5. The following are suggested as characteristic of three general

strategies of Christian education. Look at each, and do the following. (a) See if you can add other characteristics to those provided by the author. (b) Also supply additional examples of methodologies. (c) Evaluate each strategy on the basis of the arguments of chapters 6 and 7 of this book.

Three Educational Strategies

		characteristics	*appropriate methodologies*
1.	*idea to life*	begins with concept, not experience of learners	preach
		relationship of teacher to learners not of critical significance	lecture
		concepts have general application to all learners	
		application is made in words (symbols)	
2.	*life to idea*	starts with experience of the learners	role play
		relationship may or may not exist between teacher and learners	discuss movie
		learnings have general application to these learners	act out Bible story
		application is made in words (symbols)	
3.	*life to life*	starts from present experience of teacher and learner	"missions" trip
		teacher participates with learners in close relationship	intra-family conflict
		learning has specific application to these learners *now*	
		application is experienced together	(e.g., "real" experience)

8

a modeling method

THE CHURCH	IMPLICATIONS
LIFE	A WHOLE-PERSON FOCUS
LIFE'S GOAL	A DISCIPLING PURPOSE
LIFE'S COMMUNI-CATION	A MODELING METHOD
LIFE'S DYNAMIC	AN INTER-PERSONAL DIMENSION
LIFE'S TRANS-MISSION	AN OVER-FLOWING OUTCOME

To see the distinctiveness of Christian faith centered in the possession of God's life reminds us that Christian education must have a whole-person focus. To see discipleship, the growth of the person with life more and more toward God's likeness, as Christian education's task, helps us realize that transformation is related to socialization: that the whole Church teaches. To hear Jesus speak of fully developed disciples being like their teachers (Luke 6:40) points us to the method of Christian education: modeling.

As long as we think of teaching our faith primarily as communicating information, it's natural and appropriate to conceive of a teacher as one who knows. As long as we assume communicating faith is a matter of reaching persons through the mind, an essentially intellectual operation, it's natural and appropriate to develop a "school" approach to Christian education. But all this changes if we focus on teaching faith-as-life. To communicate faith-as-life means we must reach and nurture persons in their wholeness. To communicate faith-as-life means that faith's life style as well as faith's content needs to be learned, and that these need to be linked as they are being taught.

In looking for educational strategies that touch persons as wholes, that shape understanding and perceptions and emotions and values and behaviors in a united, integrated way, we have to be impressed by the process of socialization. We have to be impressed by the way a child learns a culture and a language, growing up into the orientation to the world of those around him. We have to be impressed, as well, with the fact that God has designed Christ's Body as a culture. That new believers are exhorted to "grow up into him who is the Head, that is, Christ" (Eph. 4:15). Perhaps even the significance of Jesus' remark to His disciples, that we need to "receive the kingdom of God like a little child" to enter it (Mark 10:15), reflects the need for the believer to learn *as a child does* the life style and likeness of God's children.

The nature of the Church, surveyed in chapters 1 through 5, ought to help us realize that God's discipling method is modeling rather than indoctrination.

* Upon conversion we are joined to other believers in a Body relationship. We are not meant to "go it alone."
* The Body is designed for nurture: "to make increase of itself in love."
* Every member of the Body is gifted by the Holy Spirit to enable him or her to make a contribution to growth.
* Individual and bodily growth come through that which "every joint supplies": believers functioning together promote and support the Church's nurturing task.
* The Body's ministry requires Body members to be with each other, and to minister to each other. Jesus' example in choosing twelve to "be with him" is reflected in the biblical injunction for believers not to forsake gathering together (Heb. 10:24).
* Leaders in the church are selected from those who not only can know and teach truth, but leadership requirements focus on the example they are to provide (1 Tim. 3; Titus 2).
* The stress on relationships within the Body reinforces the uniqueness of this group's existence as a distinctive community within human societies and cultures.

Our choice of socialization as an appropriate approximation of the educational strategy to be adopted by Christian education, then, is rooted not in the behavioral sciences but in theology. It is because of the nature of Christian faith, and the nature of the Church itself, that we focus on *modeling* as the key method.

What is "modeling"?

I've been suggesting that learning Christian faith should be very much like learning speech or manners, in that faith should not be communicated only in artificial situations that demand atomic modes of response, but in real situations where affect, interest, motive, perceptions, and behavior are united. This is essentially a socialization process, "by which persons acquire the knowledge, skills, and dispositions that make them more or less able members of their society" (Orville Brim and Stanton Wheeler, *Socialization After Childhood*, John Wiley & Sons, New York, 1966, p. 3). Socialization thus is viewed to include "all aspects of personality: abilities, knowledge, motivation, conscience, feelings" (Alfred L. Baldwin, *Theories of Child Development*, John Wiley and Sons, New York, 1967, p. 351). It is clear that all these are "caught" from other persons: caught in the sense that self-theorists commonly look to the pattern of interpersonal relationships experienced in youth as the origin of personality. (For typical treatments, see Don E. Hamachek, *The Self in Growth, Teaching, and Learning*, Prentice-Hall, Inc., Englewood Cliffs, N.J., 1965, and Arthur T. Jersild, *Child Psychology*, Prentice-Hall, 1960). It also has been long suggested that the deep-seated motivations and attitudes which characterize persons are essentially "caught" from others with whom one feels a strong emotional bond. Thus sweeping assertions about moral and character and personality development have been made. "The nature of a child's morality will depend upon those around him — upon, that is, the identifications he makes" (Norman J. Bull, *Moral Education*, Routledge and Kegan, London, 1969, p. 15). While this is an overstatement, it is still in general harmony with social learning theories which insist that "the social environment plays a direct molding role and important social experiences are those in which authorities supply the child with ready-made standards and act in ways that ensure the arousal of notions necessary for adapting the standards" (Martin Hoffman, "Moral Development," *Carmichael's Manual of Child Psychology*, Vol. 2, ed. by Paul H. Mussen, John Wiley and Sons, New York, 1970).

Direct instruction surely has a role in socialization. But much research has been done on another process whose role is postulated by social learning theorists: observation of adults. Bandura, Hoffman, Sears, A. Freud, McDonald, Walters, and others have shown that observation of others does have a powerful impact on behavior. Most of their research, however, has been done in a laboratory setting in which children have established few or no emotional ties with the adult, and has focused on narrow issues like moral prohibitions, guilt, and norm violation. Still it is clear from their research that the common notion that "likeness" is communicated from person to person, from model to observer, is certainly established.

In fact, it is modeling (or identification) that is fastened on as the most significant source of likeness communication. It is not so much power or rewards that shape behavior as the striving to be like another person: "a motivated attempt to resemble a specific person" (see Unrie Bronfenbrenner, "The Study of Identification through Interpersonal Perception," in *Person, Perception, and Interpersonal Behavior,* ed. by R. Tagiuri and L. Petrullo, Stanford University Press, Stanford, 1958, p. 118. See also Justin Aronfried, *Conduct and Conscience,* Academic Press, New York, 1968, p. 82).

Looked at this way, more than imitation is involved in modeling and identification.

> Identification is a process in which a person believes himself to be like another person in some respects, experiences the other's successes and defeats as his own, and consciously or unconsciously models his behavior after him. . . . The fact that there is <u>emotional involvement</u> with the other person <u>distinguishes identification from mere imitation</u> (L. Douglas DeNike and Norman Tiber, "Neurotic Behavior," *Foundations of Abnormal Psychology* (Holt, Rinehart and Winston, New York, 1968, p. 355).

In a much-quoted article Kelman (Herbert C. Kelman, "Compliance, Identification, and Internalization: Three Processes of Attitude Change," *Journal of Conflict Resolution,* No. 2, 1958), suggests three types of social influence understood in terms of three different psychological processes: *<u>compliance</u>,* produced when the influencing source has some <u>means of control</u> over an individual; *<u>identification</u>,* when influence is based on <u>desire to establish or maintain a satisfying relationship</u> with another person or group; and *<u>internalization</u>,* when <u>the content</u> (ideas and behaviors) <u>of the induced behavior is adopted as intrinsically rewarding</u>. In a real sense, identification precedes internalization. Seeing reality in another person and striving to be like him permits the testing and then the adoption of his traits, values, and character. In point of fact, exploration of identification and modeling has shown that in childhood and adolescence parents do serve as models for most types of behavior and for character (see Martin L. Hoffman, "Conscience, Personality, and Socialization Techniques," *Human Development.* 13:90-126, 1970).

Many studies indicate that mere observation of adults or others, even those with whom children have no significant relationship, can initiate changes in behavior. But identification goes beyond imitation of behavior. Kohlberg points out that "identification differs from imitation in two respects: 1) in identification the total role is learned, with the self modeling many aspects of the model (not just overt actions), and 2) identification is based on a strong emotional tie with the model" (Lawrence Kohlberg, "Moral Development and Identification," *Child Psychology:* 62nd Yearbook of the National Society for the Study of Education, U. of Chicago Press, Chicago, 1963, p. 296).

Modeling, then, is the primary mechanism through which socialization takes place. As a child lives with his parents, he grows into their culture, and becomes like them. As he grows, other models are presented as well with whom he identifies, and on whom he models his own personality and behavior. Choice and personal commitment do enter in. *But one learns his likeness through seeing that likeness lived in others with whom he identifies.*

All this Jesus said so much more simply two thousand years ago: "A disciple, when he is fully taught, will be like his teacher."

discipling

In the social sciences studies of identification and modeling have focused on relationships between adults and children. Yet studies have pointed out also that for adults as well, social anchors to personality and behavior are important. For all Christians, children and adults, who are learning to live in the culture of Christ's Body and who are developing new, Christian personalities as they move toward His likeness, the existence of models and a close relational identification with them is important. It also is important that the models be provided not only by the individual, but also by the Christian community itself. The existence of multiple models of faith's life is essential.

A study of the behavioral science literature on modeling and identification reinforces conclusions already drawn from theological considerations, and helps us describe factors in the educational situation which enhance the teaching/learning of faith-as-life (e.g., the discipling process).

1. There needs to be frequent, long-term contact with the model(s).
2. There needs to be a warm, loving relationship with the model(s).
3. There needs to be exposure to the inner states of the model(s).

4. The model(s) need to be <u>observed in a variety of life settings and situations.</u>
5. The model(s) need to <u>exhibit consistency and clarity</u> in behaviors, values, etc.
6. There needs to be <u>a correspondence</u> between the behavior of the model(s) and the beliefs (ideal standards) of the community.
7. There needs to be <u>explanation of life style</u> of the model(s) conceptually, with <u>instruction</u> accompanying <u>shared experiences.</u>

These factors help us see that instruction and modeling are not contradictory or mutually exclusive. Instead, they point us to a situation in which Truth concepts are taught, explained, and expressed in words. But they also point us to other dimensions of the teaching/learning situation which make it more likely that the concepts will be perceived as realities to be experienced rather than simply as ideas to be believed. For God's Word to catch at our hearts and be most effectively applied for transformation, we also need an intimate relationship with the teacher. We need to see ourselves (and desire ourselves to be) like the teacher. We need to know the teacher well, to have access to his feelings and his values and his attitudes and his ways of responding in life. We need to be with the teacher outside the formal learning setting, in life. And the teacher needs to be a person who *lives* his faith, and who in his own personality reflects the meaning of truths Scripture communicates in words.

For an adequate Christian education, we need also to realize that <u>each of us needs many teachers.</u> That the Body as a whole, and members of the Body individually, each will contribute something to each person's growth in Christ. Rather than thinking of "teachers" as specialized individuals who function in a classroom, we need to <u>see one another as believer-priests,</u> who are <u>*always, in every contact,* nurturing and discipling</u> one another.

We need, in short, to break out of our old molds and modes of thinking about Christian education, and begin to think about the Church's educational ministry in new and bolder . . . and more biblical . . . ways.

PROBE
    case histories
    discussion questions
    thought-provokers
    resources

1. If someone were to suggest that we change our terminology in Christian education to reflect our understandings of the nurturing process, what terms would you fasten on to replace the following:

   teaching
   teacher
   classroom
   content
   education
   instruction
   learned

2. Here's a list of some of the questions about Christian education I feel we need to examine seriously. Look them over and (a) add any others you feel should be here, (b) jot down answers to those about which you have convictions, (c) put a check mark beside any you feel are "impossible."

   a. If parents are children's primary models, why have we trained teachers but not parents?
   b. How close a relationship should exist between members of a local church body?
   c. How important is sharing our feelings to Christian growth and nurture?
   d. What difference would it make in adult classes if we actually did view each member as a "teacher"?
   e. How much interaction between Christians is needed if we are supposed to disciple one another?
   f. What is the relationship between church leaders and other believers to be if one leads by modeling?
   g. In what way do believers identify with their pastors? Or do they? Does this really make a difference?
   h. What is the advantage of a retreat over a Bible conference in church where we're taught by a lecturer?
   i. What is the place of the Bible conference (lectureship) in Christian education?
   j. What is the place of the retreat?
   k. How personal should the pastor be when preaching his sermon?
   l. Is "one hour a week" the best way to structure Bible teaching? Do we have any alternatives?
   m. What is a healthy teacher/pupil ratio in a Sunday school class?
   n. If you were going to design a church building for nurture, how would you build it?
   o. What differences does it make if children never see the adult teachers functioning in the "real" world?
   p. Is team teaching better than the single-teacher class structure we use today?
   q. What should have our priority, adult or childhood Christian education?

r. What criteria would you establish for the selection of Sunday school teachers?

s. How often have you heard the Bible referred to to explain another believer's attitude or value?

t. What is the place of instruction in Bible content in Christian education?

u. Who are the three people most likely to have a significant role in discipling a child?

v. Who are the three most likely to have a significant role in discipling an adult?

w. What are advantages of group Bible study over personal individual Bible study. Vice versa?

x. What makes you admire and want to be like another person?

y. If we could help each "layman" think of himself as a believer-priest instead of "laymen,' what difference might it make?

z. Are spiritual gifts really organizational (e.g., to fit us for a "superintendent" or "committee" or "teacher" role in a C.E. organization) or are they essentially interpersonal, to operate in all contexts in and outside of organizations? What difference would it make?

3. I've suggested in this chapter that modeling and socialization provide clues for adult as well as childhood Christian education. That is, that we need to see the total ministry of the Body as a discipling ministry, and design our whole life together for this educational purpose. Look over the following "guidelines for fellowship" developed by the leadership of Countryside Chapel, a church in Glen Ellyn, Illinois. These guidelines represent an attempt by that body to design the total church experience as an educational (discipling) time. It's a good example of a creative attempt to build on many of the same biblical principles that are being explored in this book.

BELIEVERS'
FELLOWSHIP
IN
ACTION

"Forsaking not the assembling
of yourselves together . . ."

Our guidelines for
fellowship come from

God's Word

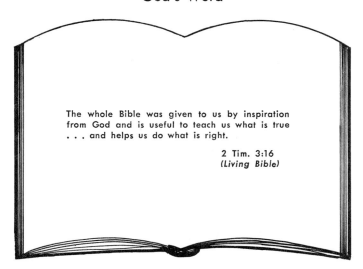

The whole Bible was given to us by inspiration
from God and is useful to teach us what is true
. . . and helps us do what is right.

2 Tim. 3:16
(Living Bible)

Countryside Chapel   Glen Ellyn, Ill

We believe God's Spirit breaks
through to us in various ways
and times.

SO . . .

Following a rigid time schedule

or an unvarying procedure

Jan. 1	Jan. 8	Jan. 15	Jan. 22
1.	1.	1.	1.
2.	2.	2.	2.
3.	3.	3.	3.

is less important than

FLEXIBILITY

(sensitivity to God's Spirit)

We believe that forms of *expression* are not as significant as *people*. People put the meaning into the forms, but some forms help to do certain things better.

Sometimes we sit where we can see many people's faces. Here we may see God's JOY and PEACE shining through.

"encouraging one another" (Heb. 10:24)

Acts 20:27

Sometimes we sit so the group can focus its attention more easily to learn the Word or praise the Lord.

We believe *all* parts of the body are
important. (1 Cor. 12:12-26)

SO . . .

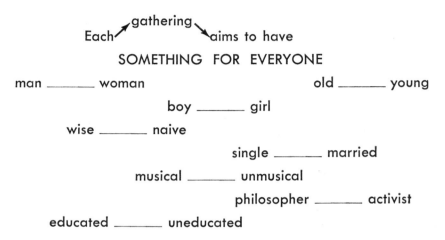

Each ↗ gathering ↘ aims to have

SOMETHING FOR EVERYONE

man _____ woman   old _____ young

boy _____ girl

wise _____ naive

single _____ married

musical _____ unmusical

philosopher _____ activist

educated _____ uneducated

We believe that *all Christians* are
God's ministers . . . though performing
different roles. (1 Cor. 12:4-11)

SO . . .

We try to give everyone "a
platform" by often sitting in
a way which encourages many
"ministers" to become involved.

"participants, not spectators"

We believe all are ministers and can
help others. God has given
each believer spiritual gifts.
(Col. 3:16; 1 Cor. 12:7)

SO . . .

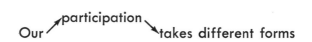

Our participation takes different forms

"You can do it!"

Some can
exhort.

Some can sing.

Some can pray
or lead in
prayer.

"Praise God!"

Some can
testify.

Some can
show.

Some
can teach.

Some can touch.

We believe everyone's insight is needed.

SO . . .

Sharing may be spontaneous

or helpfully arranged to make it easier.

We use the example of the early
Christians.

They prayed
together.
(Acts 4:24-31)

They sang together.
(Eph. 5:18b-20)

They shared spiritual insights.

(1 Cor. 12:8-11; Acts 15:35)

They ate together.
(Acts 2:46)

They studied together.
(Acts 2:42; Acts 17:11; Col. 3:16)

Early Christians worshiped in a
way that allowed many to take part.

1 CORINTHIANS 14:26: "What then, brethren? When you come
together, *each one* has a hymn, a lesson, a revelation, a tongue
or an interpretation. Let all things be done for edification."

We believe ➔ some ➔ gatherings of Christians should center on sharing (1 Cor. 14:26).

"Thank you, Jesus!"

SO . . .

People come expecting to

SHARE (as well as to receive), not to

SIT
and/or
zzzzzz

Sometimes we minister to *each other*
in our music (Col. 3:16, 17; I Cor. 14:15; Eph. 5:18b-20).

Music from all ages and cultures helps us worship.

Ps. 150:4

"Do, Lord, oh do Lord . . ."

"They'll know we are Christians . . ."

"A mighty fortress is our God . . ."

"Amazing grace,
how sweet . . ."

Ps. 149:3

Ps. 150:3

"Kum ba yah, my Lord . . ."

Ps. 150:5

"All hail the power . . ."

"Jesus loves me, this I . . ."

99

The Holy Spirit speaks to us as we speak
to and with *each other.*

The BIBLE says:

"Teach Christ's words to *each other.*"
(Col. 3:16)

"Consider how to stir up *one another*
to love and good works."
(Heb. 10:24)

"Talk with each other much about the
Lord."
(Eph. 5:19)

SO . . .

We allow those with public spiritual
gifts to share in presenting God's
Word. This may be pre-planned,
but sometimes it is extemporaneous.

When we pray, we allow for:

_____ the sharing of burdens

_____ expressions of need

(HELP!)

I Corinthians 14:15

_____ Thanksgiving and praise

We take them to the Lord

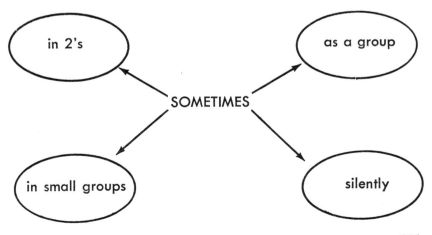

101

SO . . . *Each week* our fellowship

includes these *ingredients:*

F
E
L
L
O
W
S
H
I
P
I
N
G

- PRAYING together
- SINGING together
- RELATING together
  (testimonies, getting acquainted,
      family activities,
         small groups)

- LEARNING together
  (Bible study, exhortation, drama,
      films, sharing)

Each week has a *different* mix

and

so

a *different* FLAVOR.

Because we believe
"God is not a God of confusion but
of peace, . . . all things should be
done decently and in order."
(1 Cor. 14:33, 40)

The Elders believe that a
Believers' Fellowship requires *much*
planning

(in order to secure wide
and varied participation).

SO . . .

The   { Elders }   evaluate
        { Pastor }

regularly to insure a biblical
people-centered *planning* process
is used, based on objectives set
by the Board.

SO . . .

Come along!
Share and be blessed
as God speaks through and
to us! !

ONE MORE WORD —

This type of church meeting may be unfamiliar to you. In fact, you may feel uneasy and "on the spot" until you get used to it. And not everything will seem relevant to you — but you can rejoice that one of your brothers may be blessed at that moment (Mark 10:45).

One good way to get the feel for this type of worship is to try it with a small group. Find 6-10 other Christians and form a home fellowship group to learn and worship together around the Word of God. *Try it — you'll like it!*

an interpersonal dimension

It's clear from Scripture that intimate interpersonal relationships are vital within the Body. Modeling theory helps us see why: we need to know and to love those who disciple us toward their likeness.

Given this, we ought to raise a relevant objection. Isn't it possible to develop relationships in the classroom? Why abandon reliance on the class as the primary setting for Christian education? Does our theology really demand as drastically new an approach as this book seems so far to imply?

THE CHURCH	IMPLICATIONS
LIFE	A WHOLE-PERSON FOCUS
LIFE'S GOAL	A DISCIPLING PURPOSE
LIFE'S COMMUNI-CATION	A MODELING METHOD
LIFE'S DYNAMIC	AN INTER-PERSONAL DIMENSION
LIFE'S TRANS-MISSION	AN OVER-FLOWING OUTCOME

The idea that the relational climate is important for learning is common to secular as well as Christian education. A survey of two decades of research in this area will help us face some of our own issues.

interpersonal approaches in education

early expectations. Concern for the classroom group is hardly new in education. The early '50s produced numerous reports of experimental studies focusing on differences between "teacher-centered" and "student-centered" classes, nearly all conducted on the college level. While some apparently viewed discussion and other student-centered methods primarily as a means toward greater student involvement in learning, many had a broader conception of the role of the classroom group and higher hopes for the impact of group processes. A typical view is reflected in two late-'50s articles by Leland P. Bradford, the first of which appeared in *Adult Education* and the second in the *Teachers' College Record*. In these articles Bradford suggests that

> a group climate which reduces individual defensiveness and anxiety about exposures of one's inadequacy, and gives acceptance and emotional support to all students, will do a great deal to prevent or repair feelings of rejection, of inadequate self-image, of failure. *Such a climate is paramount in creating readiness for learning* [italics mine] and for being able to face and solve difficulties inhibiting individual and group growth and development.

On the supposition that "the teaching-learning process is a human transaction involving teacher, learner, and learning groups in a set of dynamic interactions," Bradford suggests that education must concern itself with development of "an effective learning group where members help members and where morale is high." When such a group is developed, individuals should have an important support in learning and in changing behaviors. In fact, Bradford states that

> until the thoughts, feelings, and behaviors needing change are brought to the surface for the individual and made public to those helping him (in formal learning situations the teacher and other members of the learning group), there is little likelihood of learning or change.

Thus Bradford argues for a group emphasis in education which will provide a climate for learning, an "atmosphere in the learning group" which will "reduce threat and defensiveness and also provide emotional support while the learner is undergoing the difficult process of changing patterns of thought and behavior."

research on outcomes. Many experiments have been conducted with a view to confirming the superiority of student-centered methods. The results have been far from encouraging. Dubin and Taveggia (*The Teaching-Learning Paradox,* Center for Advanced Study of Educational Administration, U. of Oregon, 1968) analyzed the data of over 140 such studies of college teaching methods, and concluded concerning the relative effectives of various approaches that when "*utility is measured through final examination:* THERE ARE NO DIFFERENCES THAT AMOUNT TO ANYTHING." While admitting that there may well be outcomes which are not measurable by examination but which are of valid concern in education, the authors point out that such measure-

107

ment is still "relevant to one of the major functions of an institution of higher learning" — and, we might add, relevant to the claims of interpersonal theorists that group approaches provide a context in which individuals will gain in cognitive measures as well as in other dimensions.

There are many discussions of such experiments in the literature. Frymier (*The Nature of Educational Method,* Chas. E. Merrill Books, Inc., Columbus, Ohio, 1965) discusses various classroom manipulations, such as lecture vs. discussion, large and small group structures, etc., and concludes that

> most of these studies are disappointing. In the main they indicate little difference in educational attainment regardless of the method employed or the objectives measured. Some of the technical reports even carry an air of defeatism when they state that such and such a procedure "apparently did no worse than" some other approach.

Even McKeachie, writing of teaching at the college/university level in the *Handbook of Research on Teaching* (N. L. Gage, ed., Rand McNally, Chicago, 1963) is forced to report that "no significant difference" in learning outcomes is found in study after study, although he does suggest that research seems to indicate that "the more highly one values outcomes going beyond acquisition of knowledge, the more likely that student-centered methods will be preferred" (p. 1140). Yet in the same publication Wallen and Travers state that even in those areas where proponents of group methods claim advantage (problem solving, application of knowledge, etc.), "there is little direct evidence" of success when there is an attempt to measure outcomes in these terms (p. 481).

However one may wish to argue the case, it is clear that concern for the learning group and use of teaching methods designed to facilitate interaction has not fulfilled the expectations of the theorists.

While experiments with the classroom group have proven disappointing, a parallel tradition, epitomized by the NTL Institute, has developed a mass of literature growing from experimentation with group process. This tradition suggests exciting functions for group experience in human relations training, in personal self-discovery, in facilitating change of various sorts in individuals and organizations. The confrontation group, or T-Group, primary tool in this tradition, has proven fruitful and suggestive for many fields. And what has been discovered about group process (about free flow of emotional as well as cognitive data, group problem solving, consensus reaching, etc.) is of great concern to the educator. Work with such groups perhaps suggests that if only educational experiments had been preceded with experiences designed to develop a cohesive group, measured results might have been different.

Unfortunately, what research evidence there seems to be does not support this notion. Torrance ("Perception of Group Functioning as Predictor of Group Performance," *Journal of Social Psychology*, Vol. XLII, Nov., 1955) early noted that effective bomber crews differ from ineffective crews "in that their members less frequently perceived harmony and more frequently perceived discord." In a study of business management gaming, "companies" were composed of members who previously had been in the same or different leaderless T-Groups fifteen weeks earlier. Those who had been in the same groups performed differently from those who had not. While the former reported less conflict, more ease of contact, and more openness, they performed very poorly, losing $5.37 million rather than showing a profit as did the multiple T-Group companies. So also Blake, Mouton, and Frucheter ("A Factor Analysis of Training Group Behavior," *Journal of Applied Psychology*, 1962) report contradictory results concerning a direct relationship between cohesion and group productivity. While evidence is sparse, such findings as these make one hesitate to accept the naive, but intuitively reasonable idea that if only T-Group training were provided for classroom groups, the student-centered class would perform as the early theorists predicted.

either/or? Cartwright ("The Nature of Group Cohesiveness," in *Group Dynamics Research and Theory*, Cartwright and Zander, ed., Harper & Row, New York, 1968) has suggested that there are two basic types of group function; those focused on (a) the achievement of some specific group goal, and (b) the maintenance or strengthening of the group itself. Little consideration has been given in education to the possibility that *within our present system* these functions are mutually inhibitory. That is, that concern for the goals imposed by our educational system blocks behaviors appropriate to psychosocial functions of a group, and conversely that behaviors of the psychosocial type are perceived by instructional groups as inappropriate in view of the ends inherent in education.

For instance, Jansen in his exploratory text, *Educational Sociology*, sees five types of relationships developing between members of instructional groups: (1) problem-solving and work relationships, (2) relationships having to do with decision-making, (3) those developing when group members attempt to influence one another to behave in one way rather than another, (4) sociopsychological relationships evolving from the need of members to express private perceptions of feelings about experience in the instructional group, and (5) those emerging when members attempt to make personal evaluations of one another. It is important to inquire whether or not certain of these are perceived by members of an instructional group as enhancing the possible achievement of individual and group goals, and others (particularly 4, 5, and often 2) as irrelevant to the reason for which the group exists.

An article by Harrison ("The Design of Cross-Cultural Training," *Explorations: Human Relationship Training and Research,* National Training Labs., Washington, D.C., 1966) is suggestive here. He argues that the methods of traditional education cannot be applied to reach the goals of crosscultural training, or for any application situation which requires ability to adapt to ambiguous social situations and to take action in such situations under stress. He points out that the classroom trains for "manipulation of symbols rather than things; reliance on thinking rather than action." The fault in traditional education as viewed by Harrison lies not so much in its content as in its orientation to life and problem solving, determined by its classroom approach. Picking up from Schien and Bennis the label "meta-goal" for such orientations, Harrison analyzes classroom education as follows:

Meta-goals of Traditional College and University Classroom	Appropriate Meta-goals for Crosscultural Training
Source of Information. Information comes from experts and authoritative sources through the media of books, lectures, audiovisual presentations. "If you have a question, look it up."	*Source of Information.* Information sources must be developed by the learner from the social environment. Information-gathering methods include observation and questioning of associates, other learners, and chance acquaintances.
Learning Settings. Learning takes place in settings designed for the purpose, e. g., classrooms and libraries.	*Learning Settings.* The entire social environment is the setting for learning. Every human encounter provides relevant information.
Problem-solving Approaches. Problems are defined and posed to the learner by experts and authorities. The correct problem-solving methods are specified, and the students' work is checked for application of the proper method and for accuracy, or at	*Problem-solving Approaches.* The learner is on his own to define problems, generate hypotheses, and collect information from the social environment. The emphasis is on discovering probems and

least reasonableness of results. The emphasis is on solutions to known problems.

Role of Emotions and Values. Problems are largely dealt with at an ideational level. Questions of reason and of fact are of paramount importance. Feelings and values may be discussed, but are rarely acted upon.

Criteria of Successful Learning. Favorable evaluation by experts and authorities of the quality of the individual's intellectual productions, primarily written work.

developing problem-solving approaches on the spot.

Role of Emotions and Values. Problems are usually value- and emotion-laden. Facts are often less relevant than the perceptions and attitudes which people hold. Values and feelings have action consequences, and action must be taken.

Criteria of Successful Learning The establishment and maintenance of satisfying relationships with others in the work setting. This includes the ability to communicate with and influence others. Often there are no criteria available other than the attitude of the parties involved in the relationship.

In brief, then, Harrison argues that there is inherent in our educational method a life style which is independent of the content taught. And these meta-goals are not supportive of those dimensions of group life which the educational theorists feel must be developed as supportive for learning and change! In fact, Harrison seems to suggest that even where behavioral goals appropriate to a particular course's content and those implicit in educational method are in conflict, the likelihood is that the meta-goals are more likely to influence subsequent behavior!

directions? In summary, then, it can be said that the expectations for a revitalization of education through development of cohesive, supportive instructional groups has not been realized. Student-centered methods have not been demonstrated superior to teacher-centered methods, particularly in cognitive outcomes. Some evidence exists that intergroup harmony may even decrease productivity. Considerations like these provide few guidelines for education — but they do generate a whole set of questions, and suggest possibly more fruitful (and certainly more difficult) lines of research. For instance, some questions that are generated are these:

> *Is the group approach to educational innovation (in which a teacher attempts to develop a cohesive group) a viable strategy?*
> *Is it possible for the two basic types of group function (achievement and psychosocial) to "mix" in education so as to support and enhance one another?*

> *Are the meta-goals of contemporary education better suited to the realities of life in our culture than those implicit in the group orientation?*

These and other similar questions focus attention on the educational *system* and force us to ask questions about its structure. Questions like the first two above suggest that our present structures exert pressures which inhibit the very effects we seek to gain through group development. Questions like the third ask value-rooted questions, probing the kind of world we are training students for — or seeking to create through education. They ask questions about life styles and orientations to life: which are to be preferred?

It is my conviction that these are the kinds of questions education must ask — and be willing to answer. We need to define the outcomes which are most appropriate to our values, and, rather than toying with components of educational process within the present educational system, to attempt a restructuring of education's basic method.

This is not an isolated point of view. In a discussion of educational method Ohio State's Jack Frymier confesses that

> perhaps it is unreasonable to hope for dramatic changes in educational effectiveness, but we need a breakthrough in education. Repeating old mistakes is not enough. What is called for is a completely new concept of educational effort, a bold new approach casting all component parts into a new mold. Tinkering with what we already do is not enough... (29, p. 285).

There are many candidates for the "new concept," ranging from CAI (Computer Assisted Instruction) to Britain's Structural Communication System and the Rogerian approach to self-reliant learning. Each candidate advances a variety of arguments. For instance, in reporting on one three-year experiment in independent study programs for highschoolers sponsored by the Ford Foundation, Dr. B. Frank Brown insists that "in a world which has been rocked by the rapid explosion of knowledge, teaching must be subordinated to learning and the school's curricula centered around:

1. Learning by inquiry.
2. Learning by doing.
3. Capturing the imagination.
4. Stimulating reason.
5. Learning by discovery, testing, and even failing and trying again.

And, Dr. Brown continues, "these objectives can be achieved only in viable independent study situations."

Yet many educators have concern for learning outcomes that will go well beyond these. As recently as 1962 it could be said that objectives in the affective domain, involving changes in student interests, attitudes, values, and appreciations (the domain of personal-social adjustment) were not classified or fully developed. Since Krathwohl's *Taxonomy of Educational Objectives, Handbook II: Affective Domain* has been available (1964), renewed consideration has been given to the place of such learnings in education. Still, a recent article in *Educational Technology* ("Instructional Objectives in the Affective Domain," Mary Harbeck, Jan., 1970) points out,

> In spite of recent emphasis on the necessity for integrating cognitive with affective processes the gap between what is known about the nature and development of thinking-feeling processes and how this is translated into instructional practices is still enormously wide.

Those who take affective learning goals seriously, however, are characteristically concerned about interactive behavior in the classroom, and persistently express the viewpoints of earlier "groups" exponents. Gorman, in an excellent book of this type, states, "the basic assumption . . . is that teaching and learning is a process of communication among individuals in a group setting." This view of teaching/learning leads Gorman to recommend working toward development of a cohesive group, on the twin suppositions that in a supportive climate people "work toward their potential and are free to concentrate on learning," and that building such a group "teaches learners to be more self-directing, happier human beings."

And so we come full circle.

The more educators view learning as an intermix of cognitive and affective outcomes, the more their concern for interpersonal relationships — and the more difficult the design of educational method.

In summary, what we seem to be discovering is that the formal school setting *itself* defines certain relationships and certain kinds of sharing (of ideas, not feelings) as appropriate, and thus rules out the kinds of relationships which are significant for discipling! This does not mean that adults or children and adults can not come together to learn. But it does imply that when they do come together, it is best *not* to define that situation as a "school." As long as teachers and learners perceive themselves to be in school, they will not develop the kinds of relationships or the kinds of sharing which are important for discipling!

Strikingly, it seems that when we adopted from our culture the formal school approach to nurture, we in fact set up the conditions under which discipling and growth in likeness are least likely to take place!

INTERESTING THOT!

PROBE
    case histories
    discussion questions
    thought-provokers
    resources

1. When our goal in developing an educational strategy is to facilitate identification and modeling it becomes important that teachers and learners (models and disciples) come to know and understand each other well. We need to know each other's feelings and motives as well as ideas and observed behaviors. An example of how easily persons can *misunderstand* each other unless motives and feelings as well as concepts are verbalized is given in Laing, Philippson, and Lee, *Interpersonal Perception* (Tavistock Publications, London, 1966).

They describe the "whirl" like this:

Peter	Paul
1. I am upset.	1. Peter is upset.
2. Paul is acting very calm and dispassionate.	2. I'll try to help him by remaining calm and just listening.
3. If Paul cared about me and wanted to help he would get involved and show some emotion also.	3. He is getting even more upset. I must be even more calm.
4. Paul knows that this upsets me.	4. He is accusing me of hurting him.
5. If Paul knows that his behavior upsets me, he must be intending to hurt me.	5. I'm really trying to help.
6. He must be cruel, sadistic. Maybe he gets pleasure out of it.	6. He must be projecting.

In this sketch the authors demonstrate clearly how easily behavior alone can be misinterpreted. We must understand other persons and their perceptions and emotions: to understand these there must be *self-revelation* and an honest sharing of feeling data as well as cognitions.

   a. How many times in classroom situations have you seen self-revelation (feeling data) shared?
   b. How many times in a seminary or local church Bible class have you seen self-revelation taking place?

    c. What do you think is the relationship between self-revelation and identification?

    d. How many of the local church Sunday school teachers did you feel you "really knew"? Where did you get to know them? How did you get to know them?

    e. Why is self-revelation so seldom a part of our classroom experiences?

2. In their book on *Interpersonal Perception* the three authors present a method to discover how well we do know others whom we are close to. The method is simply to pose a series of statements that participants are to answer for themselves, then as they think the other person would answer, then as they think the other person would think they had answered. Each statement is rated as *very true* $++$, slightly true $=$, slightly untrue -, and very untrue —. Here are a couple of examples of the pattern to look for, taken from the book.

    45. A. How true do you think the following are?
         1. She readily forgives me.
         2. I readily forgive her.
         3. She readily forgives herself.
         4. I readily forgive myself.

        B. How would *she* answer the following?
         1. "I readily forgive him."
         2. "He readily forgives me."
         3. "I readily forgive myself."
         4. "He readily forgives himself."

        C. How would *she* think you have answered the following?
         1. She readily forgives me.
         2. I readily forgive her.
         3. She readily forgives herself.
         4. I readily forgive myself.

    53. A. How true do you think the following are?
         1. She believes in me.
         2. I believe in her.
         3. She believes in herself.
         4. I believe in myself.

        B. How would *she* answer the following?
         1. "I believe in him."
         2. "He believes in me."
         3. "I believe in myself."
         4. "He believes in himself."

        C. How would *she* think you have answered the following?
         1. She believes in me.
         2. I believe in her.
         3. She believes in herself.
         4. I believe in myself.

Of course, this "test" is taken by each party involved, and then the responses compared. The result is a rather accurate indication of how well persons do understand each other, how transparent they are in their relationship, and how well each could serve as a model for the other. Obviously if one's perceptions of others are inaccurate, they cannot be an effective model if *likeness* of model and disciple is in view.

Having gotten this measurement strategy in mind, now attempt the following:

a. Select *ten* indicators (like *forgiveness* and *believing in* in the examples above) which you feel are significant dimensions of Christian interpersonal relationships and are to be modeled by believers for one another. List the ten below.

1._____   6._____

2._____   7._____

3._____   8._____

4._____   9._____

5._____   10._____

b. Next, design a question series like that above which might be administered to two people in a teaching/learning setting.

c. Select one or more pairs to give the ten-item test to: perhaps parent and teen, professor and student, pastor and parishioner, Sunday school teacher and student, husband and wife, new believer and evangelist, etc.

d. Develop a *prediction* about which of the pairs you will find the greatest accuracy of perception between. State your reasons for the prediction carefully.

e. Administer the questionnaire to the selected pairs, and compare results.

f. *If your predictions were inaccurate,* jot down a number of hypotheses to explain why this might have been. Then interview the subjects, and see what you can find out to explain the results.

If your predictions were accurate, interview the subjects to make sure that the reasons you made them were valid and related to the results you obtained.

3. If you are part of a class studying this book together, you might consider undertaking a class project, and analyzing relationships between participants in different local church education settings. Explore the possibilities. There are many!

an overflowing outcome

Christian education is a dynamic ministry of the Holy Spirit; a ministry in which He goes about His task of transforming believers through processes God has built into human nature and the nature of the Church.

Christian education is a ministry distinct from what we have tended to call "education." It produces not simply men and women who know, but men and women — and a community — who are, in this world, taking on Jesus' likeness.

It is that likeness which is the key to the believer's impact on the world in terms of evangelism . . . and justice.

THE CHURCH	IMPLICATIONS
LIFE	A WHOLE-PERSON FOCUS
LIFE'S GOAL	A DISCIPLING PURPOSE
LIFE'S COM-MUNICATION	A MODELING METHOD
LIFE'S DYNAMIC	AN INTER-PERSONAL DIMENSION
LIFE'S TRANS-MISSION	AN OVERFLOWING OUTCOME

There is an alternative to programmed evangelism: to training believers in a canned talk, and sending them out in teams on specified days to speak to strangers. There is alternative to programmed social action: to committees who meet and push and pull, and then speak or act in the name of a congregation. And the alternative is a *better* way.

Review

To understand the alternative, we need to put together the picture of C.E. that has been developing through these first chapters. With that picture in view, we can go on and look at some of the implications of our theologically based C.E. for mission and outreach.

Theological roots	Christian education implications

LIFE sets apart
   the believer
   the Church
	Christian education is to focus on
	     whole persons
	     whole congregations
	the traditional "schooling" approach focuses on cognitive, *not* whole-person or whole-people learning.

LIFE'S GOAL is
   transformation
 	
   toward Christlikeness
	Christian education's purpose is to facilitate this transformation
	
	the learning theory which best fits this goal is characteristically four-factored, and transactional.
	
	"socialization" provides a better example than "education" of how to facilitate this kind of learning.

LIFE'S COMMUNICATION is interpersonal	Christian education's method must be interpersonal: *discipleship* as contrasted to *schooling* identification between learner and model(s) is critical. Scripture needs both to be explained and demonstrated as a lived reality. Information processing techniques cannot in themselves produce a disciple.

LIFE'S DYNAMIC
   is relational.
 	
   The Body is marked
     by love.
     by intimacy.
	Christian education must always pay attention to Body relationships.
	
	Developing love is a primary (not secondary) concern of C.E.
	   love between teacher (model) and learner (disciple)
	   love within the Body (groups)
	
	Coming to know other believers intimately is
	   a necessary part of this relationship
	   necessary if modeling is a viable method.

Noting the above, we have said that the formal school setting as it is perceived by teachers and learners in our culture does not encourage or permit development of the kind of relationships which Christian education demands. Nor does it provide a context for real-life involvement with a teacher-model. This does not mean that we can never meet together in a school setting, or for schooling. It does mean that we cannot *rely* on schooling as *the* strategy in Christian education. It means that we need to develop a multi-strategy approach to Christian education. It means that we need to help Christians think of teaching and learning, and to understand their role in nurturing children and one another, in ways that do not necessarily imply a "class!"

It means, too, that we no longer can think of "Christian education" as a *part* of the church's ministry expressed through "educational" (e.g., schooling) agencies. Instead, we need to begin to see the total life of the Church, *all* the interactions of believers, as part and parcel of the Church's educational (discipling) ministry. As a theological discipline, Christian education demands that we come to understand how growth takes place, and that we develop strategies and approaches to ministry which in fact facilitate the transformation process.

Growth

This view of the Church challenges the conviction held by many that the church is designed by God essentially for evangelism. We have been looking at the Church as an organism designed by God for discipling. There is a great difference; a practical as well as theological difference. A church organized for evangelism will take on different forms and activities than a church organized for discipling. In the one, meetings will tend to be designed for the non-Christian or for exhortation. In the other, meetings will tend to be designed for the believer and for sharing. In the one, smaller groups will tend to be action-oriented: committees whose task is to plan outreach or other programs. In the other, smaller groups will tend to be person-oriented: believers will meet to build one another up in Christ. In the one, the church will tend to evaluate success or failure on numerical grounds (conversions, baptisms, Sunday school size, dollars given). In the other, evaluation will tend to focus on personal spiritual development, love's expression, etc. In the one, church leadership will tend to feel a responsibility to plan and organize evangelistic and social action ministries. In the other, church leaders will tend to encourage individuals to take responsibility for evangelism and social concerns as God leads.

In looking at these tendencies we need to resist the temptation to charge the "evangelistic church" party with a lack of concern for Christian growth and nurture. And we need to resist as well the temptation to charge the "nurturing church" party with a selfish unconcern for the lost. I am convinced that both are concerned with spiritual growth, and that both are concerned with evangelistic outreach. *The difference between them is essentially a difference in strategy — and that difference is rooted in ecclesiology.*

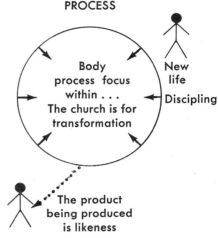

PROCESS

Body process focus within . . . The church is for transformation

New life

Discipling

The product being produced is likeness

OUTCOME

The disciple

and the body

How does the nurturing church view the relationship of "making disciples" to evangelism and social concerns? This way. The Church is designed by God for the ministry of transformation: for communicating and nurturing the development of Christ's life to men. Relationships within the Body are essentially *discipling* ones. Whenever the Church gathers as the Church (as the two, or three, or as the hundreds), the concern is nurture.

As the discipling and nurturing processes God has designed into Christ's Body operate, both the individual and the local group undergo progressive transformation. Love becomes a visible mark of Jesus' presence. The fruit of the Spirit is produced within individuals.

Because of likeness will witness to Christ in their own world and culture.

Likeness to Jesus increasingly produces in the individual and the local body concern for others . . . both for their "spiritual" and their "natural" needs. The Holy Spirit coordinates these maturing disciples, and through them brings others to Christ and expresses His concern for every need of all men.

We might summarize it like this:

   * The "evangelistic church" party tends to believe that in a

church which focuses on evangelism spiritual growth will automatically take place.
* The "nurturing church" party tends to believe that in a church which focuses on discipleship, evangelism will automatically take place.

The critical question is this. Does either of these positions find greater support in ecclesiology? Does one more accurately reflect what God has revealed about the purposes of the Body, and the functions of the Body? Does one more accurately reflect the nature of Christian faith-as-life?

It is a temptation, of course, to seek a middle position, and say that the Church is both a discipling and evangelizing organism. This is acceptable if by "both/and" we mean that through discipling the church accomplishes God's purposes in the world as well. But if we mean that we are to structure the local Body both as a discipling fellowship and as a task-oriented organization, we are almost certain to lose sight of the distinctive processes the Scripture reveals as those through which church functions to accomplish God's purposes. Strikingly, as we will see, there seems to be as deeply rooted a conflict between *church management* leadership and *servant* leadership, between *task* oriented and *person* oriented groupings, and between *numbers* and *nurture* evaluation criteria, as there is between *schooling* and *discipleship* education.

I am personally convinced that we do not have to attempt to have it both ways. By becoming the Church that God intends, I believe every goal of His and ours will be reached.

* As we become like Jesus, we will come to care about others.
* As we come to care about others, we will sacrifice to become involved with them.
* As we come to care about others, we will share Christ with them.
* As we come to care about others, we will reach out to meet *all kinds* of needs.
* As we come to care *for* each other, we will provide a living example of a people among whom God dwells, awakening the hunger of those who do not know Him.
* As we become like Jesus, in our growing maturity as disciples, we will reproduce both His love for people and for justice.

Building a nurturing church frees us from the necessity of urging babes to attempt to reproduce themselves. Building a nurturing church assures a growing maturity which will naturally express itself in the communication, and reproduction, of God's life in others through the living communication of His Good News.

PROBE
case histories
discussion questions
thought-provokers
resources

This has been an especially short chapter, primarily because it isn't my purpose to contend for the "nurturing purpose" understanding of the Church, but rather to explore what such an understanding means for us in Christian education. At the same time, it's probably important to provide some example of what I mean by suggesting that the outcome of nurture is overflow. That is, when we pay attention to accomplishing God's discipling and transformation ministries through the Church, both evangelism and expression of social concern are a natural outcome.

1. Here's a column from *Action* magazine which reports on a Seattle, Washington, church which I visited. This ten-year-old ministry demonstrates how God has led a congregation that does stress discipleship to ministries in which individuals and groups of its laymen have been called apart (under the authority but not the direction of the church board) for ministries that have both social justice and evangelical dimensions.

"One of these days you're likely to hear of SKY CLUB. Or Survival Bible Training. And possibly you've already heard some of the tapes produced a few years ago by the Electric Message.

When you do hear, perhaps you'll remember something of the story I want to tell here: the story of the church behind the ministries.

Ten years

The story goes back about ten years to a group of men who felt God wanted them to form a new church in the pacific Northwest where they lived. After talking with Ray Stedman of Peninsula Bible Church and his board, the church took shape, and a young pastor was called to its ministry. There were years of struggle for the small church . . . perhaps half its life was spent seeking the unique shape God the Holy Spirit intended for it. When that shape began to emerge, it was through an emphasis that has been associated with "church renewal"; an emphasis you've run into often in this column. The young pastor began to realize more and more fully that Jesus' Church is a church composed of *believer-priests*. Not laymen. Not clergy. Believers who are each one priests; priests with a ministry of service to one another and the community.

For five to six years this concept has taken deep root in the personalities of the membership, and in the local church's understanding of its identity.

All of its ministry has been focused on developing the God-given gifts and capacities of believer priests to minister: capacities turned into realities as God's truth in His Word is taught and studied, and Jesus' love experienced within the Body and shared freely with all.

Today?

It was exciting for me this last December to visit this church, and see what God has been doing through its members. Here's a brief catalog of the Spirit's workings.

The grapevine is a ministry to young people in need. I talked with four young ex-drug addicts, all who had been on heroin, who came to know Christ at the grapevine and who lived there as they became established in their new relationship with the Lord. I talked with four: there have been many more.

The country store. Widows in the church are given a significant (and biblical!) role in the life of the congregation. One ministry of the widows is the operation of a store next to the grapevine, where a variety of things are sold — including much the widows themselves create. Funds are used to support the grapevine ministry: and the women themselves have had a tremendous impact on the youth they often spend time with.

Study center. Realizing the need to disciple and build young people who have just come to know the Lord, some through the grapevine and others from nearby colleges, live-in study centers (the only property the church owns) have been established. A tough, four-hour a day study program is administered and the young converts discipled by the pastor and the church board.

The electric message. This early ministry focused on communicating with youth culture through media. Early efforts showed a need to strengthen the content mastery of those in ministry: communication was important — but so was what is to be communicated! Recently the young man who spearheaded the electric message has developed and tested *Survival Bible Training.* SBT is a tough, high cost (in terms of time and commitment) study program designed to train in the how of Bible study, with a survival task attached to the completion of each unit that leads the students to apply what has been learned in a real-life situation.

Sky club. Several pilots were in the membership of the church. One of them had a burden for ministry to boys eleven to thirteen. Out of this burden came SKY Club, which now uses flight to bring about 20,000 boys in contact with Christian men who care about them.

Art center. In the planning stage is a ministry to Christian kids that God has gifted as artists, who want to develop their talents and think through the meaning of their ministry. I'm excited about this one — my own son, Paul, is an excellent painter who majors in Fine Arts at ASU.

And there is more in mind — more in vision.

How?

How did all these ministries evolve? The pastor shared his basic approach. The church seeks in a variety of ways not only to see that each member is a growing Christian, but also seeks to help each member as a believer-priest develop his spiritual gift. As gifts are discovered and developed, God lays burdens of ministry on the laymen themselves (though usually the young pastor and board have already had a preliminary vision!). Then the church leaders advise and support the believer-priests in taking responsibility for the ministry, and in developing it. The ministries are not "programmed" or "imposed from above." As God gifts and directs the believer-priests, the ministries grow out of their lives.

A sermon?

Whenever I run across a church like this one (and there are a growing number of churches that God is giving His own distinctive flavor to) I can hardly resist a short sermon. But I try. And I rejoice to share what God's been doing because we do need concrete examples of how biblical principles do work out in the life of God's people. So often as calls to evangelical renewal have been given, and New Testament principles presented (like the simple principle that there are no laymen — simply a company in which all are believer-priests), we have tended to hang back. "It's so idealistic" are words I've heard tens of times.

But it is not idealism: it is God's realism! And this is why it's so exciting for me to find pastors and peoples who have together taken God so completely at His Word — and discovered how utterly practical even the most amazing truth of the Word is. It's encouraging for me — as I'm sure it must be for you too, to realize that God keeps giving us such signposts to let us know that we can move on.

Oh, by the way. I didn't mention the name of the church or the pastor. They like it that way. They don't want to be held up as "ideal" — the men are very aware that they have not yet "arrived." If you should go looking for the church you can find it. But one word of warning. Don't look for impressive buildings. Don't look for a church that is dramatically different from your own. The membership this year is around 190.

The lives they touch?

Thousands."

2. An example of "natural" evangelism comes through a small group of which I've been a member for a year or so. We began with four people in a home next door, with a strictly nurturing purpose. After a time, God began to add others to the group (which was sponsored by our local church but not limited to its membership).

One of the early couples to join was Charlie and Barbara, a couple in their late twenties. "Religious" when they joined us, they did not yet have Christ's life. We welcomed them, loved them, and treated them just as the other brothers and sisters. In time both received Christ as personal Savior, and His life was born in them.

After nine months or so the group became too large for the home in which we met. After real soul-searching, we finally divided the thirty-five or so regulars and started three groups. My wife and I joined Charlie and Barbara in their home as the nucleus of a new fellowship.

124

We met with just the four of us for some six or eight weeks. Then God began to bring people in to join us. Among them were several who did not yet know Jesus or have His life in them. In the past six weeks, six of these people have become Christians: three through Charlie's influence at his office, and two (children of one couple) through their parents' influence. In several of these cases the Phoenix Billy Graham crusade crystallized decisions which already were essentially formed.

To give an insight into overflow evangelism, I've asked Barbara to share how her journey to new Life took place, in a group that did not meet as an evangelistic group at all, but as a discipling group, concerned with the transformation of its members. Here's her story:

After my brother died I had an overwhelming need to know where he was and why God had taken him. One minister explained to me that God really hadn't had control in the operating room: the doctors had. My heart just couldn't believe that there was such a powerless God, and that the whole world was the victim of arbitrary fate. Two years later a "mixed up" friend told me how powerful God is, and that He is in complete control of the world and people's lives. I felt better about God for the world's sake, but why did God let a wonderful, clean-cut nineteen-year-old die?

My friend didn't give up. He dragged me to his church, where a man said the Second Coming was coming soon (in six months!) and that if we weren't Christians, we weren't going to get to heaven. Heaven was my big concern. I wanted to believe my brother was there, and that I would go there too.

Since my brother's death I'd been searching my heart and our church to find God. In my church I never felt good about who God was, and, as I look back, I am amazed to see that I could make a habit of such an empty experience. Anyway, when I went to my friend's church, I felt that I had to have what the people in that church had, and from that first Sunday I was no longer content to continue passively looking for God. My husband hates pressure tactics, but I needed someone to say "the hour of decision has come."

My faithful, mixed-up friend and I dragged my husband to that church the next Sunday, and we heard a speaker (the author of this book) that my husband could identify with. A Bible study was being held at the speaker's house on Tuesday and we decided to go.

We sure felt uncomfortable with this group of committed Christians. We'd never been with people who knew they were going to heaven and rejoicing in it. We felt uncomfortable — but there was something there that we knew we wanted. We kept coming back. Since everybody was a Christian, nobody talked much about how they became one. They just talked about how God was acting in their lives, and I could see that being a Christian was very different from being Barbara D. Boy, was it great to learn about God's love and see the love and joy in these people's lives. From my first church service in April until mid-October I tried to be a Chris-

tian. I prayed, we said grace, I tried to show the joy and peace which I could see my Christian friends had, and I tried to turn people to God.

On October 18 we had one of the couples in the Bible study over for dinner. He was a minister. I asked Bill what you had to do to commit yourself to God. By this time I had been convinced that the Second Coming wasn't when I had first heard it was — so I no longer felt any pressure for an immediate commitment to God. I had come to the point where I wanted to commit my life to God — even if I knew I didn't have to worry about salvation for fifty years.

Salvation didn't convert me. I just wanted to live a peaceful, joyful, loving life down here, and change the quality of my whole style of living. I had come to see that what I thought was bringing happiness was really shallow, impermanent, unstable. I knew that I was vulnerable to life's blows because I'd already lost a brother. Because of the love, joy, and peace in the people in our Bible study I was seeing a living heaven on earth.

Bill said that all I had to do was invite Jesus into my life, commit myself to the Lord and instantly I would be filled with the Holy Spirit. The Holy Spirit had been guiding me, but I had never known it, since I hadn't invited Him to.

The next morning when I was cleaning up the dining room I decided that the time had come to commit myself to the Lord and do what Bill had told me. Holding onto the edge of the dining room table, I asked God and Jesus to fill me with the Holy Spirit and I committed myself to them. At that very moment I felt filled with joy. I had done it! I had the Holy Spirit right inside me.. The awareness of this new fact really made me want to burst. It was wonderful to feel so good, so joyous, and to know the love that existed between God and myself.

For two years and eleven months since my brother's death I had been searching, and all my life I had wanted someone to guide and protect me. That someone I now realized had to be God, a supernatural being, because I was a strong, independent, self-sufficient person who wasn't about to rely on any peer. All of a sudden I didn't have to be alone any more, and someone knew me totally without my having to confess my faults or share my thoughts. The most powerful being in the universe was now part of me.

Since then I don't have to imagine. I know the peace that passes all understanding when you become a Christian.

PART II: Implementing Christian education
in the local church

Building the Body

11. the Servant Leader
12. the pastor, in pulpit and person
13. the lay leadership team
14. implications for seminary training

Childhood education

15. present approaches: a critique
16. guidelines and limitations
17. the home as nurture center
18. an alternative system

Adult education

19. the nature of ministry
20. conditions facilitating ministry
21. educational strategies: one to one
22. educational strategies: the small group
23. educational strategies: Body Life
24. educational strategies: worship
25. educational strategies: the preached Word

building the body: the servant leader

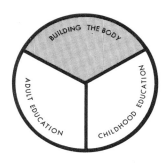

Earlier we saw that the Body itself has been designed for discipling. We need then in Christian education to have a deep concern for bringing members of the Body into ministering relationship with each other.

And we need to probe. What are critical factors in building the Body of Christ into a unit which fulfills its ministering purpose?

* the servant leader
   the pastor, in pulpit and person
   the lay leadership team
   implications for seminary
     training

It's always exhilarating to look at "how to" in Christian education. We find so many different ways the Church's educational (discipling) ministry can be carried out. The Holy Spirit seems to delight in bringing each local church to unique expressions of the principles of Body Life expressed in Scripture. "How to" thus plunges us into realm of possibilities: and there are so many possibilities! Later in this book we'll look into "how" as we examine various strategies in Christian education. But for now, in this section, we have to keep on probing principles. We have to see if the concepts of discipling, identification, modeling, and so on, have implications for what we do as the Body gathers to "build itself up in love, by that which every joint supplies, when each part is functioning" (Eph. 4:16).

visualizing the body

It is helpful for us to visualize the Body as we approach the issue of building it. Often visualization brings into the open hidden assumptions and images which affect our attitudes and ideas. I suspect that if the average believer were to visualize the Body, he might see it something like this: first of all, the church is viewed as the pastor. (How often do we say in speaking of a local body that it is "Pastor Garland's church, downtown"?) Second, the lay members of the body are visualized as they are normally seen, seated

in rows, facing the pastor, ready to be ministered to. Then we might add the lay leaders, off to one side because, except for monthly board meetings and the times the men serve communion, the board members are not visible to the congregation, nor is their role understood.

This visualization brings into focus the role-images held by many today. The pastor: minister. Laymen: not ministers, but those ministered to. Lay leaders: present, but with an uncertain function. The problem with this common image of the Church? *It does not cast each member of the Body as a minister.* And it distorts the role of church leadership as well.

mutual ministry. It is critically important as we think of the Body of Christ as a discipling community to recognize the Bible's teaching that each believer has a spiritual gift. Through this gift each believer makes a *ministry contribution* to the edification (growth) of other individuals and the group. This teaching of Scripture is well recognized. It is through every joint's contribution that the Body grows (Eph. 4). Each believer is to use the gifts given him (Rom. 12:5). The apostle Paul felt no fear for the Roman believers because he was sure that they were "able to instruct one another" (Rom. 15:14). While there are many varieties of spiritual gift enablements, each believer has a gift to use within the Body for the "common good" (1 Cor. 12:7). In the Body each part is "indispensable" (1 Cor. 12:22). No wonder when the early church assembled opportunity was given for each to be involved in ministering, and "all things" in the gathering were to be done "for edification" (1 Cor. 14:26-33). Our image of the Church must reflect this active, ministering, believer role. Rather than accept an active-passive dichotomy of the Body, like that implied in "minister" and "layman," or in "pastor/people" classifications, the New Testament insists that we come to see *each believer* as a minister. For each believer does have a priestly, ministering role in the Body.

How might we visualize the Church if our image is to reflect this concept of the believer's role? The circle at the right might be appropriate. Here we see the believers gathered, not focusing attention on a lone "minister," but on one another. Each is ready both to give and to receive. We do have special individuals marked off in the Body. 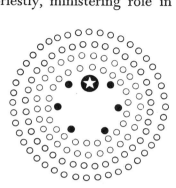 We'll continue to show the pastor by a star. And we'll continue to show local lay leaders — elders, deacons, the board — however you wish to designate them. But in this image of the church, they have a position which reflects their biblical function. That position is one of high visibility — and of closeness — among the other members of the Body. As we move on, we'll see that leaders are the key to building the Body into a functioning, ministering community. But first we *must* realize, and *commit ourselves to the understanding of the local Body as a ministering fellowship. We must give fullest commitment to the Bible's teaching that there are NO "laymen": that each of us is a believer-priest.*

Only when we realize that each believer is both to be discipled and to disciple, to be ministered to and to minister, can we understand the role of leadership in the church. And only when we understand the role of leadership can we begin to structure our local congregations as educating communities of faith.

the servant leader

We want to begin our exploration of leadership and its role in the Church with Jesus' instruction to His disciples, recorded in Matthew 20. It is important to focus our understanding of leadership in the Church through concepts drawn from the New Testament. This is not because we reject the Old Testament. Or because there are no insights into the nature of leadership there. It is because the New Testament defines the way leadership principles are applied to the Body.

For instance, we might define "leadership" in a general way. But if we were writing a manual on leadership for the military, it would certainly differ from a manual on leadership for business. Or for parents in the home. *There are different situations in which leadership principles are applied differently.* And leadership principles are applied uniquely in the Church of Jesus Christ. Leadership principles for the church are unique because of the way the Body is structured and functions.

So let's look at Matthew 20, and the teaching which grew out of a misunderstanding of leadership by James and John. These two brothers, eager for status and power, had their mother approach Jesus to ask for "left and right hand" positions in Jesus' coming kingdom. They wanted to be the top two men! Hearing of it, the other members of Jesus' discipleship band were upset and angry. Using this real-life situation as a time for teaching, Jesus called His disciples to Him and said,

> You know that the rulers of the Gentiles lord it over them, and their high officials exercise authority over them. Not so with you. Instead, whoever wants to become great among you must be your servant, and whoever wants to be first must be your slave — just as the Son of Man did not come to be served, but to serve, and to give his life a ransom for many (Matt. 20:25-28).

conflicting models. The first thing we note is that there are two conflicting models of leadership here. One, the Secular Ruler model, portrays leaders as men who *exercise authority over others.* There is nothing wrong with this model of leadership in the secular world. Jesus is not saying that such leadership is itself wrong. But He is saying it is wrong *in the church.* As for the disciples, it is to be "not so with you!"

Jesus then presents a counter model. Strikingly, His kind of leader, suited for greatness among disciples, is presented as a Servant. Among disciples in the Body of Christ, leaders are not *over but among,* not rulers but slaves, not takers but givers. If we are to understand the nature and function of leadership in the Church, we *must* take the Servant model with complete seriousness.

dimensions of servanthood. It's helpful to take a group of local church leaders and present these contrasting models to them, and ask them to draw implications from the two. Each group with which I've done this has found many. Three areas however are of particular importance.

(1) The servant relationship. The servant is a person who is *among,* not *over* those whom he leads.

There are many interpersonal implications of this relationship. One who is *over* us (an employer, an officer over enlisted men in the service) is normally perceived as "different from" us. The *over* relationship makes it easy for directives and cognitive kinds of data to be passed and processed, but very difficult for personal, affective kinds of data. (How many of us share our problems and feelings with our boss?) The *over* relationship also means that communications are normally through one-way channels. That is, the one *over* normally communicates directive-type data *down,* the one *under* normally communicates response-type data *up.*

On the other hand, an *among* relationship places persons on the same level. When we see another person as on our level, we normally perceive of him as "like" us. This makes it easier for all kinds of data to flow: we can share ideas, feelings, thoughts, attitudes, etc., knowing that we stand equal with the other and have his respect. Communication channels are now open to two-way flow. Either party can initiate, either respond. Either party can share. In a church context, either can minister, either respond.

An *among* relationship means that each person perceives the other as like him, and that each freely shares in the give and take of self-revelation and mutual ministry.

(2) The servant task. A servant among the disciples is, like Jesus, to expend his life on the behalf of others. The servant task is to serve others *in that which is important to God.* Jesus' gift of life, as we have seen earlier, has goal and direction. God's life, implanted in us as we come to trust Jesus, is to grow and transform us more and more to His image.

The Christian leader, called to serve as Jesus served, enters into this transforming purpose, and gives himself to build others as disciples. *His primary concern and ministry is the building up of the Body and its members.*

(3) The servant method. It is at this point that confusion often arises. "Leaders" are seen in our culture as directive. Their task is to *tell.* But a servant is unable to command. The man who is a servant does not "lord it over" others. Somehow the way that the secular ruler exercises authority is cut off from the Church by Jesus' words, "Not so with you."

How then does the servant lead? How does the servant exercise his authority? [And we must never make the mistake of visualizing Christian leaders as weak men who neither lead nor have authority!] We find an answer first of all in the servant role: <u>a servant does not command, he *does*. A servant does not direct others, he sets an example.</u>

This theme is picked up by Peter in his first letter. Writing to other elders who are to be "shepherds of God's flock that is under your care, serving as overseers," Peter tells them how God wants them to serve, "not lording it over those entrusted to you, but being examples to the flock" (1 Peter 5:1-5).

<u>The servant's method of leadership is to provide an example, and by virtue of example leaders bear a powerful authority. As models, leaders are used by God to move others to become like them.</u>

harmony with theology

In the first chapters of this book we looked at principles of ecclesiology which guide us to understand the distinctive educational (discipleship) principles on which Christian education must be based. Strikingly (and expectedly!) what we've seen of leadership thus far parallels these principles and concepts.

educational principles	*leadership principles*
the teacher is a model	the leader is a model
the learner is a disciple becoming like his teacher	the believer is a priest becoming like the leader
modeling and identification are the principle methods by which transformation takes place	modeling and identification (example) are the principle methods by which leaders lead
the relationship between teachers/ learners is transactional	there is an "among" rather than "over" relationship between leader/led which is transactional

If we can accept a biblical understanding of the believer as a priest and the church as a ministering community, then we can begin to understand the role and the purpose — and the method — of local church leadership. Then, too, we can begin to understand *how to organize the church for discipling through the whole community.* What are the critical principles? Those we've begun to look at in this chapter:

> ■ Each believer *is* a minister, a believer-priest, who has an active ministry role in the Body (not a passive ministered-to role).

There is no essential difference between "ministry" performed by a pastor or another church leader and ministry performed by a believer-priest. Each uses His God-given spiritual gift to build up others in the Body.

The specific task of leaders is to "serve" Body members, and through their service equip others for their ministering work (cf. here Eph. 4:12).

Spiritual leadership is to function in a *different way* in the Body than do secular rulers in society. There is a difference between the Body as a living organism and society as an association of individuals.

Spiritual leaders, by ministering "among" the Body, set an example which the Holy Spirit uses (through the educational processes of identification and modeling) to help other believer-priests become more and more like them.

Spiritual leaders who minister in this way have no need to worry about their "authority." God will open hearts in the Body to respond to them (cf. 1 Peter 5:5).

Unless we begin our thinking about leadership and organization of the Body with these concepts and principles, we are certain to fail to build the church into an educating, ministering, discipling community.

PROBE
  case histories
  discussion questions
  thought-provokers
  resources

1. As we began probing the organization of the Body for discipling, we looked at relationships between believers and leaders. The chapter suggests that essentially "leaders" are to be viewed as "teachers," in that leaders are to provide models for Body members, and are to develop an "among" relationship within which identification and modeling processes can take place.

    To examine this idea more thoroughly, you might want to study the following passages of Scripture. What does each have to say about the basic concept expressed above?

    a. Review Bible passages dealing with "imitate," "example," and "follow."

    b. Look at Philippians 4:9 ["Whatever you have learned or received or heard from me, or seen in me — put it into practice. And the God of peace will be with you."] How many parallel thoughts can you find in the Gospels or the Epistles?

    c. Examine the qualifications for leadership given in 1 Timothy 3 and Titus 1. How do you explain the criteria Paul gives to govern leader selection? Why is there not more skill or talent focus?

d. Look at two chapters of letters written by Paul to young leaders (1 Timothy 4 and Titus 2). How does what he says relate to the concept of leadership which we've begun to explore?

e. Do a thorough study of 2 Corinthians to get a portrait of Paul's leadership style, particularly the relationships he encourages with the people of this church.

2. In her book, *Focus on People in Church Education,* Dr. Lois LeBar, my friend and co-worker for seven years at Wheaton College Graduate School, includes the following paragraph on leadership education. Read the paragraph and interact with it. Is what Dr. LeBar says compatible or incompatible with what we've been saying about leadership in the church? How would you describe the assumptions underlying this paragraph? Would you, if you were a Minister of Christian Education in a typical local church, write on the same issue differently? If so, how, and why? If not, why not?

> *The church's leadership education program is planned and supervised by the standing committee on leadership education as one of the major functions of the church; or, if there is no leadership education committee, by the Board of Christian Education. The leadership education committee is composed of six or seven mature people who know the inner workings of the church and who have a burden for competent leadership upon their hearts. They oversee the leadership file which contains information about the gifts and backgrounds of new converts, as well as up-to-date cards of old members. They work out job descriptions for all the educational positions and set up qualifications in terms of a covenant for all workers and specific requirements for specialized ministries. They seek to fit the available people to the existing needs. Annually, they appoint and dedicate the next year's workers. They afford continuous training opportunities in terms of training classes, workers' conferences and other types of in-service training. They also supervise the extending of calls to prospective workers.*[1]

3. Case history.

In Our Heritage Church, Scottsdale, Arizona, the pastor, Bob Girard, developed an extensive writing and speaking ministry beyond the local congregation. This caused some conflict in Bob's own life, as "switching hats" gave him a sense of disorientation to the happenings at the church.

After considerable discussion and prayer, the elders felt that Bob's

---

[1]From *Focus on People in Church Education* by Lois LeBar. Copyright 1968 by Fleming H. Revell Co., Old Tappan, New Jersey. Used by permission.

gifts were such that he should be freed to minister to the Church at large as well as the local congregation. The elders thus recommended that Bob be "given" to the Church as a gift by the local congregation for three months out of the year. During those three months, he would be free to write and speak, and the church would continue his support as their "missionary." Ministry in the local body would be supervised by the elders while the pastor was absent, with the elders and other members of the local body leading in worship and ministry of the Word.

This recommendation was presented to the entire board (made up at Our Heritage of elders and deacons), and after discussion and prayer the leaders unanimously agreed on this course of action.

The next Sunday pastor Girard spoke on the Church and its mutual ministry, and informed the congregation of the decision of the board. The following Sunday, one of the elders shared more of the reasons behind the decision, the need for each member to accept responsibility for ministering, and the expectancy with which the board looked forward to discovering more about Christ's headship during these months.

As part of this service, the congregation was divided geographically with elders and deacons from each locality meeting with the members to talk over the decision, to listen to feelings and ideas, and to ask for suggestions, advice, or warnings about the coming time of Bob's absence.

Looking over this situation, which happened as described in July of 1974, evaluate particularly the following:

(1) How did the elders show leadership?

(2) How was "making the decision" rather than calling for a "vote" in harmony both with the biblical description of church leaders as "rulers" (or "overseers") and the concept of the servant who gives the example rather than demands?

(3) What potential problems do you see with this approach to decision-making . . . especially when a critical issue like the one described is concerned?

(4) What was the value of the "discussion groups" after the elder's message on Sunday?

(5) What steps do you believe the church leaders should take now to prepare for the upcoming three-month period?

(6) Under what circumstances could you reasonably expect the approach described above to *fail*?

building the body:
the pastor, in pulpit and in person

Christian education must concern itself with the Body, for discipling is a ministry of the community as well as a ministry for individuals with special "teaching" gifts. To develop a ministering Body, involvement of each member as a believer-priest is essential. Leaders are called by God to set the tone, and to bring members into a ministering relationship with each other.

Once we grasp the purpose and servant character of spiritual leadership, we can clearly see the pastor as an "educator." In fact, we see him as the primary Christian educator in the contemporary local church.

the servant leader
* the pastor, in pulpit and person
the lay leadership team
implications for seminary
   training

There is a great deal of strain these days on men in the ministry seeking to define their role. This strain is typical of many professions in our age. When I went to seminary the role was defined quite simply. The pastor is a "pastor-teacher," who equips the believers for ministry by teaching them the Bible. And "teaching them the Bible" meant essentially by speaking to them Sundays and on other occasions from the pulpit.

Shortly after my graduation, there was a swing toward the idea that the pastor is a counselor. Pastoral counseling became the big department in many seminaries, and many men envisioned their primary role as "minister" to be one of comforting and correcting those whom life had disturbed.

Today there seems to be a trend toward viewing the work of the pastor as essentially administrative. Church management seminars are flourishing. The image of the corporate executive who organizes the church and its members to accomplish tasks — particularly tasks that lead to church growth — seems attractive to many.

The confusion is understandable. It stems from our failure to begin with theology, and to ask what the *Church* is. Once we see the Church as a ministering Body, as a transforming community, we are on the track of discovering the pastor's identity. He is not an instructor of listeners (the old "pastor-teacher" image). He is not a bandager of the bruised (the pastoral counselor image). He is not a manager of the Church's human resources (the church administrator image). Instead, the pastor is one charged with leading disciples into ministry. The image which fits him is that of a servant: a servant who leads by example.

We've seen elements of this role in the last chapter which describes some of the principles common to all spiritual leadership in the Church. How does a pastor in a local church need to see himself?

* as one of many ministers.
* as one *among* the many.
* as one who senses God's direction, and sets the example for the many.
* as one activating others to minister.
* as one whose ministry is not *different from* the ministry of the many but whose ministry is essentially *like* theirs.

With this understood, a number of practices in ministry are suggested ... practices which have educational significance for the Body, and which suggest the kind of leadership pastors are to provide.

the pastor and the pulpit

In a later chapter we'll look at a theology of the preaching. For now we'll not be concerned with the *content* taught the Body, but with ways that a pastor might express his identity as a servant leader through the church's pulpit ministry. Noting that each practice can find its roots in understanding of the *relational, exemplary,* or *activating* functions of leadership, here are a number of possible ways that the pastor might *lead* in his pulpit ministry.

sharing the pulpit. There are many ways to do this. In some churches, such as Newport Beach's *Mariner's Church,* board members take all parts of the service but the morning sermon. In others a "God at work" segment features the pastor chatting with a member of the congregation whose life God has touched that week. In other churches members of the congregation — particularly lay leaders — have regular preaching responsibilities. Dialogue sermons provide another possibility — the pastor may begin a message, then move into dialogue with a prepared layman.

Even in very traditional churches, there are simple ways to increasingly involve other believer-priests, and by this involvement communicate nonverbally that pastor and people are ministers together.

sharing response. Increasingly these days the importance of response to God's Word is understood. And many are taking steps to facilitate response.

There are many methods. They range from placing probing questions in the bulletin for families to talk over at home, to having open sharing in the congregation after a message. In Phoenix's *Trinity Church,* pastor Joel Eidsness has a discussion class after the message in which meaning is explored (in this church, Sunday school follows the regular morning service). In another church, members regularly move to the "fellowship" room for a meal and for discussion of the meaning of the Scripture taught. Such fellowship table-talks may be led by elders or deacons. In other churches, like the one I attend, opportunity for sharing and Body ministry is given the whole congregation following the pastor's teaching. Questions are raised, comments made, insights shared, as all the members of the Body accept the responsibility to teach one another.

preliminary involvement. Dave Mains of Circle Church regularly meets with groups of believer-priests before he preaches. He shares with them the purpose sentence of his sermon (summarizing the one main Bible truth he hopes to communicate), outlines the passage, and invites their feedback. They explore the purpose sentence, and raise questions, give suggestions as to the passage's applications, and in general help David construct the message. Thus the preaching ministry is not only an expression of David's gifts, but also of the gifts of the Body. By rotating groups, all members of the congregation have the opportunity to be involved in the pulpit ministry of the church.

Other ministers have found other ways to involve believers. Some will infrequently use survey questionnaires to give members opportunity to express needs and interests which can be reflected in coming messages.

being personal. One of the things I was told about preaching in seminary was to avoid illustrations from my own life, or from others in the congregation. I've come to believe that this was probably one of the most incorrect things I was told! It's vital, for modeling to take place, that teacher (pastor) and disciple (believer-priests) be able to identify with each other. For identification not only a love relationship but also transparency — a *knowing* of one another — is vital. As the pastor shares in the pulpit, and shares too the experiences of brothers and sisters [of course it's right to ask beforehand if you can share something], the modeling process is enhanced, and truths are viewed in a life, rather than intellectual framework. "He is a man like me" is one of the greatest compliments that believers can pay to their pastors. Such an awareness shows that the sacerdotal gap between "minister" and "laymen" is perhaps being bridged.

Now, these illustrations are not meant to be exhaustive, but they do show that the pastor *can* in his pulpit ministry take definite steps to model for the congregation who he is and who they are. By providing an increasing and varied role for members he can help each believer-priest see himself or herself as "minister." He can break the passive pattern, and gently guide each believer to a clearer understanding of who he is to be in the Body.

It is particularly important that this kind of thing be done in churches where the pastor is *preaching* about renewal and Body ministries. *The preached Word must always be lived out to have its fullest, compelling impact.* The pastor who tells his people that they are ministers, but who fails to step aside in his pulpit and involve them in ministry, will always find that the congregation's understanding grows slowly, if at all. It is a fact that the critical method of spiritual leadership is example. If no example is given, it is likely that spoken words will be ignored.

the pastor in person

It's important to see the pastor as a leader through his pulpit ministry, for it is in the pulpit that most of the people of a congregation relate to him. But over the long run, a "pulpit image" is one the pastor needs to take steps to eliminate. Instead, the pastor needs to be viewed — whether in the teaching role or out of it — as a person.

It becomes very important then for the pastor of a local church to come to know and to be known to his congregation personally.

sharing. One way, already noted, is to share himself when he preaches or teaches. This often is looked at with concern by pastors. There is fear that sharing will be misunderstood. Fear that in sharing, weaknesses might be revealed, and that if others know one's weaknesses "respect" will be lost.

It's true that sharing will reveal weaknesses. But it is also true that <u>self-revelation is a strength, not a weakness, in spiritual leadership.</u> The reasons for this are basic, and are rooted in theology.

* We are to be examples . . . not of perfection, but of a *process*. We can afford to remove the veils because we are being transformed: progress is being made (2 Cor. 3:13).
* <u>We are to reflect the gospel.</u> And the gospel is not "accept Christ and become perfect." The gospel presents Jesus as the continual answer to man's needs. "Without me you can do nothing" (Jesus' words from John 15:5)reflects <u>our continued weakness and need for divine enablement.</u> If we misrepresent ourselves as so "strong" that we do not need Jesus, we misrepresent the gospel of God's grace.
* <u>We are to be models with whom others can identify.</u> Strikingly, it is our weaknesses rather than our strengths that most help others see themselves as like us.

None of this detracts in any way from the pastor's responsibility to be a man of God: to set a *good* example in godliness (Titus 2:6-8). But it does cut us off from being hypocritical; it eliminates the need to pretend when we hurt. In sharing ourselves, in being real with others, they may well see our weaknesses — but they will also see Jesus' strength. And they will be encouraged that the transformation Jesus has been working in us can be worked in them as well!

meeting. <u>It's important then for the pastor to meet with the believer-priests of his congregation in a variety of settings so they can come to know him.</u> This might often be in carrying out his ministry. David Mains' people come to know him better as they hammer out a coming sermon together at his home.

But additional relationships are important. For example, some pastors meet weekly in their homes with four or more couples from the church, rotating the group each time. These times are not "spiritual" ones, but are designed simply to help people get to know each other and to know the pastor. One pastor uses Lyman Coleman's *Serendipity* materials on occasions like this, with good effect.

A number of pastors these days have seen the need to develop a special discipling relationship with men of the congregation. Gib Martin of Seattle meets weekly with seven men for a breakfast discipleship class that continues over a two-year period. The men study during the week, do reports and projects, and in the close association with Gib are discipled into deeper dedication and become better equipped as ministers.

visitation. This of course is another opportunity to come to know members of the congregation and to be known by them. But visitation needs to be viewed as having deepened relationships as one of its purposes. Visitation of the sick (remedial visitation), as significant as this may be, is not really as significant as getting to know members of the congregation as persons. Often traditional visitation does not help in this purpose: when viewed as a "pastoral call" both pastor and hosts are sometimes uncomfortable. It's far better to keep visitation informal — and consistent.

Dropping in on a member to say hello as he or she works at a lunchroom counter, having a meal with a downtown businessman, dropping over with some tomatoes from the garden, picking up the phone to express appreciation for a favor, and to chat — these informal contacts are the ones that help build personal relationships with people.

And it is the personal relationship that is vital to good pastoral leadership.

modeling. Often special situations provide opportunities for modeling the personalness that the pastor wants to encourage between himself and others and, as an outcome, encourage within the congregation as well. One Fresno, California, pastor provided "fellowship training" for ten couples for eight weeks on a Sunday evening. Then he took ten more couples, and repeated the course. Over two years, some one hundred and fifty members of this church not only got to know him and each other better, but also learned relational skills which helped bring the congregation closer as a family.

More than one pastor sees as a critical part of his ministry launching small fellowship groups for home Bible study or prayer. After spending a few weeks with a new group, he moves on to launch another, infrequently visiting the old, or being available should questions arise.

In all these ways the pastor can be pictured as *facilitating the development of personal relationships in the local Body.* In the process others come to know him as a person. In the process he sets the relational tone, becoming a model of the freedom to know and be known that Jesus gives us within His family.

education?

In the traditional sense, the things we've looked at in this chapter may not be viewed as "education." There are no classes described here. No content or curriculum. The classroom setting is not in view. The pastor is not even seen here in his traditional teaching ministry role.

But in the most significant sense what we have described is education: education for discipleship. What we've been looking at are elements of *nonformal education:* education conducted through the ways people live together in their shared identity as a local body. *It is this kind of nonformal education which is the most significant education for the Church.* And we can make no mistake. The way the pastor lives with a people *does* educate. In fact, *if the model provided by the pastor is a counter model to the concept of the ministering Body, then that local church will not develop as a ministering fellowship.* Until that pastor changes, or leaves.

When we break out of our old suppositions about education and realize it is not a formal but an informal thing, not a class-room but a life-context proposition, not an information-processing but a dynamic, whole-person, transactional experience, then we realize that the way pastoral leadership models biblical principles of Body life in every interaction with the members of a local body is perhaps *the* critical factor in Christian education. Transformation and education for discipleship operate on principles of modeling and example. Because this is true, the example set by church leadership is, bluntly, *the* key to understanding the ministering church, and the whole ministry of Christian education.

PROBE

case histories
discussion questions
thought-provokers
resources

Building the Body: The Pastor, in Pulpit and in Person

1. This is a good time to do a little stretching. So see if you can find two or three books in each of the following areas. Skim them, and find out what their presuppositions are. Then write a brief paper covering the questions following each category.

   A. *Christian education*

   Locate three books on Christian education, preferably written from different theological perspectives. Look particularly at the table of contents, then skim the most significant areas. From your review, record your impressions about:

   (1) How does each book view "education"?

   (2) What processes are suggested for educating?

   (3) Who are viewed in the book as educators?

   (4) Does the book seem to reflect a learning theory?

   (5) How does each approach education — as a theological or a philosophical issue?

   (6) How does each compare and contrast with the present text?

   B. *Church leadership*

   Locate three books on Christian leadership, preferably written from different theological perspectives. Look particularly at the table of contents, then skim the most significant areas. From your review, record your impressions about:

   (1) What does each consider the most significant aspect of leadership?

   (2) How does each suggest that the leader lead?

   (3) Who are viewed in the book as "leaders"?

   (4) How great a role does theology play in the definition of leadership tasks and methods?

   (5) Is any distinction made between "organizational" leadership and leadership of the Church as a Body?

   (6) How does each compare and contrast with the present text?

   C. *Pastoral ministry*

   Locate three books on the pastor and his ministry, preferably written from different theological perspectives. Look particularly at the table of contents, then skim the most significant areas. From your review, record your impressions about:

   (1) What does each consider the pastor's primary role to be?

   (2) How does each suggest the pastor minister?

   (3) Does each suggest ways the pastor is the same as or different from ministering members of the Church?

   (4) What view of the "laymen" and the local church itself is implicit in the suggestions of the books?

   (5) What is said about the pastor's servant role and its meaning in ministry conduct?

   (6) How does each compare and contrast with the present text?

2. A resource pastoral students or pastors will want to explore is the *Fingertip Consultant,* produced by Step 2, Inc., a Chicago-based, not for profit organization serving the local church and encouraging its renewal through application of basic biblical principles of church life.

The following is a section from a training manual that is included with the *Consultant.* In it, David Mains sets before pastors the task of meeting with a lay team for sermon preparation. (For those interested, the *Fingertip Consultant* can be ordered from Step 2, 1925 N. Harlem, Chicago, Illinois, 60635, on approval.)

This is your first week to work with a group of your parishioners on a sermon. In order that the experience be most helpful let's return to one of our previous formats.

BEFORE YOUR MEETING WITH GROUP Y

1. We need you to project one final time. Write out a list of five people in your congregation who you feel would be open to helping you prepare for Target Sunday C on (month)_____ (date)_____ (WEEK TWELVE). Include among the five at least one church officer, if none has been involved to date. Also, put down the name of a person in the congregation who can be expected to oppose change. Lastly, attempt again to balance the group by getting a cross section of the various people in your congregation. Write the names down.

   Group Y names

   1. _____
   2. _____
   3. _____
   4. _____
   5. _____

2. Spend time *now* thanking God for the people of Group Y with whom you are meeting tonight.
3. *After you have prayed* . . . set a reasonable "official" end time for tonight's session. (We will stop at_____.)
4. Read through the seven points of the suggested agenda under the next section "During Your Meeting With Group Y." Decide on how much time should be given to items two, three and five, writing this information on the line before each number. (The other four items require a total of 30 minutes.)
5. Review your thoughts about the sermon for Target Sunday B. Are they in Key Truth form yet? If not, the people of Group B will still be of help, so *don't panic!* Can you state clearly the need you see about which you would like to preach? For an added bit of inspiration read J. H. Jowett's comment on Key Truth preaching which you'll find behind tab "Reference Thoughts."

DURING YOUR MEETING WITH GROUP Y

2 minutes

1. Tell the group the "Official" end time of the meeting. Let them know they are welcome to stay longer; however, at the time stated the meeting will be "officially" ended. Also, make sure everyone knows each other.

15 minutes

2. Let the group discuss their reaction to the tapes they have heard. Remind them that Step 2 is only using Circle Church of Chicago as an illustration of its Program Guidelines. These Guidelines are (1) In planning a church service *Let's Get Coordinated* and (2) In preparing the sermon around which the service is built, *Let's Say One Thing Well.* It is not intended that you copy how Circle Church puts these Guidelines into operation. Encourage those who have not listened to all of the tapes to do so by next week. Inform the group that you will need all six tapes returned to you the next time you meet and that this is important.

15 minutes

3. Allow the people of Group Y to talk about last Sunday's service. Can they remember the thrust of the sermon? What hymns were sung? Can anyone recall the Scripture reading? Has the service brought about any specific change in the life of someone in Group Y? (Note — especially be aware of the response of your key layman!)

3 minutes

4. Explain that in order to be coordinated on a Sunday morning, Step 2 stresses the importance of building the entire service around a single Key Truth. The purpose for this meeting is to have their imput regarding the single sentence you are in the process of preparing for two weeks from Sunday (month)_____ (date)_____ (WEEK NINE). Explain that one of the suggested steps is to discuss what people of the congregation feel about sermons while they are still in the planning stage.

15 minutes

5. Share with Group Y where you are in your thinking to this point. If you can give a Key Truth sentence . . . fine! If you are able to describe the theme . . . do that. Maybe you are only capable of pinpointing the problem that concerns you. Possibly you are so blank you can only ask their help in suggesting a theme. One way or the other, solicit their comments. Do they see the same need? Would a sermon like this be where they live or beyond them? What questions do they have? Would they like the Key Truth changed? *Do not* allow

yourself to become defensive! If it helps, pretend you are leading a discussion about a church other than your own. And, be sure they are doing most of the talking . . . not you!

15 minutes

6. Try to come up with a strong Biblical Key Truth that relates to the total of the conversation. Put the words on paper so the thought does *not* escape.

10 minutes

7. *Ten minutes* before the "official" quitting time stop the discussion for a period of prayer. Let everyone know how appreciative you are that they have come. Ask them to think about the discussion between now and the next time you get together. Remind them of the date and time. Encourage each person to call you if they come up with further ideas. Let them know you will not be able to use everything suggested, but it will no doubt be of help in understanding the topic.

Stand *up* at the end of the prayer time so they will know the session is "officially" over.

AFTER YOUR MEETING WITH GROUP Y

1. While the thoughts are fresh in your mind and you are now alone, try to work out a final Key Truth sentence. If possible, settle on a scriptural text as well.
2. Step 2 will be waiting to meet with you an hour before your meeting with your friends next week.
3. Between now and the next time we are together use the following space to write additional thoughts regarding your sermon for Target Sunday B.

May God fill your heart with gratitude for the people of your congregation . . . not only that you can significantly touch their lives, but that they can reach out and touch yours as well.

building the body: the lay leadership team

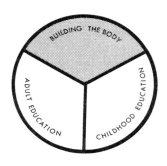

Because the Body is composed of believer-priests who are all to minister, no one person can be a sufficient model. Because there is a corporate as well as individual dimension to the Body, there is to be a corporate as well as individual model(s).

When we understand the nature of the Church and the nature of its transforming (discipling) ministry, we see clearly why God planned for each local congregation a multiple lay leadership team.

the servant leader
the pastor, in pulpit and person
* the lay leadership team
implications for seminary
   training

Over and over the New Testament speaks of recognizing "elders" in newly planted churches. Prior to A.D. 70 the term "elder" was used in Jewish synagogues to denote leaders. It was used also of members of the Sanhedrin. This title used in the Church reflects both a Jewish and Gentile heritage: the "old ones" were those older and more advanced in the faith, who had earned respect and demonstrated their capacity to model. In the Jerusalem church there were both apostles and elders (Acts 15 and 16). The elders are mentioned throughout Acts (11:30; 14:23; 15:2, 4, 6, 22f.; 16:4; 20:17; 21:18) and also in the Epistles (Titus 1:5; James 5:14; 1 Peter 5:1; etc.). According to early Christian literature elders, like the "bishops" (a term stressing one's role as overseer), had exhortation and preaching roles in the church's services. This role is reflected also in the

Pastoral Epistles, where, among the qualifications for ordination as a deacon or elder, is listed ability to teach.

Yet it is striking that the primary concern in recognizing men as elders is that their character and behavior be exemplary. They are to show a distinct work of God toward transformation. This concern with *who the elder is as a person* focuses our attention again on the primary role leaders are to play. Leaders in the Church of Jesus Christ are to be examples of Christian living (1 Peter 5:4).

It also is significant to see that wherever terms for leaders (elders, bishops, deacons) are used, the user has in view many rather than one! Each church is seen as having deacon*s*. And elder*s*. The leadership of the church is to be multiple . . . not singular.

Why is this important? It is important not merely because an individual may be more easily mistaken than a group. It is important not merely because unanimity is a sign of the Spirit's communication of His will, and thus *agreement* is a significant concern in church decision making. It is important not merely because where there is multiple leadership the leaders will be open to correction and ministry from each other, while a lone individual might purposely or inadvertently cut himself off from the ministry of others. Each of these is a factor, and a part of the reason for multiple local leadership in the Body.

The central reason for multiple leadership moves us back again to theology. The Church is a Body. Not just the individual, the Body's local experience as a unit is of concern to Christ. The Body, as well as the individual, is to grow and "make increase of itself in love." There is an identity for each local body, as well as many identities for members within it. As each individual is to be responsive to Christ as his Head, so the Body is to be responsive to Jesus as its corporate head.

It is because there is a corporate identity for each local body that multiple leadership is necessary. Just as individuals are to be transformed as they grow in Christ, so are local bodies. The local body is to grow in love. The local body is to grow in ability to use members' gifts. The local body is to grow in capacity to mirror Christ's character to the world around.

Now, how is a group of believers to learn to function as a body? *In the same way that all learning takes place within the Body. Through being discipled. Through becoming like a model which exemplifies a pattern of life the whole Body is to develop.*

Who then can be a model for the Body?

The pastor can't. He is an individual. He can be an example for individuals, but not for a Body.

But a *group of leaders* can model in their relationship with each other, and their ways of working together, how the whole Body is to live and relate. A group of leaders, servants to the congregation, called to set an example of Christian living, can model Body Life!

This group of men in the local congregation is the educational key to the development of the Body's life — just as the pastor is key to helping members of the Body discover their identity as ministers. A church's lay leadership team is critical in helping the local Body discover its identity as an organism.

principles and practices

In chapter 11 we looked at some principles of servant leadership. We pinpointed these:

* the servant leader does, and by doing sets the example.
* the servant leader is among the people, encouraging them to know him.
* the servant through his ministry equips others to minister as well.

These principles help us understand the role of lay leaders in the local church, and also suggest practices which facilitate their functioning as corporate models.

the first responsibility. The first responsibility of a lay leadership team is to become a functioning "body." It is always central to leadership that leaders *be becoming* what other members of the body are to become.

At Our Heritage Church in Scottsdale, Arizona, the elders meet each Saturday morning for three hours, from seven till ten. The times together are not primarily times for discussing church business. They are times for mutual ministry, to share what is happening in one another's lives, and to study the Bible together. Often church concerns do come up, and are studied, talked, and prayed through together. Each contributes his own viewpoint and gift, and in time God gives unanimity. When the board shares decisions or recommendations with the Church as a whole, the men speak with a unified voice, with each fully understanding and reflecting the other. The unity of the Body is something they can portray to the Body because they have grown together and have come to experience unity.

It is important, then, to get rid of the image of church leaders as having primarily a *business* function. The primary responsibility of local church leadership is to develop a "body" relationship between themselves, that they might model what a body is to the congregation. It also is important that the pastor be viewed as *a part of* and not *different from* this lay leadership team. He may enjoy full-time support, and have special responsibilities, but he is to be always a member of a team. In fact, the development of church leaders into a lay leadership team is one of the most critical tasks a pastor can undertake.

Church board meetings, then, change their "business" character and become times for ministry, sharing, discipling one another, and growing as individuals and as a group. This kind of growing together costs in time and commitment. Personally I believe it requires *weekly* time together. Commitment to one another, a vital factor in the functioning of the Body as a whole, must be demonstrated first by the leadership of the church with one another. If the church leaders do *not* take time to grow together in a vital unity, there is little likelihood that unity will come to characterize the local body as a whole. *We reproduce what we are.* The servant does lead by example . . . and the example he sets is the one which will be followed.

representing unity. For an example to be followed, it must be seen. This demands exposure of lay leadership to the congregation. Elders and deacons should have roles in regular services. Pastoral prayers, sermons, and personal sharing might well be offered by lay leaders.

The division of a congregation into geographical localities and discussion of body concerns with elders and deacons, described on page 137, permits leaders to meet with the people and also to reflect the unity of the leadership team. Some churches have made geographical divisions a basis for lay leaders' ministries, and involved elders in visitation in their district.

What is important here is that the elders be recognized by the congregation, be viewed as working together in ministry areas, and reflect in the process the unity which they have developed with one another.

among the people. This factor is like the above, but has a different emphasis. Lay leaders, like the pastor, need to be involved personally with the members of the congregation. They need to be known as persons, and identified with.

In practice, they develop this kind of "among" relationship just as the pastor must: by being personal and self-revealing when they share in a congregational gathering, by getting together informally with members of the body.

In one Phoenix church, each board member is involved in one or more "little churches." These little churches are small groups that meet during the week for several hours, to share, study the Bible, and pray. Thus board members build relationships with congregational members as well as each other. In another church, board members invite groups from the congregation to their homes monthly. These groups rotate, and are designed to give members a chance to get acquainted with each other and the leader. When discussion groups are used following services, having elders and deacons head up each one also facilitates building relationships. In churches where Body Life type sharing takes place, church leaders will often have a significant role and thus become known in this setting as well.

Actually, each local church will develop its own style of meeting and ministry. In each, different patterns for communicating the leadership team's example will develop. *Where there actually is a leadership team, the "how" will come naturally.* People will increasingly sense the strength of the local church's leaders, and confidence in them will grow. With confidence, there will be increasing freedom to follow the example set, and grow closer to others in the Body. In many churches this process will be almost unrecognized. As with other informal education experiences, the process is so natural that it takes place almost without awareness.

But for it to take place, there must be a leadership team. Leadership of the local Body must involve more than "name only" leaders, elected in some balloting process to fill organizational slots. A leadership team becomes a team by growing into one another's lives; by spending time together and in the Word, working together toward that unity with which the Spirit sets apart the functioning body. Without the development of actual unity, of actual example, there will be little impact on whatever plans we make to use church leaders.

PROBE

case histories
discussion questions
thought-provokers
resources

1. A pastor of my acquaintance was enthusiastic about his plan to involve elders in his church's ministry. *Evaluate the chances for success or failure of his plan.* The plan: Take the newly elected church

board, and divide the congregation geographically. Give each elder or deacon one geographical unit as his responsibility. Give each elder or deacon an outline of responsibilities (visit each family twice a year, check up on those who drop out over six weeks consecutively, etc.). Set aside Tuesday nights for thirty minutes of training, then to go out to do the visitation required.

In addition, as time passes, each elder or deacon is to take on counseling responsibilities for people in his area. Phone numbers will be published in the church bulletin, with the direction that anyone wanting pastoral care call the appropriate lay leader.

2. It's clear from what's been said in the past two chapters that *communication* is a primary concern in the church's functioning as a Body. Most books on organization and administration tend to present a *control function* organizational structure. That is, the church is organized to facilitate the communication of *directives down,* and *reports of responsibilities fulfilled up.* Look, for instance, at this typical chart.

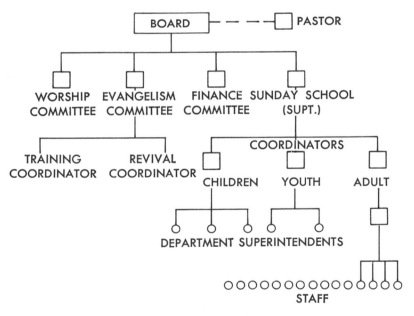

"control" organizational structure

This kind of organization stresses task accomplishment. Persons tend to come together only to perform work. Also this organizational structure stresses differentiation rather than identification. The "superintendent" is above the teacher or worker. He is responsible for the worker's perform-

ance, and is in turn responsible to the board or person above him for his performance. In such a performance or "control" structure, the kinds of personal relationships we have explored as significant in the church tend to be viewed as inappropriate to "getting the job done." Note also that the "jobs" for which the organization is designed have only indirect relationship to transformation. That is, task groups do not meet to edify each other, but to design formal structures in which it is assumed edification will take place.

Is it possible to design a different kind of organizational chart which will stress communication rather than control functions within the Body? That is, a chart which will structure the church around transformation rather than task meetings? That will stress identification rather than differentiation? That will have a direct rather than indirect relationship to ministry?

In an earlier book I suggested one model of the Church's organization which attempted to do this kind of thing. It was misunderstood by some who failed to see that in it communication rather than control was at issue. I did not then and do not now see this model as *the* way to organize a local church. But it is at least one other way than the traditional: one that I believe is in closer harmony with the Church's nature and the nature of ministry than the normal organizational charting taken, quite obviously, from the business world. Here it is:

"Communication" organizational structure

This kind of organization stresses interpersonal ministering. Persons are with each other for upbuilding. Each member of the various groups share a common identity: rather than being "above" the others even the five "supervisors" represent the groups of which they are members. Each is responsible to and for the "growth cell" of which he is a part, and through each leader (who is known intimately by his smaller group) each individual has a share in charting the life of the local Body. The gatherings of each of these groups ("growth cell," "counselor," and "supervisor") are for ministry, not for the design of formal "educational" programing or structures.

This kind of organization looks then at an organism and at interrelationships between persons: not at an organization and at the interrelationships between jobs.

Looking over the two charts, try your hand at the following.

(A) Do your own analysis of how lay leadership would function in each setting.

(B) Do your own analysis of the kinds of relationships each setting would tend to promote.

(C) Do your own analysis of the effect of each kind of organization on the flow of affective (feeling) data.

ORGANIZATION OF THE RE-FORMED CHURCH

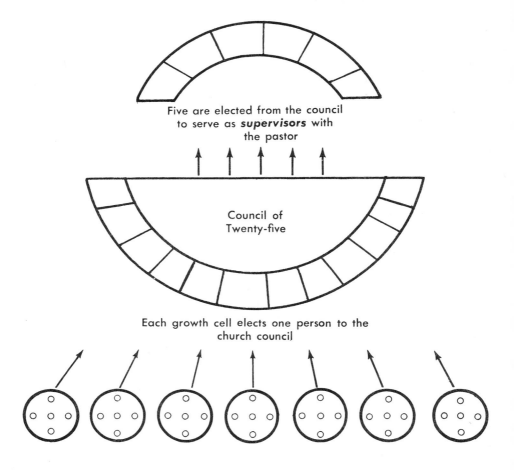

Five are elected from the council
to serve as *supervisors* with
the pastor

Council of
Twenty-five

Each growth cell elects one person to the
church council

(D) Do your own analysis of the *kinds of example* which would tend to be given by leaders in each setting.

(E) Develop a third and different model of church organization which stresses communication functions rather than control functions.

3. One of the criticisms of a "communication function" organizational approach is that it is not adapted to accomplishing tasks. Thus, even though a communications oriented organization might facilitate involvement in mutual ministries, the argument goes, it would not permit effective functioning of something like a Sunday school. "It's a nice dream but it wouldn't *work,*" is a common complaint.

   Is this a valid criticism? See if you can design a total educational ministry for Junior Highs [not, for now, involving the home] by using the principles fo discipleship teaching/learning presented in this book. One hint: remember that in your design "teachers" will function in the same way "elders" do in the local Body. Your educational design should reflect the same basic principles that are reflected in the operation of the Body as a whole.

4. One last task. In this and preceding chapters you've seen several suggestions for getting pastor and leaders in closer relationship with believer-priests, and also suggestions for ways they might model. By yourself or with others;
   A. List twenty ways leaders and people might come to know each other better.
   B. List twenty ways a leader's practices might demonstrate to other believers that *they* are expected to be actively involved in ministering.

14

building the body:
implications for seminary training

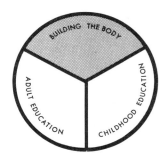

Training needs to be purposive. It needs to have in focus the product it is designed to produce.

When we understand the nature of spiritual leadership for the Church, we're able to define the kind of persons pastors, missionaries, and other "full time" or "professional Christian workers" are to be. We are also able to better define the kind of training seminaries need to provide.

the servant leader
the pastor, in pulpit and person
the lay leadership team
* *implications for seminary training*

I confess to a bias as we look at the question of training for professional ministry. It's a bias which has grown through the years of my own seminary training, my ministry in a graduate school preparing young people for ministry, and years of working with church renewal. It's a perspective that has grown as I've researched an experimental "internship" design for ministry once planned for Wheaton College's Graduate School. The bias has been a reflection of theological conviction rather than experience: I thoroughly enjoyed both my training and my teaching in the formal learning setting.

However, once teaching is understood as a discipling process, a whole-person concern that involves identification with a model like whom the disciple becomes, the luxury of enjoyment can no longer be afforded. I may enjoy the seminary's classical approach to training . . . but I must find a better way to equip men for ministry.

Part of the difficulty experienced by men moving into local church ministry grows out of the fact that example leadership *does* reproduce itself. Seminaries *train* as well as teach. The "hidden curriculum" of the learning setting has a greater impact on the learner than the "content" curriculum which is being taught in the instruction.

What is involved in the hidden curriculum of most seminary (as other formal learning) programs?

* *conceptual structuring of content.* Biblical truths are communicated in logical sequence, organized in categories which are essentially impersonal. This is not to say that content taught is untrue, or irrelevant. It is simply to say that the biblical material interacted with is related to the cognitive. It is not viewed as valid in the seminary classroom to deal with how truths make one feel, the present experiences they relate to, etc. The classroom teaching process does *not* attempt to tie Bible truth to the total — the psychological, sociological, interpersonal, etc. — personality. As a result, students are trained to study and master Scripture in an intellectual rather than personal or relational way.

* *impersonal learning setting.* There is no time in the classroom setting to come to know the teacher or other learners personally. As a result an impersonal style of ministering is "caught," and is likely to be reproduced in the seminarian's church ministry.

* *"learning" is viewed as "knowing."* Grading and other forms of approval hinge on cognitive mastery of biblical data which can be expressed on papers or in examinations. A premium on having Bible information is unconsciously transferred to ministry, so that those with information rather than those who are examples are likely to be selected for leadership roles in the local church.

* *learning is individual.* Testing, grading, assignments, all are given with an assumption of individual achievement. The tendency to view persons as those who ought to be able to stand on their own is reflected in a priority on the minister's "private" study time, and in the organization of the church to encourage personal but not group Bible study. The idea that the "teacher" is one who goes home and

studies the Bible and then tells others what he has learned is an expression of this orientation.

* *competitive rather than cooperative.* The seminary setting, like the secular school, tends to throw individuals into academic competition with one another. This encourages interpersonal distance rather than closeness. It also makes it difficult for a person schooled in competitive behaviors (which insist he be *better* than others) to take the lead in a Body in which he is called to model *cooperative* behaviors and attitudes!

It is possible to go on. But not necessary. The point I am making is simply this. *If Christian learning is essentially a discipling, "becoming like" process, then training for a life of ministry must itself be based on these processes. To equip a person for ministry in the Body, that person's training must be like the ministry he is being trained to undertake.*

realism

Realistically speaking, our present approach to training for ministry simply cannot be restructured to permit fulfillment of this ideal. (For an outline of the "ideal" see PROBE 2.) But we certainly must take steps to insure that a counter-model (expressed above as the "hidden curriculum") is not presented in ministry training.

It may be objected that the seminary's function is not to do *everything* needed to equip a person for ministry. Perhaps the seminary's function is simply to "teach the Word," and let the interpersonal and other dimensions of personality and leadership style be developed by the seminarian's own local church. The problem with this objection is that it is totally unrealistic. In teaching the Word the seminary *does* present a model: a model that the future minister will in fact tend to follow! It becomes vitally important that the seminary "teach the Word" in some semblance of the way that the minister will be expected to perform that function in his local church!

Looking then at the "hidden curriculum" items listed earlier, we can see ways to reverse their present directions. What we would have then would be:

* *a personal learning setting.* At least part of the seminary's courses would be taught out of the classroom, with personal relationships between teachers and students as developed.
* *a "growth" orientation to learning.* Less stress would be

160

placed on grading as a way to evaluate learning. Recognition of personal growth and growth in others would be encouraged, with ministry to others in the educational community valued.

* *team learning emphasized.* Rather than treating students as isolated individuals, learning teams might be set up when a student enters seminary. The required courses in the curriculum could be studied cooperatively by these teams, with guiding based on group projects and evaluation of one another. These learning groups might also be expanded to include wives for certain courses and activities.

* *cooperative behaviors would be encouraged.* The learning team approach should involve training on building a Body relationship with others, and involvement in mutual ministries. Over the years of seminary training members of learning teams would learn valuable lessons on how to accept, minister to, and be ministered to by others.

These are simple, yet basic, suggestions. They grow out of a theological appreciation of what the Church is, and what learning in the Christian context is to be. As long as our idea of preparing professional leaders for the local church includes time set aside for seminary, some steps like these *must* be taken. Otherwise we will continue to see men entering the ministry with an idea of what the ministry should involve — but without the example needed to make them the kind of men who can lead the Body. They will continue to be disciplers who have never been discipled!

a challenge?

It seems to me that the understanding of Christian education explored in this book raises even more basic questions about our approach to preparing church leadership. For the moment, I personally will be satisfied if those responsible for seminary training recognize the impact of the hidden curriculum, and begin taking steps to restructure the training process.

But in the long run, I think we will have to reconsider our total selection and training process.

For instance, isn't it suggestive that Jesus spent three years *with* His disciples before they were ordained to their ministries? Isn't it suggestive that that men like Paul involved youths like Mark and Timothy and Titus *with them* before these young men were moved out into their ministries? Shouldn't we perhaps see equipment for ministry as a *growing into ministry by involvement in ministry,* with a leader by whom one is being discipled?

The medical profession in the early 1900s attempted to train doctors through an entirely academic program. Today it is recognized that there is a vast difference between dissecting dead bodies and working with living tissue: between working with descriptions of disease and checking symptoms in a living patient. Today *all* medical training *increasingly* recognizes the fact that internship and like learning experiences are vital in training doctors to treat living people. Is theological training any less of a *living* concern? Do we really believe *academic* training alone prepares young men to work with, lead, and disciple individuals and the Body?

And what about our selection process? How can we tell if a young man of eighteen or twenty-two has the requisite gifts for ministry in the Body? He tells of a call? He is recommended by his pastor? Isn't it more significant as an indicator of an individual's being set aside if his gifts are recognized by a local Body where he has had an opportunity to develop them through ministry in that Body? Why do we rush to train men so young for church leadership? Isn't there some significance in the title "elder" beyond position and function? Certainly there are leadership roles for the young (like Timothy). But our whole understanding of how the Body functions to transform indicates that before a person should be set aside as a leader he needs time to grow up as a believer-priest. We sometimes question missionary candidates: "Do you witness now?" If the answer is "No" we ask, rightly, "Then what makes you think going overseas will make any difference?" Shouldn't we ask those applying for professional ministry training, "Are you ministering in the Body now?" To ask a person who has no significant input to a local Body's life — and who is not recognized by them as gifted for leadership — why he thinks going to seminary will make him a leader for the church seems just as fair . . . and important.

Now, none of this is to suggest that we cut people off from going into the ministry. Certainly if God has called and set a person apart, He will see to it that that person finds his place in the Body. But why not give our young men more time to mature? More time to confirm the call they feel?

Some will argue that this will, in effect, keep many from going into the ministry. They'll graduate from college, marry, start a family, and soon be unable to take training because of their responsibilities. What a small vision of God we have! How strange of us to worship Him as Almighty, and then to worry that His will will be thwarted by economics!

I personally am convinced that as the Church rebuilds, as it is today in evangelical renewal, God will increasingly call leaders out of local churches who have experience in Body ministries. A new generation of far stronger leaders than those we have today will emerge. If we build on biblical and theological principles, this *will* happen.

For the distant future, it's possible that healthy bodies will develop leaders for the Church without seminaries. Today we see an increasing number of churches taking on young men as interns to train them for ministry. Many of these men will never go to seminary. It may be that this is a first move indicating what that distant future holds. I certainly cannot say.

But I am not concerned. What I am concerned about is bringing every dimension of the Church's life today into harmony with biblical principles of her life and growth. This concern requires us all to pay close attention to the training of leaders for the Church.

We need to train men to be models.

We need to train men who will lead as servants.

We need to train men who understand how the Body grows, and who can lead members of the Body to discover their identity as believer-priests.

We need to train men who realize that the health of the Body as a corporate entity is critical in fulfilling the Church's transforming mission — men who know how to build people together into a unity that reflects the unity we actually enjoy in Christ.

If the seminaries of today will not be responsive and provide this kind of training, then God will raise up something new, and through it Christ will continue to build His Church.

PROBE
   case histories
   discussion questions
   thought-provokers
   resources

1. Recently Joe Bayly remarked to me, "The only similarity between Jesus' way of training men and the seminary's is that each takes three years."

   Do you feel the comment is justified? Are there other similarities? What are differences?

NEAT IDEA!

2. In the chapter I promised a description of an "ideal" ministry training program. Here's a model I suggested to a California seminary I visited as a lecturer.

The model hinges on the ability of each faculty member to lead in some local church ministry. Most members of the faculty would serve as pastors; others as education ministers, or, in one case, as a special lecturer covering various Bible books.

Students entering the seminary would be assigned as interns to one of the faculty churches. They would "team" with other interns and the pastor/faculty member. Some of the traditional courses would be taught in this local church setting by each professor. Other courses involving a specialty of one of the men would see the whole seminary family coming together. These courses might be taught in intensive three to five-day "retreat" settings, over a two-week "intercession" period, or in a twice a week "class" over a quarter or semester.

During the first year interns would participate in the life of the church as members, involved in the same kinds of ministries other believer-priests perform with each other. In a second year, discipled and discipling roles would be taken: each intern might work closely with an elder of the church, and then with a teen or other young person(s). During the third year more visible leader roles (like those given the elders) might be given, provided the first two years give evidence of personal and spiritual growth and equipment.

This model is far from ideal, and very sketchy. Look it over and respond to it.

A. List the strengths of the model.

B. List the modifications you would want to make to strengthen it.

C. List the drawbacks to the plan.

D. List the weaknesses inherent in the model.

E. Develop your own "ideal" model, developing it as completely as possible.

3. One final task.

If you're not a seminarian, look over various seminary catalogs. What do you observe about their program? What educational assumptions do you believe their training approaches reflect?

If you are a seminarian, what would you like to see done *now* in your own seminary program to strengthen it? (Be sure you stay in the realm of the possible.)

childhood education: present approaches

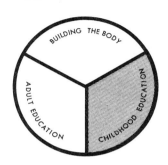

It would be wrong to criticize present childhood education on the basis of stereotypes. True, some of the stereotypes do hold forth each Sunday morning in children's classes. But today there are challenges to "good" teaching in our Sunday schools and other church agencies.

It's important to take time to look at some of these critiques . . . even those with which we can't fully agree.

* present approaches
guidelines and limitations
home as a nurture center
an alternative system

Stereotypes of children's Christian education are so easy to suggest.

*   Mrs. Wilson is teaching the Book of Zephaniah to her four- and five-year-olds. They are memorizing one verse from each chapter, especially verses with words like "wrought" and "righteousness" and "meekness," which the children can't understand. She works hard to keep them quiet (so she can "teach"), and when they get too unruly she has them sing songs which have cute motions like "Give Me Oil in My Lamp." And, of course, at the end of each class she gives an invitation.
*   Carla Friend is an "activity" teacher. She keeps the kids busy coloring Bible pictures most of the hour, hurries through her weekly Bible story, and chats with her teenage

helper Mary while the children go back to cutting or coloring. She thinks the Bible story is a good thing, but that children really "learn by doing," so she finds plenty to keep them busy.

* Harry Croft feels that moral training needs to begin early, and that there is no better way than by coming to understand God's Word. He mostly uses stories from the New Testament — stories that point up acceptable behaviors and good, Christian attitudes. He makes sure the children master Bible facts first; then he makes sure that they understand the values of truth, sharing, helping, honesty, consideration, kindness, and so on which the stories teach.

It is easy to stereotype. But even the fact that people like Mrs. Wilson, Carla, and Harry, are teaching in our Sunday schools hardly provides a valid basis for evaluation of the Church's approach to childhood education.

A valid critique ought to involve analysis of the *best* that is being done: not of the worst.

For this reason, we need to begin our thinking about childhood education with a sketch of effective teaching. We need to see the good — and evaluate to see if it cannot be better.

good childhood Christian education

A recent book by Elsibeth McDaniel (*You and Your Children,* Moody Press) reflects the best of the conservative approach to teaching children. In this book Miss McDaniel, Children's Editor at Scripture Press Publications, and long an active teacher of children, begins her thinking about how children learn with the concept that learning involves experiencing Bible truth. She writes:

> The Christian teacher has some particulars to think about in a discussion of how children learn or experience Bible truth. He must consider:
>
> 1. That the definition of <u>learning means experiencing abstract principles (biblical truths)</u> which are hard for a child to grasp.
>
> 2. That Bible stories, often the vehicle for teaching, describe events from a different culture and are difficult to present as reality.
>
> 3. That the whole atmosphere of Christian education has a right/wrong implication. Most children want to be right — to do right, to give right answers, to be accepted as right-acting persons. This is fairly simple to illustrate in a secular sense. The date of the War of 1812 is 1812. If you know the date, you are right; there can be no argument.

However, if a child expresses his idea of cheating, he is so concerned with the rightness-wrongness aspect that he is tempted to give the "right" answer even though he may personally think there are times when cheating is O.K. Do you see how the right-wrong atmosphere may confuse a child and perhaps give him a sense of guilt because he has not given his honest answer?

Noting that others in Christian education have observed these problems and concluded that the Bible is not for children, Miss McDaniel rejects their solution: "To teach only what they believe the child can understand: (1) Bible stories, often treated as fiction, with no life relevancy; or (2) social action based on biblical principles and equated with Christian living." This solution is unnecessary to her because of the Holy Spirit's teaching ministry, and because Scripture *is* relevant and essential in the child's spiritual and personal development.

Miss McDaniel presents a defense of the role of the Bible in children's curriculums as follows. Today's curriculums present parts of the Bible trained Christian educators believe to be suitable for the ages being taught, and relevant to them *now*. In addition, Bible facts and information are important.

> When someone says we are not to teach Bible facts, he overlooks a basic truth: an accurate and intelligent understanding of what the Bible says must be based on the facts that the Bible gives.
>
> The teacher wants to teach the Bible as reality, but is that all he will teach? No, there will be other material: (1) How was the Bible put together? (2) Who are Bible people? (3) Who have been some of the great Christians of the past? (4) What are the great hymns of the church saying to us? (5) Who are some of the people God has used? (Missionary heroes and denominational leaders have a contribution to make to the lives of boys and girls.) (6) And from what we teach must come some definite concepts about God, salvation, sin, man, and the world.[1]

All in all, the book Miss McDaniel wrote presents good conservative classroom teaching of the Bible. Relationships are not ignored. Children are viewed as active. Methods are appropriate to discovery. The class process recommended moves from the learners' interests and concerns to Scripture and back again to life. Personal response to God, now, is encouraged. The errors highlighted in the stereotypes of teaching are avoided . . . the absolutist teacher, the presentation of information beyond a child's capacity to grasp, the indoctrination methods, and so on.

[1]From *You and Your Children* by Elsibeth McDaniel. Copyright 1973 by Moody Press, Moody Bible Institute of Chicago. Used by permission.

But according to some critics today, even "good" teaching of children is in fact bad!

the developmental imperative

The work of Jean Piaget and his theories of cognitive development has had an increasingly great impact on secular education, and is having impact on religious education as well.

Writing in *Does the Church Know How to Teach?* Robert P. O'Neil asks the critical question:

> In the area of moral learning, it appears that the basic question has not been asked. Is there any evidence to justify the formal introduction of moral concepts such as sin or personal responsibility to God in the preadolescent years? To phrase it another way, does the formal presentation of moral concepts at the preadolescent level make a significant difference in the moral behavior of religiously educated children as contrasted to children reared in a non-religious environment? . . . The answer to the first question is, from one point of view, a qualified no. This rests on the evidence that moral development, like other parts of the personality, is age related and sequential.[2]

It is the *sequential* character of the development of moral thought that fascinates such thinkers. Children cannot handle concepts like "kindness" (often a concern for those who want to teach Bible *principles*) in such a way as to see that abstraction expressed in specific situations. One might teach a young child that it is "kind" to let dad sleep late on Friday, but he would be totally unable to generalize that behavior to letting another child use his tricycle. In Piaget's terminology, he cannot *conserve* the concepts of kindness across situations.

Noting this, religious educators have found that most of the concepts about God and man we find taught and illustrated in Scripture share a similar abstractness. Sin. Truthfulness. Omnipotence. The majority of theological concepts that fit together in the adult believer's belief-system are, it is said, simply beyond (and therefore meaningless to) the child!

John Stewart describes the developmental stages, and says of "the traditional-authoritarian" approach to moral or religious training, "How can much of what a child is taught in this approach have any meaning for him? The acceptance of adult concepts, values, and methods is, in many cases, a complete impossibility for the child. Of particular note on this point

[2]From *Does the Church Know How to Teach?* ed. by B. K. Cully. Copyright © 1970 by Macmillan Publishing Co., Inc., New York. Used by permission.

would be the highly complex and abstract beliefs and values that adults demand that children accept and understand that have to do with religion."

How then does one explain the apparent "learning" of moral and theological concepts? Stewart notes something called *psittacism* (the tendency to "parrot" adult terminology), and finds it easy to explain how children, who are especially receptive to the desires of adults, will make real efforts to do and say what adults do and say in certain situations. In addition there is a tendency on the part of adults to "read into" children's behavior and talk adult perspective (a tendency called *adultomorphism* by Piaget and Inhelder).

Much research has been invested in the past decade to discover how children do process biblical and moral concepts. In England Ronald Goldman (writing from a liberal religious perspective) explored children's processing of Bible taught in the the public schools, and criticized the "unrealistic dominance of the Bible in teaching religion to the young." His study led him to conclude that "the Bible is not a children's book, that the teaching of large areas of it may do more damage than good to a child's religious understanding and that too much biblical material is used too soon and too frequently" (see *Readiness for Religion,* Seabury Press, New York, 1970 [first edition, 1965]).

Recent work by Lawrence J. Kohlberg, of Princeton, has included a far more devastating critique. Kohlberg, building on Piaget's cognitive-structural work, believes he has discovered parallel moral development stages; stages which are, like the cognitive stages, rooted in the developing structure of the human mind. That is, just as a child does not have the *ability* to *conserve* clay from one form change to another, many today are convinced that children do not have the *ability* to understand and process biblical and moral concepts!

This thinking, carried further, leads to the suggestion that morality is *internally derived.* That is, Kohlberg and others do in fact discount the existence of an "absolute" truth or morality that exists outside human experience. Where then lie criteria by which we can evaluate and choose certain moral ideas as "better" and reject other moral ideas as "worse"? The answer implied in the structural approach to development is that those moral ideas in harmony with the higher cognitive and moral processes (higher, because they are later developments in a maturational sequence) are "better." The measuring stick of value then is not to be sought in an external set of standards, or even in a revealed set of principles. Instead the measuring stick of value is rooted in the nature of man himself.

These two possible implications of Piaget and, more recently of Kohlberg, are at the root of the "basic" questions being asked about childhood religious education today. If the child cannot process biblical truths and concepts in an adult way, shouldn't we avoid teaching them until children are grown to adolescence, when they can begin to understand? If in fact moral and character development are essentially structural, shouldn't we pay less attention to the *content* of morality, and more to facilitating the development of the moral structure implanted within?

Clearly, if we accept the findings of Piaget and Kohlberg *and these two implications,* our entire approach to Christian education — and particularly to the use of the Bible in Christian education — will shift dramatically. Rather than be concerned about the communication of Bible truths, we may be concerned only about environmental conditions which stimulate internal development. And, because such internal development *is* sequential and progressive across childhood and into adulthood, we probably will have to agree with Goldman that teaching the Bible to children really is not terribly important after all.

give up the ship?

It's characteristic of dichotomistic thinking that every issue must be seen in contrasts, as either/or. There *are* contrasts between the assumption of "good" childhood Christian education and the assumptions of the Piaget/Kohlberg school. Most obvious contrasts are those that exist between factors like these:

"Christian education"	*Piaget/Kohlberg*
Absolutes do exist	Absolutes do not exist
True content has priority	Internal development (structure) has priority
Growth essentially involves integrating truth (reality) into one's personality	Growth essentially involves restructuring one's perceptions as new cognitive structures develop, creating one's own reality
The Bible is important in this process	The Bible is not important for this kind of process . . . but may be harmful!

It would be easy to take the dichotomistic route and affirm one pattern as a whole, and reject the other. For conservatives, it would seem that theological commitments (which lead us to affirm God's existence, His right to judge truth and morality, and to communicate them through revelation) would lead us to reject the whole approach of Piaget and Kohlberg. For those whose epistemology is more in harmony with the naturalistic assumptions of the *skema* on the right it would seem that experimental evidence would lead them to reject the whole approach of traditional Christian education!

But this is true only if we insist on a strict dichotomy. It is true only if we can not integrate truths discovered through the behavioral science's experimental approach with truths revealed by God's Spirit. I believe we have to accept truths validated through either source. We do not accept truths from either source as the *whole* truth, or *exhaustive* truth. There is always more understanding to be gained of what the Bible teaches, and of what experimental approaches uncover. Our task is to *integrate* truth from each source: to integrate it into a system which we do not hold to as absolute itself, but as the best approximation of reality our limited data and our limited abilities enable us to make.

Rather than reject what either Christian educators or behavioral scientists are saying about important factors in religious and moral development, we need to examine all positions critically, and, as God permits, work toward an understanding of the whole.

What then have we seen in this chapter to help us work toward that "understanding of the whole"?

First, we've seen "good" contemporary Christian education of children. It is sophisticated, sensitive, and committed to teaching God's Word in such a way that the child discovers the Person and presence of God, and begins to respond to Him.

Second, we've seen the basis from which criticism of the content dimension of most religious education is being launched. Empirical studies have shown that children's capacity to understand and process biblical and moral concepts *is* limited. These limitations must not be overlooked; their implications for a meaningful ministry to children must be grappled with.

From this point, we can move on to explore in more depth the concepts of the contemporary, and see if there is any "fit" between them and a Christian education which is theologically rooted in an understanding of faith as Life.

PROBE
case histories
discussion questions
thought-provokers
resources

1. Before going on to the next chapter of this text, you may want to explore various approaches to Christian education for children as well as the work of the critics. At least one of the following "research" suggestions is something you might wish to do.

   a. Survey the following Christian texts. Get in mind their under-lying assumptions about the nature of C.E. How might each author respond to the Piaget-Kohlberg "school" as the author has described it?

      Wayne R. Rood, *On Nurturing Christians*, Abingdon Press, Nashville, 1972.

      Robert Arthur Dow, *Learning Through Encounter*, Judson Press, Valley Forge, PA., 1971.

      C. Ellis Nelson, *Where Faith Begins*, John Knox Press, Richmond, VA., 1971.

   b. It is important for an educator to have some understanding of Piaget. You might want to start with these books, in sequence:

      Mary Ann Spencer Pulaski, *Understanding Piaget*, Harper & Row, New York, 1971.

      Jean Piaget, *Science of Education and the Psychology of the Child*, Orion Press, New York, 1970.

      Jean Piaget, *To Understand Is to Invent*, Crossman Publishers, New York, 1973.

   c. If you are unfamiliar with various theories of childhood develop-ment, you might sample:

      Alfred L. Baldwin, *Theories of Child Development*, John Wiley and Sons, New York, 1967.

   d. The Christian educator also needs to be familiar with Kohlberg: far more familiar than is possible through the brief discussion in this text. Here then is a Kohlberg bibliography which may prove helpful.

      (1) Kohlberg, L., "The Development of Modes of Moral Think-ing and Choice in the Years Ten to Sixteen." Unpublished doctoral dissertation. University of Chicago, 1958.

      (2) Kohlberg, L., "Moral Development and Identification," in H. I. Stevenson (ed.) *Child Psychology: 62nd Yearbook of the National Society for the Study of Education*. Chicago, U. of Chicago Press, 1963.

(3) Kohlberg, L., "The Development of Children's Orientation Toward a Moral Order: I. Sequence in the Development of Moral Thought," *Vita Humana,* 1963, 6,11-33.

(4) Kohlberg, L., "Development of Moral Character and Ideology," in M. L. and L. W. Hoffman (eds.), *Review of Child Development Research.* Vol. 1, pp. 383-427. New York: Russell Sage Foundation, 1964.

(5) Kohlberg, L., "Cognitive Stage and Preschool Education," *Human Development,* 1966a, 9, 5-17.

(6) Kohlberg, L. "Moral Education in the Schools: a Developmental View," *The School Review,* Spring, 1966.

(7) Kohlberg, L., "Moral and Religious Education and the Public Schools: A Developmental View." In T. Sizer (ed.), *Religion and Public Education,* pp. 164-183. Boston: Houghton-Mifflin, 1967.

(8) Kohlberg, L., "The Child As a Moral Philosopher," *Psychology Today,* 1968, 7, 25-30.

(9) Kohlberg, L., "Early Education: A Cognitive-developmental View," *Child Development,* 1968, 39(4).

(10) Kohlberg, L., "Moral Development." *International Encyclopedia of the Social Sciences,* Crowell, Collier and Macmillan, Inc., 1968c, 489-494.

(11) Kohlberg, L., "Stage and Sequence: The Cognitive-developmental Approach to Socialization." In D. Goslin (ed.), *Handbook of Socialization Theory and Research,* New York: Rand McNally, 1969.

(12) Kohlberg, L., "The Moral Atmosphere of the School." In N. V. Overly (ed.), *The Unstudied Curriculum: Its Impact on Children,* Washington, D.C.: Association for Supervision and Curriculum Development, 1970.

(13) Kohlberg, L., "Education for Justice: A Modern Statement of the Platonic View." In N. F. and T. R. Sizer (eds.), *Moral Education: Five Lectures.* Cambridge: Harvard U. Press, 1970.

(14) Kohlberg, L., "From Is to Ought: How to Commit the Naturalistic Fallacy and Get Away With It." In T. Mischel (ed.), *Cognitive Development and Epistemology.* New York: Academic Press, 1971.

(15) Kohlberg, L., "Stages of Moral Development as a Basis for Moral Education," in C. M. Beck, B. S. Crittenden, and E. V. Sullivan (eds.), *Moral Education: Interdisciplinary Approaches,* New York: Newman Press, 1971.

(16) Kohlberg, L. and Gilligan, C., "The Adolescent As a Philosopher: The Discovery of the Self in a Postconventional World." *Daedlus: Journal of the American Academy of Arts and Sciences,* Fall, 1971.

(17) Kohlberg, L., "Cognitive-developmental Theory and the

173

Practice of Collective Moral Education." In M. Wolins and M. Gottesman eds.), *Group Care:* an Israeli Approach *The Educational Path of Young Aliyah,* New York, Gordon, 1971.

(18) Kohlberg, L., "Indoctrination Versus Relativity in Value Education," paper presented at the 18th summer conference of the Institute on Religion in an Age of Science, Star Island, New Hampshire, July 31-August 6, 1971.

(19) Kohlberg, L., "A Cognitive-developmental Approach to Moral Education," *The Humanist,* November-December, 1972, XXXXI(6).

(20) Kohlberg, L., (with Phillip Witten), "Understanding the Hidden Curriculum," *Learning,* December, 1972.

(21) Kohlberg, L., "The Implications of Moral States for Problems in Sex Education." Paper for Sex Information Council of the United States Conference, December, 1971.

(22) Kohlberg, L., "Continuities in Childhood and Adult Moral Development Revisited." Cambridge, Mass.: Laboratory of Human Development, Harvard U., 1973.

(23) Kohlberg, L., *Collected Papers on Moral Development and Moral Education.* Cambridge, Mass: Laboratory of Human Development, 1973. (Sixteen Kohlberg articles are collected in this one book.)

(24) Kohlberg, L. and Mayer, R., "Development as the Aim of Education," *Harvard Educational Review,* 1972, 42,4.

(25) Kohlberg, L., Scharf, P., and Hickey, J., "The Justice Structure of the Prison — a Theory and an Intervention," *The Prison Journal,* Autumn-Winter, 1972, Vol. LI, No. 2.

(26) Kohlberg, L. and Staff, *Standard Scoring Manual.* Cambridge, Mass.: Laboratory of Human Development, Harvard University, 1973.

(27) Kohlberg, L. and Turiel, E., "Moral Development and Moral Education," in G. Lesser (ed.), *Psychology and Educational Practice,* Chicago: Scott, Foresman, 1971.

e. Some of the most significant work being done with the Piaget/ Kohlberg concepts is through the Values Development Education Program at Michigan State University (202 Erickson Hall, M.S.U., East Lansing, Michigan 48824). The program is sponsored by the Lily Endowment Foundation and directed by Ted Ward and John S. Stewart. You'll want to keep alert to what comes from their studies, and their efforts to apply these concepts to both public schools and Christian education.

2. Here are quotes from three authors, each of whom is saying something which helps us either react to or raise questions about the contemporary critique.

Look over each quote, and write a response *from each author's probable point of view,* to the dichotomy presented on page 170.

A. What Piaget is saying is that social transmission can never be effective unless the child is ready to receive it in the sense that he has developed the cognitive structures to which he can assimilate the message, or to which he can accommodate. For example, you could never teach calculus or Einstein's theory of relativity to a six-year-old child. Most socialization agents, like parents and teachers, realize this and do not try. However, this realization seems to be inoperative when it comes to matters relating to values; e.g., religious beliefs and feelings, family relationships, and moral principles. Somehow the child who cannot understand the theory of calculus is supposed to understand complex theoretical and abstract principles like God, the holy trinity, sin, redemption, the Golden Rule, the mutual responsibilities of community members, honor, tradition, lines of authority, the fine points of lying, society, democracy, communism, and all the other concepts that end up on the list of virtues, vices, and rules taught in the family, the school, and the church to young children. One of the salient advantages of the developmental approach to values education is that it can provide guidelines for the readiness of children to assimilate information from the environment [John Stewart].

B. One of our goals is to influence the student to think about, learn about, talk about, and *do something* about our subject some time after our direct influence over him comes to an end. . . .

- Learning then is for the *future;* that is, the object of instruction is to facilitate some form of behavior at a point *after* the instruction has been completed.
- The likelihood of the student putting his knowledge to use is influenced by his *attitude* for or against the subject; things disliked have a way of being forgotten.
- People influence people. Teachers, and others, *do* influence attitudes toward subject matter — and toward learning itself.
- One objective toward which to strive is that of having the student leave your influence with as *favorable* an attitude toward your subject as possible. In this way you will help to maximize the possibility that he will *remember* what he has been taught, and will willingly *learn more* about what he has been taught (Robert F. Mager, *Developing Attitudes Toward Learning,* Fearon Publishers, Palo Alto, Cal., 1968).

C. Education is the learning of culture. The various activities that we in Western industrialized societies refer to under this rubric are only part of the whole educational process. Education, although mostly the concern of the child, is a continuing process throughout the lifetime of any person. And, of course, it includes far more than the narrow program of formal training that we usually think of when we talk about school activities. These matters form part of any educational program in any society, but the proportion of a program devoted to them varies from one society to another, as do the importance and meaning given them. Yet the major parts of any educational program concern the inculcation and understanding of cultural symbols, moral values, sanctions, and cosmological beliefs. In our own society we separate out these parts from 'formal'' education and leave them mainly to families, friends, priests, psychoanalysts, and guides and advisers of many kinds. But most societies, as the essays in this volume show, do not separate these various aspects of the total educational process (John Middleton, in *From Child to Adult: Studies in the Anthropology of Education,* The Natural History Press, Garden City, N.Y., 1970).

childhood education: guidelines and limitations

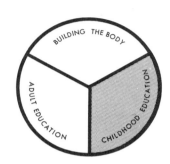

We often react defensively to "attacks" on our assumptions and our practices. We have no need to. Our faith rests on far too secure a foundation. It is just because we have such confidence in God and the biblical revelation He has given us that we can freely examine each new theory or discovery of men. We can freely examine our own practices. And we can judge: both ourselves, and others.

present approaches
* guidelines and limitations
home as a nurture center
an alternative system

In examining the work of men like Piaget or Kohlberg it is helpful to distinguish between their discoveries and implications drawn from the discoveries. We can accept, for instance, the fact that young children see cause/effect relationships between unrelated events. We do not need to accept, on the other hand, the derived notion that somehow it is not helpful to teach theological concepts like "sin."

But before we move on to see if recent discoveries do indeed give guidelines for and place limitations on our Christian education of children, we need to sketch some of the discoveries of Piaget/Kohlberg which we can (tentatively) accept as "givens." And we need to reaffirm some of the theological givens as well.

the givens: theological

There are several theological ideas which are challenged directly or indirectly by the Piaget/Kohlberg school of thought. Among them are several *givens;* several concepts which simply are not open to question, because they are integral to the Christian faith itself as it is understood by conservatives. The specific area of challenge here has to do with absolutes and with reality. Piaget and Kohlberg both assume in their theories that "reality" is a construct reflecting transactions between the human organism and his social and physical environment. There is no "truth" *outside* this framework which is revealed to man or is to be discovered by him. This assumption does cut across a concept integral to Christianity: that ours is a *revealed* religion. Thus we must take a stand here and affirm as true several concepts which will affect our understanding of teaching/learning.

Revealed truth. This is of course the keystone proposition. We are committed to the belief that God has spoken, through the prophets, in His acts in history, with finality through His Son (Heb. 1:1-3), and that true information from and about God has been given us in words which the Holy Spirit taught and which are recorded accurately in an inspired Scripture. It is true that God has revealed *Himself* in Scripture. It is true also that God has revealed true information. This is one of the givens which Christians cannot abandon without surrendering that which is basic to the faith. (For an extended discussion of *Revelation,* see chapters 1-5 in my book, *Creative Bible Teaching,* Moody Press, Chicago, 1970.)

Revealed truths: theological. Among the implications of revelation is this. We do have truth about God, man, and the universe He has placed us in. We are not in the position of groping after God. We *know* what He is like. We *know* what sin is and does, the impact it has on persons and societies. We *know* God's way of dealing with sin, of the forgiveness and love which are rooted in His character and expressed in His grace. We *know* the universe is His creation, and we *know* that human beings, shaped for eternity, have an eternal destiny described for us in the Word.

To say that "we *know*" in no way is to claim perfect knowledge, or exhaustive knowledge. Certainly our understanding is imperfect: Scripture says that our knowledge is always incomplete (1 Cor. 13:10). But incomplete knowledge is not to be despised because it is incomplete! We know *enough* to develop a unique biblical world and life-view. We know enough to respond to God, and in responding to bring our lives and personalities into harmony with what God says is real and true.

Revealed truths: moral. This too is part of the meaning of revelation. Paul the apostle encourages believers to focus their attention on "whatever is true, whatever is noble, whatever is right, whatever is pure, whatever is lovely, whatever is admirable" (Phil. 4:8). Even given some cultural definition of these factors, the apostle clearly expects believers to be able to distinguish between actions and attitudes which are just and unjust, pure and impure. Certainly too the New Testament epistles (in harmony with the Old Testament) not only speak of loving others as man's sole responsibility to his fellow men — they also clearly define certain behaviors as "loving" and others as never "loving" (cf., for example, Col. 3).

While the Bible does not absolutize all behavior (in fact, there are amazingly *few* absolutes in the moral realm), it is clear that there are moral absolutes which are defined, not by man's culture or the structure of his mind, but by God.

Correspondence with reality. In affirming revealed truth we want to avoid always the notion of "imposition." There is a peculiar assumption people tend to make that God's revelation of theological and/or moral truths is essentially restrictive. The notion is that the universe affords an infinite number of possibilities, but that God has (meanly) selected out a single set and labeled them "good" and others "bad" — just to plague and restrict us, or, by making us toe the line, to reassert His rights as God. This thinking reflects an image of God that is far different from the loving and concerned Person Scripture reveals Him to be.

Instead, revealed theological and moral truths need to be viewed in the perspective of God's character as a moral Person. Truth, justice, purity — all are rooted in His character. Because His creation reflects His personality, there is a moral order in the universe and a moral order in human affairs ... and a corresponding order in human nature! In revealing theological and moral truths, God has not *limited* men to one set of ways by *fiat*. Instead He has opened the door to the one way of life that brings freedom: freedom because it is the one way of life in full harmony with who God is, what the universe is like, and what mankind is and is to be.

The childhood story of the little train that wanted to go rolling off across the meadow is in point here. When he did jump his tracks, the old storybook tells, he became bogged down. He discovered that trains are made to run on tracks.

This is a rather accurate picture of man (and possibly was

meant to be). We too have been made to run on a track. Only when we do, do we find freedom. God's revelation, enabling us to see those tracks and to follow them, is a deeply expressive indication of His love.

What I have been saying, then, is that to understand revelation we must realize that Truth is true, not just because God says it, but because revealed truth has an *intrinsic correspondence with reality*. Our universe, moral and physical, has as intrinsic a structure as does the human personality. There should be no wonder at all if men's cognitive structure (described by Piaget and Kohlberg) should have a distinctive "fit" with the moral order of creation. And there should be no hesitation to affirm that truth and purity *are;* defined not by human cultures or the way the human mind interacts with the environment but by God's character itself the sole standard by which every idea of the true and the pure is to be measured.

And they can be measured. For God has spoken; God has revealed.

(For an extended discussion of revelation as a portrait of reality, see my book *Creative Bible Study*, chaps. 1-9, Zondervan, Grand Rapids, Mich., 1971.)

the givens: anthropological

The work of Piaget and Kohlberg says nothing about the theological givens. Instead, it focuses on an understanding of man. Using empirical methods, a number of insights into how children think and grow have been gained. If we accept the work done by them (and we should note here that there is no necessary *conflict* between our theological commitments and their discoveries), there are a number of understandings about children's thinking which have implications for childhood Christian education.

Piaget's contributions. They are many. Only a few of the most salient (to us) can be sketched here. Key concepts include these:

(1) *cognitive structures*. We're all aware that a child of three cannot be taught to catch and pass a football as a high-schooler might. No matter how much *training* we might provide the three-year-old, the development of his muscles and coordination is such that he *cannot* learn these skills. The physical structure of the child prevents development of this ability: he must grow before he can learn.

Piaget has exposed a similar *mental* phenomenon. There are a number of things that a young child simply cannot learn or understand because his cognitive structures prevent him. He must grow before he can understand (grasp) some kinds of things. For instance, one significant cognitive limitation on young children has to do with *conservation*. Pour water from a fat glass into a tall thin one before the eyes of a young child, and ask him which glass had more water in it. He'll choose the tall thin one! He cannot grasp the fact that the amount of water is the same . . . he cannot mentally "conserve" the water through its changes of form. You can *tell* him the amount of water is the same, and get him to give you the right answer. But you can't make him *understand*.

(2) *invariant sequence*. Piaget's studies across cultures have led to the conclusion that the cognitive structures grow and change in a sequence that remains the same for all human beings. In some cultures we may find one structural stage in children at a younger chronological age than in other cultures. But all children will go through the same stages, and in the same sequence.

Thus Piaget has apparently discovered something basic in human nature; something that has not before been so clearly stated about the kind of being man is. Cognitive growth through structural stages in an invariant sequence is a new and significant understanding.

(3) *equilibrium process*. Piaget points out that children are *actively* involved with their social and physical environment. They process new experiences and information; they assimilate and accommodate. This constant process of maintaining internal balance is a key to learning: it is the process by which the human mind constructs and reconstructs its portrait of reality, and regulates the person's interaction with the environment. Piaget notes that this mechanism is particularly observable at the time of transition from one stage to another. When new cognitive structures have developed, old perceptions and new data no longer seem to "fit" with the child's earlier way of grasping reality. The imbalance causes a series of active compensations and adjustments, until a new balance is achieved at the higher structural stage.

This process is viewed as going on at all times. But only when structural growth permits will the process enable a child to discover the new perspective, the new picture of reality.

(4) *learning theory elements*. It should be clear that this view has significant implications for learning theory. Accepting equili-

181

bration as the internal process involved, Piaget notes these three elements in human learning.

* *structural stage (maturation).* Learning is subordinate to the individual's level of development. He cannot learn that which his cognitive structures have not developed sufficiently to accommodate.

* *experience in the physical environment.* Learning involves doing, touching, seeing, feeling, playing, etc., in the physical environment.

* *experience in the social environment.* Learning involves social interaction as well; hearing and using language, being angry, being the object of anger, being loved, etc.

Of this last factor, Piaget writes, (in "Piaget's Theory," by Jean Piaget, in Mussen [ed.], *Charmichael's Manual of Child Psychology*).

> The third classical factor of development is the influence of the social environment. Its importance is immediately verified if we consider the fact that the stages mentioned in Section III are accelerated or retarded in their average chronological ages according to the child's cultural and educational environment. But the very fact that the stages follow the same sequential order in *any* environment is enough to show that the social environment cannot account for everything. This constant order of succession cannot be ascribed to the environment.[1]

Learning, then, according to Piaget, involves the child's physical and social environment. But these are not determinative. That is, how much a child can learn through these factors is clearly limited (and to some extent determined!) by the stage of cognitive development.

Kohlberg's contributions. The work of Lawrence J. Kohlberg was stimulated by the work of Piaget, and applies a number of Piaget's insights to moral development. Kohlberg's work has implications far beyond the education of children. For instance, he has adapted some of his theoretical orientations to prison reform. At Michigan State University Kohlberg's concepts are being adapted to public schools. Asbury Seminary's Donald Joy is exploring their meaning for Christian education of children. The theory is one that has the broadest sociological and societal implications.

Again, only salient points can be sketched here. Further re-

[1]From *Charmichael's Manual of Child Psychology*, Vol. 1. Copyright 1970 by John Wiley and Sons, Inc., New York. Used by permission.

search (see the bibliography on last chapter's PROBE) is recommended.

What, then, are significant findings for us as we think about a childhood Christian education ministry?

(1) *cognitive (moral) structures and stages.* Kohlberg believes he has distinguished levels in moral thought which are parallel in nature to Piaget's cognitive structural levels. That is, the inner structures of the mind limit and determine not only ways persons understand things like water passed from glass to glass, but moral concepts as well!

(2) *invariant sequence.* Kohlberg believes he has isolated moral stages of thought which progress in invariant sequence like the cognitive stages of Piaget. This does not mean that a person moves through all stages as he matures. In fact Kohlberg believes many adults never go beyond the third level (Stage II, Level 3). It does mean however that progress from one stage (way) of thinking about moral issues will follow the other, sequentially, as far as a person does develop.

(3) *egocentrism/social role-taking.* "Egocentrism" is a term coined by Piaget to describe the young child's inability to perceive others as existing independently of himself . . . to see that they have perspectives, beliefs, feelings, and experiences different from his own.

This is particularly significant in terms of moral development, because morality (secular or religious) does have significant self/other implications. The Christian is to "look not only on his own things, but also on the things (concerns) of others." The Golden Rule requires us to put ourselves in the other's place, and to determine how we would want to be treated in his place. Thus social role-taking is significant in moral growth . . . in fact, is *necessary* to it.

But what if a child is *unable* to see the perspective of others? Obviously the way he processes moral concepts and teaching will be significantly affected.

4) *equilibration process.* Kohlberg sees moral growth as coming through this process, even as Piaget sees it as the heart of learning. The growing child, his capacities limited by his cognitive development, will use data in his physical and social environment and develop moral (and theological) ideas through equilibration . . . through taking in, interacting with, and developing a "reality" picture in which all (to him) "fits."

Thus Kohlberg sees moral training not so much as bringing the content of morality to the child's attention, or indoctrinating

OVERVIEW OF KOHLBERG LEVELS AND STAGES

Level/Stage	Name	Approximate Earliest Age	Piaget Stage Required	Prerequisite Cognitive Tasks
Level 0	**Premoral Period**			
Stage O-A	Amoral Stage	Extends to 4	Sensorimotor and Preconceptual Sub.	
Stage O-B	Premoral Stage of Egocentric Judgment	To about 6	Preconceptual Sub. and Intuitive Sub.	
Level I	**Period of Preconventional Morality**			
Stage 1	Punishment and Obedience Orientation	No earlier than 5 or 6, 7-8 likelier	Transitional from Intuitive Sub. to early Concrete Op.	Categorical classification
Stage 2	Instrumental Relativist Orientation	7-8 earliest 9-10 likelier	Concrete Operations	Reversibility (logical reciprocity)
Level II	**Period of Conventional Morality**			
Stage 3	Interpersonal Concordance Orientation L sount relationships	10-11 earliest 11-12 likelier	Formal Operations Substage 1	Inverse of reciprocal; mutual simul. reciprocity
Stage 4	Law and Order (or Conscientious) Orientation	12-14 earliest 14-16 likelier	Formal Operations Substage 2	Able to order triads of propositions or relations
Stage 4½	(Stage of Cynical Ethical Relativism beyond conventional, but not principled)	H.S. earliest College likely	This is not true stage insofar as not part of invariant sequence. Only few go through it.	
Level III	**Period of Postconventional, Autonomous, or Principled Morality**			
Stage 5	Social Contract Legalistic Orientation	Early 20s Mid-late 20s likelier	Formal Operations Substage 3 Self-resp. exper.	Hypothetico-Deductive Reasoning. All poss. comb. of variables. Sys. relations.
Stage 6	Universal Ethical Principle Orientation	Unlikely before late 20s Early 30s likelier, if at all	Sustained resp. for welfare of others; irreversible real-life moral choices; high level cognitive stimulation and reflection.	

Prepared by John S. Stewart
Research and Development Program for Values Development Education
College of Education, Michigan State University
East Lansing, Michigan

him in it, but as helping the child grow from one stage of moral development to another as he is ready. We help children by encouraging them to question, probe, and think (e.g., by introducing disequilibration) when they are developmentally ready for transition to a higher stage and by providing a moral climate in which they can grow. Thus moral development, like all learning, involves not so much *what we transmit* to others, but what the environment encourages them to *discover* as cognitive structures expand and change.

response

It is, essentially, on the basis of these elements of the discoveries of Piaget and Kohlberg that the challenges to Christian education for children described in chapter 15 have been based. The critics note that children *cannot understand in an adult way* the theological and moral concepts of Scripture. Moreover, they note that often children will seriously *distort* or *misunderstand* a truth simply because they are unable to comprehend it. The conclusion suggested is that because a particular truth cannot be grasped accurately or adequately, children should not be introduced to it.

Without committing ourselves to a classroom approach to teaching theological and moral concepts, we still must respond to this argument. And reject it.

"exhaustive" versus "true" meaning. Sometimes the possibility of knowing Truth is rejected because we cannot know all the Truth. But it is not necessary to know Truth perfectly to know truth. Certainly a child cannot "understand" omnipresence. But he can understand that "Jesus is always with me." The vast Truth of omnipresence has come to have true meaning for him . . . however limited his understanding of "Jesus," of "always," or of "with" may be.

We need to be careful here. Understanding of biblical truths is *always* limited by our ability to perceive. What adult really "understands" omnipresence? We can have an idea. We can have an idea that has personal meaning (application) for us. But we cannot and will not understand "omnipresence" as God does.

We can say the same with moral concepts and ideas. What does it mean to "forgive"? Possibly to a child no more than to stop showing anger. To an adult it may mean little more than "saying nothing more about it." But the Bible says that to God "forgive" means "forget" — that "their sins and iniquities I will

185

remember against them no more" (Heb. 10:17). Should we never introduce the concept of forgiveness until a child is old enough to have an adult perspective? Or until an adult has grown enough to at least have a dim grasp of what forgiveness means to God? I think not.

I think instead we ought to introduce theological and moral concepts to children as they grow up with us, and as the concepts are experienced as part of our life together as Christians. I do think we must be careful, and never demand or expect adult understanding, or adult application, of Bible truths. Instead we ought to encourage children to respond *on their own levels* to biblical truths, remembering that it is the intention of the heart, not the act itself, which is of greatest significance to God.

equilibration. The description of the learning process which Piaget and Kohlberg espouse shows us another reason why we need to *provide* (not prohibit) biblical information and truths to children. According to this theory, learning takes place as children transact with their social and physical environments and fit data from them into a construct of reality appropriate to their developmental stage. As a child becomes ready, disequilibration stimulates him to reorder the data he has, and to fit it plus new data into a system appropriate to the new cognitive ability.

This process of reconstructing one's perception of reality *from the data possessed* continues as the child grows from one stage to another. *But data which is not possessed* (and by "data" I mean concepts, terms, symbols, etc.) *cannot be handled in this restructuring process! The child will build a world view with the data he has . . . and if theological and moral content is not part of his data bank, his construct of reality will leave it out!*

Thus a *late* introduction of concepts *foreign to a child's view of reality* is hardly desirable. Instead, it is better to communicate, through the social environment, all the terms, symbols, concepts, meanings, etc., which can become and remain part of his construct of reality throughout the developmental process. At each stage Bible truths, like all other data a child possesses, will be reprocessed, and new and more significant understandings will grow.

These two arguments alone seem to me sufficient response to those who want to rush toward a blanket acceptance of the Piaget/Kohlberg system and an immediate application of the implications some have drawn.

For truth to be valuable to us, it need not be known exhaustively. Experience of God and of the meaning of biblical truths *is* open to even young children.

And, since a restructuring process is involved in learning, it is important to provide theological and moral concepts (and Bible facts as well as truths) so that the child's constantly reshaped perception of reality will *always* involve, as an integral dimension of reality, the fact of God.

PROBE
case histories
discussion questions
thought-provokers
resources

1. I'm convinced that there is validity in the work of Piaget and Kohlberg, and that their findings do help us evaluate our childhood education practices. From the description in this chapter, can you list:
   A. *Ten guidelines for C.E. of children (do's).*
   B. *Ten limitations on C.E. of children (don'ts).*

2. Lest you worry about the fact that the work of Piaget and Kohlberg is done outside a biblical framework [some people do feel that if something is not in Scripture it cannot be true, or at least cannot be safe], there are two lines of biblical research that may be interesting.
   A. Look up the Hebrew terms for children. You'll find several which seem to distinguish between stages of development! Find out all you can about them, and see if there are any implied relationships with what we've been thinking about here.
   B. Read this quote from a commentary on the Old Testament written by Hebrew scholars C. F. Keil and F. Delitzsch, long before anyone was talking about a "developmental" understanding of children. The quote is from their discussion of a famous verse, Proverbs 22:6, which says, "Give to the child instruction conformable to His way; So he will not, when he becomes old, depart from it."

   Here is the entry from Volume II, pages 86 and 87, of the K. & D. commentary.

   The first instruction is meant which, communicated to the child, be עַל פִּי, after the measure of his way, i.e., of the nature of the child as such. נַעַר דַרְכּוֹ is the child's way. The instruction of youth, the education of youth, ought to be conformed to the nature of youth; the matter of instruction, the manner of instruction, ought to regulate itself according to the stage of life, and its peculiarities; the method ought to be arranged according to the degree of development which the mental and bodily life of the youth has arrived at.

3. Here is a series of statements with implications for childhood Christian education. Write a response to five of them.

   (1) The Bible is an adult book.

   (2) Children should not be expected to understand Bible truths.

   (3) The biblical "age of accountability" (see Num. 14:29) indicates, with Kohlberg (see page 184) that children are not responsible for their moral behavior.

   (4) Among the biblical concepts I would want to teach children are forgiveness, God's love, Jesus' deity, and salvation through faith in Christ.

   (5) Among the biblical concepts that I would not want to teach children are sin, the second coming, Bible history, and salvation through faith in Christ.

   (6) It is best to teach Bible concepts in a formal classroom.

   (7) It is best to teach Bible concepts in a life setting.

   (8) The socialization approach to teaching faith has no "fit" with what Piaget and Kohlberg are saying.

   (9) The "good" classroom teaching of the Bible described in chapter 15 is clearly shown to be irrelevant by what Piaget and Kohlberg are saying.

   (10) It should be possible to use the insights of Piaget and Kohlberg to prepare a list of significant truths which should be introduced to children at various stages of their development.

4. Evaluate the following class "lesson plan." How would the "good" Christian educator probably view it? How would Kohlberg or Piaget probably view it? How do *you* view it?

   The lesson is on John 15, the vine and the branches. Involved are about eighteen children, from ages six through twelve. The lesson time begins with three older children, arms outstretched, acting out the role of branches. They move around the room, grimacing to show great effort, but produce nothing. Then the adult leader, taking the role of the vine, enters. The branches come and link hands with him, and from a hidden basket bananas appear in their hands. The younger children are given the bananas, and eat them as the leader reads and explains John 15. He tells them that *they* are branches, and that if they stay close to Jesus, they too will produce fruit.

   Next the children are involved in looking at Galatians 6 and the list of fruit there. Love, joy, peace, and patience, with the others, are explained. The children are asked to give examples of each from their homes or weekday school lives. Then, for activity, the children cut out fruit designs from prepared construction paper sheets, label the fruit shapes with one of the terms from the Galatians passage, and enjoy putting the fruit each has prepared on a large poster-picture of a vine hanging on the wall.

Concluding the lesson, the children are divided into smaller groups and talk with teaching helpers about which fruit each would like to have in his or her own life. Why would one like love, another joy, another peace? The lesson closes in prayer, and with the reminder to each child to ask Jesus to produce the specially desired fruit in his life during the week.

childhood education: home as a nurture center

In the last chapter we looked at several theological and anthropological (man related) "givens" that we need to consider in thinking about childhood Christian education. We also looked at (and rejected) several implications others have drawn from Piaget/Kohlberg as to whether to teach the Bible to children.

This was not done in defense of "good" Christian education of children as it is now conducted. In fact, our present approaches need criticism too!

present approaches
guidelines and limitations
* home as a nurture center
an alternative system

Our contemporary approaches to teaching children in the Church are, without question, "classroom" approaches. While we now and then may hear sermons on the home, and while as I write the family has become a growing concern (revealed in the spate of books on the Christian home, in the tapes on the subject, and in increasing talk about "home relating" our teaching), the fact is that our educational efforts still focus on the Sunday class. It is our classroom education that is supported by a *system* (curriculum, "teachers," recognized patterns of time, method, etc.).

We can and should make distinctions between poor classroom teaching and "good" classroom teaching. Certainly the kind of teaching that stresses student activity, student involvement, working from life interests and concerns to Scripture and back again, and so on, is a better kind of classroom teaching than that which casts the teacher as a dispenser of words and the children as empty vessels to be filled. But to recognize something as better than something else does not mean it is best . . . or right! The point stressed over and over in the first ten chapters and their PROBE activities is that the classroom setting itself has dangerous implications for Bible teaching. *In our culture, classroom treatment of any subject matter tends to clue learners to process that content as academic. And the academic is perceived as "unreal" in so far as present experiences, feelings, attitudes, and values are concerned.* This is particularly tragic for Christian education. We communicate a revealed truth that must be perceived as life and integrated into life. If our method of communication is not in harmony with the message communicated, we distort the message itself.

How then do we respond to classroom teaching? Is it always bad? Is there a better way? How do we build a childhood Christian education ministry? To answer questions like these, we have to go back to our learning theory, and to one other dimension of the Piaget/Kohlberg approach which I believe needs criticism.

learning theory

We noted in the last chapter (and in chap. 7) that Piaget seems to present a three-factored learning theory. Viewing man as an active organism in whom an equilibration process is always going on, Piaget focuses on cognitive structure, and on the physical and social environments which provide data with which the person transacts to construct reality. Others following his theory have accepted this description. They tend to place stress on the structural, the equilibration process itself, and the physical/ social environment . . . *as if the latter actually presented the individual "raw" data from which to develop his constructs!*

The problem here is with the notion that either physical or social elements in the environment exist as "raw" data! In fact, *everything* in the environment is essentially processed data. The environment itself is *essentially social.*

What I mean by this is that no one "starts from scratch" with even the most concrete of physical objects. Even blocks of wood have previously been defined in the culture as "square" or "triangular," or as painted "blue" or "red" or "green." Each person starts life in a world that is in basic ways the same world for all others. Yet in every culture there are significant ways in which perceptions of space, distance, time, and so on, differ. Not surprisingly, these differences are not differences in *individual* perception, but in cultural perception.

The point is, of course, a growing individual does not have transactions with the raw data of his environment, but with the previously structured perceptions of environment already extant in his culture. Thus it seems to me the complaint of Middleton (in *From Child to Adult*) is valid: that the educational psychologists who study the actual process of learning from culture to culture and find striking similarities "almost all ignore the social contexts" (p. xvi). The process of learning may well be in part a function of the structure of the developing human mind. But learning is *not* the discovery or creation of reality from transactions with the environment's raw data. Learning is better understood as the creation of a personal reality from transactions with environmental data *as that data is perceived within the individual's culture.*

Let's take several examples. First let's take the letter A and let it stand for any data in the child's environment. At first, according to cognitive-structure theory, the child will have a distorted (from the adult point of view) perception of the item. It may be just unrelated marks to him. When someone says "A," he will have no notion of the meaning. Later he may notice a relationship between the lines, and associate them with "A," but really know nothing more than that they are somehow supposed to be associated. Still later, as structural development enables him, he will recognize the A and as an "A," and also as part of a larger system. He may by this time take great pleasure in childish "mastery" of the system, saying the alphabet (with which he has now firmly associated "A") over and over again. Later, again as cognitive growth permits, his perception of "A" will change. He'll see the "A" as a sound, as a word, as part of words. Ultimately he may go on to the highest level of understanding "A," as a linguist and philosopher of language! But at no stage will he be dealing with *raw data* from his environment from which *he* constructs a private reality. At each stage he will be dealing with "A" as "A" is perceived in his culture. The "reality" which "A" represents is not an individual but a social/cultural phenomenon!

Take the Japanese term "kami." It has religious significance, and was mistranslated by early missionaries as "God" or "gods." But the concept "kami" has a far different connotation than the Judeo/Christian "God." How does the Japanese child develop his understanding of kami?

At first it may be a meaningless sound he hears spoken by his parents. Later the sound may be associated with visits to a shrine, and the child may point to a pagoda roofed building and shout "kami, kami," much as my children when they were young delighted to shout "truck, truck" on the highway. As the child grows, and cognitive development permits, new understandings will gradually grow. Ultimately the child may grow into an adult who is a philosopher of religion, and who explores the deepest roots and meanings of "kami" in Japanese culture and history. Yet whatever happened in this learning process, the child did *not* construct an individual reality as he grew in which kami had a special meaning only to him. Instead the child's perceptions were shaped and channeled by his culture. He came to understand (perhaps deeply) the social reality expressed by "kami." *All the processes of learning described by educational psychology must ultimately describe how a child learns not raw data from his environment but social constructs of that data!*

Now, all this affirms that in developing an understanding of any data at all, the critical cues are found in the way that data is defined by the cultural (e.g., social) environment.

What are the implications for Christian education? Biblical concepts too will also be perceived by growing children as those concepts exist in his social environment! If Bible truths are *treated by us* as beliefs to be accepted intellectually, but without affective or conative (decisional) meaning, then the child will tend to perceive and integrate these concepts into his growing personality in the same way! No wonder the Bible insists, "these words which I command you this day shall be upon your heart; and you shall teach them diligently to your children, and shall talk of them when you sit in your house, and when you walk by the way, and when you lie down, and when you rise" (Deut. 6:6, 7, RSV). *Scripture must be communicated as a lived and livable reality!* Its truths must be communicated by those who have integrated them into their personalities and who, in the shared experiences of life, talk of the Word and words of God with their children. The *critical location* for Bible teaching is not the classroom but rather the household; the walk, the sitting together on the porch, the snuggling into the warmth of bed, the joy of rising to a new day. It is in life itself, where Bible truths are to have meaning for us as whole persons, that their communications must center.

And this kind of learning is rooted, not in "education," but in the socialization process.

This, then, is the major problem with even "good" classroom Christian education. If that is *all* we have, we are going to be communicating truths in such a way that their import *must* be distorted. If that is all we have, we are in our method of teaching going to shout to children that the Bible is an academic book; that the theological and moral truths it communicates are "unreal" as far as living is concerned. My concern for Christian education is that we will continue in our approach to teaching to isolate what is to be lived truth from life, and thus fail to communicate it in that context of shared experiences in which its whole-person meaning can be seen and shared by a model in whom God Himself does live.

Does this mean there is *no* place for a classroom teaching of the Bible to children? Not necessarily. But it does mean that the role we give the classroom must (1) be clearly understood to be a part, not the whole, of what we are doing in children's ministry; (2) to be integrated with the whole so that it supports and is supported by what is happening elsewhere; and (3) be designed so that teacher and learner roles, the ways concepts are communicated, etc., actually do fit in our total approach, and contribute to the socialization process.

This is not a particularly easy task. But we'll look in the next chapter at one way it might be approached.

the home

If we accept socialization as more appropriate than "education" for communicating Christian faith as life, we are immediately forced to look to the home when we consider Christian education of children. There is no question that parents still are the primary socialization agents for young children. This does not mean that they are [or should be] the *sole* socializing agents. Other adults can be significant in a child's life, including a Christian teacher. At the same time, the role of parents is *primary*.

This may be one reason why organized "schooling" in Christian faith for children is of relatively late appearance. In the Old Testament, the whole life of God's people was organized to teach . . . the festivals, the laws, the daily patterns of work and worship. And it was to parents that God said, "you" shall teach "your children." [For a good description of Hebrew education, see Barclay's *Train Up a Child.*]

The New Testament makes no change in this basic strategy.

194

Paul is recorded to have established no Sunday schools. The Epistles add nothing new to the Old Testament injunction that leaves parents with responsibility for training of their own children. The community surely had an impact. A young girl was with the adults in the prayer meeting for Peter (Acts 12) ... and like young people today, was given the task of running to see who was at the door! The families of church leaders are to show that they have been well trained (1 Tim. 3:4). Timothy himself learned the Scriptures well from mother and grandmother. It is clear that nurture was a family affair.

And it still is.

This, of course, poses a challenging problem for the Church. We know so much about how to "educate" children in the classroom. But we know so little about how to help parents understand their socializing roles. How *do* we shift the focus of childhood education from the formal to informal learning setting? How do we help parents understand the divinely designed process by which *they* are to bring up their children in the faith? How do we equip parents and encourage them in that task? How do we reverse the dependency on church agencies which has grown up over the years? How can we support parents as they nurture? We have curriculums for the classroom. Do we need an "at home" curriculum?

These, and many other problems, face us if we take seriously the need to shift our method of communication from a classroom to a socialization one. Personally I am convinced that they are problems we must face ... and can. We need never fear challenge. What we do need to fear is our own unwillingness to commit ourselves to what we believe is right and true, and, whatever the cost, to trust God to lead us (as Abraham) to a "land we know not of."

PROBE
  case histories
  discussion questions
  thought-provokers
  resources

1. To interact with some of the concepts presented in this chapter and their implications, you might enjoy trying one or more of the following:

  A. Write a bulletin insert designed to help Christian parents understand their role in nurture.

   B. Write an article on "family devotions." (Before you do, however, decide whether you're for them or against them.)

   C. Sketch out an approach to a "parents' training class." What would you want to acccomplish? What would you want to communicate? What specific parent behaviors would you want to see as an outcome?

   D. Now design an educational process to achieve the goals listed above . . . without having a formal parents' *class!*

   E. Look over curriculum from publishers who promote a "family" emphasis. What do they mean by family emphasis? What values/weaknesses of their approaches do you see?

   F. Draw up a presentation for a publisher of Sunday school materials showing how they might better relate their present publications to help parents teach (socialize) their own children.

2. The problems facing us as we seek to implement a childhood education ministry growing out of a socialization concept of learning faith are far more complex than appear on the surface. One of the problems has to do with developing a parent support system. Do we prepare an "at home" curriculum? What are the implications of a planned curriculum as to its "fit" with the nature of socialization?

   The following is a section from my Ph.D. dissertation at Garrett Seminary/Northwestern University, Evanston, Illinois. In it I discuss this particular problem. Read it, and afterward try putting in your own words answers to these questions.

   A. Why is "curriculum" a problem?

   B. What should the real goals of an educational system be?

   C. What place does a curriculum play in terms of reaching the system's real goals?

   Here is the section. Read it, and respond (in writing) to the questions above.

Earlier in this chapter it was noted that meta-goals of an educational system should be in harmony with the explicit goals of the education. Thus the stated assumptions about the nature of Christian faith and its communication have great significance for development of the proposed church/home educational system. The system itself, as well as what is taught in it, must support and facilitate the teaching of faith-as-life.

This requirement for the system creates nearly insurmountable difficulties when it is realized that socialization provides the best model for Christian education. The difficulty hinges primarily on one issue: that of control and sequencing of learning experiences.

I noted earlier that our present educational system operates on a classroom model, suited and designed for the transmission of information and of those concepts the society sees as significant. This model may be represented as a flow, originating in a body of content (information and concepts from a field or discipline), with the logic of the content determining the sequence and nature of educational activities.

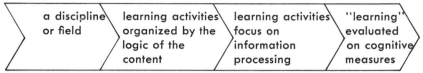

Figure I-1. Traditional Classroom Education

The roles of teacher and student, the character of the curriculum, the nature of testing and evaluation, all are defined by reference to the system content-transmission goals, and by the system flow, originating in the logic of a particular content and controlled at each point by content-transmission considerations.

Today many serious attempts are being made to link the cognitive and affective in education. Normally the approaches seek to bring affective and value data into the classroom setting. In all such innovation an attempt is made to change the role of the teacher to specifically explore value implications of a field, and to open up the classroom to a freer flow of affective data. The classroom teacher sees his task as linking the information processed about a field to the motives, values, and personal perceptions of his student.

But all such innovation, no matter how healthy or creative, does not fundamentally change the control function of the content. It is still the content, and the logic of the content, which determine the sequence and nature of the educational activities.

cognitive	discipline or field		learning sequenced by logic of the content		learning activities information processing		learning evaluated on cognitive measures
		class		class		class	class
affective	motives, values, experiences, personal perceptions						

Figure I-2. Contemporary attempts to link cognitive/affective dimensions of learning.

It is clear, however, that in its pure form the socialization model operates very differently. Life itself, and the experiences shared by model and learner, controls and sequences the education. The content (concepts, information) is organically related to experience and to the attitudes and behaviors appropriate in organizing and responding to situations. The teacher communicates far more than information: he communicates a way of perceiving and experiencing life.

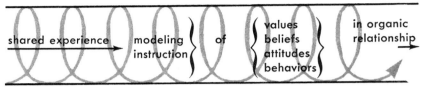

Figure I-3. Socialization education.

In this pattern, controlled as it is by life's natural sequencing of experiences, the teacher's role, the role of content [concepts and beliefs now become a way of structuring reality and guiding responses in real situations], the learner's role, and the way learning is evaluated, all are strikingly different from both the traditional and the modified classroom education.

This brief analysis highlights the central problem in seeking to develop a Christian education system on a socialization model for the communication of faith-as-life. *The very concept of "educational system" implies an external control and sequencing of learning activities. But the socialization process operates as it does just because what is communicated is already an integral part of the organic life of model and learner.*

In Christian education, as in secular education, control has been exerted through the logic of content. Christian faith does have a belief-content, "truths" which can be conceptualized and expressed as cognitions. Conservatives, with their great respect for Scripture as God's revelation of truth about Himself, man, and the nature and purpose of life, are particularly concerned that biblical teachings be communicated in any Christian education approach. But if a curriculum is developed for a Christian education system, that system would seem forced into the control patterns of present educational systems. Certainly the free flowing, spontaneous expression of faith-as-life as a response to the ongoing experiences of life cannot be systematized. And certainly too such response is at the heart of the socialization process, and at the heart of the educational process the author's assumptions demand.

It seems from the above that no church/home educational system can be devised which directly implements communication of faith-as-life on the socialization model. But it may be possible to develop a system for *indirect* implementation: a system in which the ultimate goal is to facilitate the communication of faith-as-life; a system in which other concerns (such as the transmission of beliefs) are subordinate to and at the same time designed to encourage achievement of the primary goal.

Such a system, designed to encourage and facilitate development of communication of faith-as-life on a socialization model, meets the following requirements:

198

(1) Shift the primary focus for communication of faith-as-life from church agencies to the home.

(2) Equip children's primary natural models, their parents, for effective communication of faith-as-life.

(3) Shift the role of in-church staff from the traditional "teacher" role to that of model and friend.

(4) Relate faith's belief-content in an organic, meaning-sharing pattern rather than transmit it merely as information to be believed.

(5) Free children and adults for expression of affective as well as cognitive data in all relationships that develop [parent-child; leader-children; children-children].

3. One excellent educational tool is most often used solely for evaluation. It's a questionnaire. A well-designed questionnaire can stimulate thinking and can introduce in an unobtrusive way concepts a person hasn't thought of before. If we want to look at it in Piagetan terms [or in terms associated in our country with Festinger's cognitive balance theory of attitude change], such a questionnaire can introduce disequilibrium [cognitive dissonance], and thus stimulate learning and change.

Here's an older questionnaire on family life developed by the Lutheran church. It is *not* a good questionnaire, partly because it permits "yes/no" answers rather than asking the taker to evaluate along a continuum. It's far better to scale responses along five possible responses ranging from "very satisfied" to "very unsatisfied" or from "effective" to "ineffective." Another reason the following is not a good questionnaire is that it often asks either the wrong questions, or else it picks out as indicators stereotypical behaviors. For a questionnaire to be valuable as an educational or an evaluative tool it needs to carefully define (explicitly or implicitly) the concepts it is seeking to measure *and a range* of behaviors which are *appropriate* indicators.

Even though the questionnaire is a poor one, it gives us a starting point. And it's easier to react to something already done than to start from scratch. So, taking this questionnaire as a starting point, try the following:

A. Evaluate the questionnaire itself and each item.

B. Define the concepts you would like such an instrument to explore.

C. List indicators which would reveal the functioning or nonfunctioning of the defined concepts in the home.

D. Develop your own "family" questionnaire . . . and if you can, give it to a test population.

A SELF-ANALYSIS CHART FOR THE HOME

The home is the foundation of the state and the bulwark of the church. Positive Christian homes, in which boys and girls are brought up in the fear of God, are not only an ornament and an asset to the church, but they are the hope of the nation. Moved by the mercies of God in Christ, parents who recognize the importance of their homes will earnestly desire to build them Christian. In order, however, to carry on an effective program of home training, they will have to adopt methods that can be followed consistently and that promise to yield the desired results.

The following analysis chart is to help parents locate and define weaknesses in the conduct of their homes and undertake improvements in specific areas of life in the home. Because of the wide range of varying circumstances in our home life, it would be out of the question to devise a chart that would apply equally to all families. The chart will be most helpful to parents whose children are still in the formative period of physical, mental, and spiritual development and who are urgently in need of instruction, guidance and supervision.

A twofold use of this chart is suggested: (1) by parents; (2) by discussion groups (parent-teacher leagues, parents' Bible classes, couples' groups).

(1) Read each statement carefully. If the statement is true in your case, place a + on the blank space. After you have checked a section, add up the points and place the total in the box. For example, if you have checked four statements in Part I, A, your score is 4. When you have completed the analysis, add up the totals, and you will have the sum total of the score.

No home can have a perfect score. Even if that were possible, the score would not report perfection, but would only reveal a high degree of success in the efforts of parents to maintain a real Christian home. Whatever success we may have is ours only by the grace of God. There is no room for pride and self-righteousness in a Christian home.

When you have finished your study of the chart, reread the statements you have not marked with a +. Then work for improvement. After several months of effort, place a + before the statement which you can now honestly check. The improved score will be an incentive to you to work for further improvement.

(2) To get the greatest good out of this chart, use it as the basis of a 4- or 5-lesson Bible study course or parents' class. The fuller study of related Biblical texts and practical discussions will give depth and relevance.

You will not be expected to show the result of your analysis to anyone

---

"As for me and my house, we will serve the Lord," Joshua 24:15

I. The Ideal Christian Home

A. Relationship of Husband and Wife

"As being heirs together of the grace of life," 1 Peter 3:7

1. _____ We try to make ourselves worthy of respect, knowing how necessary mutual respect is for a happy, God-pleasing marriage.
2. _____ We are kind and forbearing toward each other, endeavoring with the help of God to give love and receive love.
3. _____ We settle disagreements privately, never in the presence of those who are not concerned.
4. _____ We cherish Christ in our hearts and home, and we live as in His holy presence.

5. _____ We cultivate a home atmosphere which encourages self-restraint and peaceable behavior. ☐

B. The Devotional Life

"Let the Word of Christ dwell in you richly," Colossians 3:16

6. _____ We pray often and earnestly for each other.
7. _____ We have a prayer at each meal.
8. _____ We observe family worship at least once a day.
9. _____ Husband and wife each has a daily period of devotional reading and private worship.
10. _____ We sing hymns in our home.
11. _____ We pray with and for our children and teach them to pray.
12. _____ We lead our children into the Bible through the use of a Bible story book and the Bible.
13. _____ We teach our children to cultivate their religious life by private Bible reading and prayer.
14. _____ We teach our children reverence for God's Word and for all that is holy.
15. _____ We often discuss practical problems of Christian living with our children.
16. _____ We give our children religious books to read. ☐

II. The Home as a School

A. The Children

"Bring them up in the nurture and admonition of the Lord," Ephesians 6:4

17. _____ We both participate actively in the religious training of our children.
18. _____ We teach our children to honor and obey Father and Mother as God's representatives.
19. _____ We train our children to live according to God's commandments.
20. _____ We try to be impartial in the treatment of our children.
21. _____ We command and forbid as little as necessary, but in every case we insist on obedience.
22. _____ We try not to make threats or give promises which cannot or will not be carried out.
23. _____ We do not anger our children by harsh rebukes and unjust treatment.
24. _____ We avoid shouting, but depend on the quiet yet firm assertion of authority to secure obedience.
25. _____ We withhold privileges and we use the rod, if necessary, to enforce obedience.
26. _____ We refrain from calling children names which should never be applied to a baptized child of God.
27. _____ The aim of our training is that the child may be motivated by the fear and love of God in everything he does.
28. _____ We are aware of individual differences among our children and we adapt our training methods accordingly.
29. _____ We apply Law and Gospel as they are needed.

30. _____ We try to gain the confidence of our children so that they will come to us with all their problems.
31. _____ We teach our children thrift, encouraging them to spend money wisely as stewards accountable to God.
32. _____ We observe the habits of our children and give them the necessary interpretation of sex. ☐

B. The Youth

"Let them first learn their religious duty to their own family and make some return to their parents," 1 Timothy 5:4 (RSV)

33. _____ We try to be sympathetic with our adolescents without relinquishing our authority, because we know they are passing through a critical period of life.
34. _____ We avoid nagging and harsh rebuke, because we believe it hardens young people.
35. _____ We encourage initiative and a healthy spirit of independence, coupled with a strong sense of personal responsibility.
36. _____ We help them keep Christ and the Gospel central in their lives, and to grow up into Christ in all things.
37. _____ We try to help our young people decide upon a suitable life vocation.
38. _____ We believe that prayer, earnest counsel, mutual respect, and open discussion are of primary importance at this period.
39. _____ We participate in school activities with our children to show our interest.
40. _____ We try to make the church the central interest in the lives of our young people.
41. _____ We teach our young people to stand up bravely for right, even at the risk of incurring ridicule.
42. _____ We encourage our young people to bring their friends to our home.
43. _____ We know where our young people are at night, and we do not permit them to keep unreasonably late hours. ☐

C. The Example of Parents

"I will walk within my house with a perfect heart," Psalm 101:2

44. _____ We see the need of constant parental self-discipline.
45. _____ We do not curse or use questionable language in the presence of our children, or at any other time.
46. _____ We act on the conviction that a bad example may undo all we try to achieve by means of instruction.
47. _____ We reprove and cheerfully accept reproof, just as we ask forgiveness and offer it to one another for Christ's sake.
48. _____ We try to practice the same courtesy and friendliness in the home as we display outside the home. ☐

D. Culture and Amusements

"Walk worthy of the vocation wherewith ye are called," Ephesians 4:1

49. _____ We train our children for profitable use of leisure time.

50. _____ We provide entertainment with a view to keeping our children interested in the home.
51. _____ We encourage play because of its constructive and health values.
52. _____ We carefully choose books for a home library and advise the reading of none but wholesome literature.
53. _____ We supervise our children's movies, radio, TV programs, and other amusements.
54. _____ We teach our children the love of nature and encourage the outdoor life.
55. _____ We try to awaken and cultivate in our children a fairly wide variety of interests.
56. _____ We give our children an opportunity to develop their talents.
57. _____ We take as much time as possible to be with our children. ☐

III. The Home and Church Relationships

A. Church Attendance

"Lord, I have loved the habitation of Thy house," Psalm 26:8

58. _____ We regularly attend church, considering public worship a sacred duty and also a blessed privilege.
59. _____ We train our children to attend church, and we help them understand worship and make it a regular part of life.
60. _____ We often discuss with our children the meaning of church and the priceless blessings God gives us through the church.
61. _____ We try to awaken in our children a true love for the house of God.
62. _____ We discuss the sermon in our home, bringing out its meaning for our everyday life.
63. _____ We train our children to be quiet, reverent, and well behaved in church.
64. _____ We train our children to say a prayer when they enter church, and to participate in the worship services.
65. _____ We try to make the influence of Sunday carry over into the rest of the week.
66. _____ We encourage all confirmed members of the family to partake of the Lord's Supper frequently for growth in faith and the new life in Christ. ☐

B. Educational Agencies

"These words . . . shall be in thine heart; and thou shalt teach them diligently unto thy children," Deuteronomy 6:6f.

67. _____ We believe in the Christian elementary school and high school and send our children (if such a school is available).
68. _____ Our children attend Sunday school as soon as they are old enough.
69. _____ Our children are prompt and regular in their school and Sunday school attendance, and we work with their teachers.
70. _____ Our children attend Saturday school and vacation Bible school (if such schools are available).

71. _____ We help our children study their religion lessons and their regular school lessons.

72. _____ We consider ourselves responsible for the children's education even though they get their formal schooling outside the home.

73. _____ We help train our children to give generously toward the support of the church.

74. _____ We co-operate with the Sunday school and other educational agencies to the best of our ability.

75. _____ Parents and confirmed members of the family attend parents' classes or Bible classes regularly. □

C. Church Work

"We are laborers together with God," 1 Corinthians 3:9

76. _____ We acquaint our children with the work of the congregation and often emphasize the importance of church work.

77. _____ The father and eligible sons are voting members of the congregation and attend meetings faithfully.

78. _____ We give generously to the support of the church and to charity.

79. _____ We encourage our young people to give liberally of their earnings or of their allowance to the Lord.

80. _____ Our children realize that we have an active interest in all the work of the congregation.

81. _____ We subscribe to and read at least one church paper and discuss its contents in the family circle.

82. _____ We are members of church organizations, such as the men's club, ladies' aid society, couples' club.

83. _____ We gladly serve our church in one or more activities such as Sunday school, choir, mission visits, boards and committees.

84. _____ We cultivate in our children a live interest in missions and in the work of the church at large.

85. _____ Our confirmed young people are participating members of a young people's organization. □

IV. The Home and Social Relationships

A. Neighborliness

"If God so loved us, we ought also to love one another," 1 John 4:11

86. _____ We try to maintain friendly relations with our neighbors, avoiding anything that might cause race or class prejudice.

87. _____ We are respected as a family group that lives up to its Christian profession and thus sets a good example.

88. _____ Our family is always ready in Christian love to aid neighbors who are in trouble.

89. _____ We seek the welfare of our neighbors, avoiding undue intimacy and involvement in injurious neighborhood gossip.

90. _____ We do not allow our children to talk ill of neighbors or to quarrel with their children.

91. _____ We witness to our faith and seek to win unchurched individuals and families for Christ.

92. _____ We permit our children to associate exclusively with children who are morally good and well behaved.
93. _____ We instruct our young people with respect to sex and warn them against the danger of improper association. ☐

B. Community

"Seek the peace of the city," Jeremiah 29:7

94. _____ We co-operate in projects undertaken to improve the community.
95. _____ We avail ourselves of our right to vote and use the right to put reputable persons into office.
96. _____ We unite with other citizens in efforts to improve and maintain the moral standard of our community.
97. _____ We teach our children as Christians and as patriotic citizens to respect persons in authority and to obey the laws.
98. _____ We discuss local and national issues with our children.
99. _____ We help our children to realize that God blesses the nation because of the righteousness of the individual.
100. _____ We believe a well-reared family is the best contribution parents can make to the community, the nation, and the world. ☐

childhood education: an alternative system

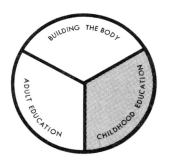

Theology isn't the stuff of "impossible dreams." Theology is instead completely practical, the very stuff of reality.

For us this means that we can work toward the development of a practical way to support and develop a socialization-based Christian education ministry to children. To me, it also means that we must.

present approaches

guidelines and limitations

home as a nurture center

* an alternative system

In 1971 when I left my teaching position in Wheaton College's Graduate School, one of the projects on my priority list was the development and testing of an alternative approach to the Christian education of children, one which might help shift the primary location of our educational ministry from the classroom and help parents develop as effective communicators of faith-as-life. This was not to attack the Sunday school, but rather to attempt to go beyond what the Sunday school is doing, and to integrate the Sunday learning time with a more significant weekday process of learning faith. To communicate to believers that this approach is not an attack, the name "Sunday School, PLUS" was given to the system. The traditional Sunday morning hour is retained. But much is added . . . to it, and to the time beyond.

We are still engaged in the testing process, and expect to be for several years. But it may be helpful to share now several of the hypotheses on which our approach has been constructed, and some of the learnings from early testing. So in this chapter I want to share some of the hypotheses which can be derived from the socialization theory I've stressed in this book on which to base a design for a Christian education system: a system to support the nurture of children in faith-as-life. The following is taken from my dissertation, and may at times sound a little academic.

discussion of hypotheses

In the last chapter the theoretical considerations pointing to the need for a new Christian education system were discussed. The point was made (see PROBE, 2, p. 196) that no system can be devised which *directly* implements communication of faith-as-life on a socialization model. But an educational system may theoretically encourage such communication *indirectly*. Requirements for a system designed to facilitate and encourage communication of faith-as-life in the home were stated:

1. Shift the primary focus for communication of faith-as-life from church agencies to the home.
2. Equip children's primary natural models, their parents, for effective communication of faith-as-life.
3. Shift the role of in-church staff from the traditional "teacher" role to that of model and friend.
4. Relate faith's belief-content in an organic, meaning-sharing pattern rather than transmit it merely as information to be believed.
5. Free children and adults to express affective as well as cognitive data in the various relationships [parent-child; leader-children; children-children].

It is the purpose of this chapter to briefly discuss hypotheses guiding operationalization of the Pilot program of an alternative Christian educational system seeking to meet these five requirements. Hypotheses are related to the three major system elements: curriculum materials, the in-church experience, and the parent-child relationship in the home setting.

curriculum materials

1.1 A curriculum for broad use should be developed. In education by socialization, the educational flow and process is structured around experiences. In a primitive society, where the whole community moves together through shared experience of seasonal and ritual activities, life itself stabilizes and unifies the educational experience. In our culture, where each family's and individual's experiences are organized around multiple roles in a highly diversified and fragmented society, church-sponsored educational programming must seek a different organizing principle if it hopes to unify the educational experiences of the church community.

Traditionally this unification has been sought through published curriculum, or through projects and activities in which youths or adults might be involved together. Each of these unifying approaches has been church-centered: each has been viewed by developer and user alike as education which takes place "in church," and for which the church is responsible. Denominational attempts to involve the family through "church-home" curriculum materials have been failures.

Still a viable alternate Christian educational system which has any possibility of broad application to the Church must have a way to unify the educational experiences of groups of people. In our culture this seems to demand external-to-the-situation structuring of curriculum. Some kind of curriculum materials would seem to have the greatest potential to unify the educational experiences and at the same time to aid in the shift of the primary location of learning from the church to the home. However, such curriculum materials must be distinctively designed to provide a basis for meaningful interaction at home and in the in-church setting.

1.2 *Faith's belief-content should be taught*. The biblical revelation does place emphasis on faith's belief-content. While the Christian is not to "fight wordy battles, which help no one and may undermine the faith of those who hear" (2 Tim. 2:14, Phillips), he is still to "keep my words in your mind as the pattern of sound teaching, given to you in the faith and love of Christ Jesus" (2 Tim. 1:15, Phillips). And so we hear an echo of the Old Testament's voice: ". . . these words which I command you shall be on your heart, and you shall teach them diligently to your children. . . ."

The danger in communicating faith's belief-content, however, lies in communicating it as something which can be accepted intellectually without commitment or response. In a recent book by the author, the danger of attempting to communicate biblical truth isolated from its action consequences was highlighted:

> We need to communicate reality so that people not only come
> to understand it intellectually, but so that they subjectively

accept and act in harmony with it. To attempt to communicate Scripture in the way we attempt to communicate true but irrelevant information (so that it might be accepted as true without demanding decisions and response) is to violate the essential nature of the Scripture itself, God's Word must always be communicated so as to demand and invite decision to act.

Thus, while the curriculum of an alternate Christian education system will deal with faith on a cognitive level, it can never isolate the cognitive from the affective or other dimensions of a person's experience of life, but must rather consciously seek to interrelate them.

To attempt a broader linkage of faith's belief-content seems to indicate a need to teach biblical concepts rather than biblical data. Most conservative Christian education curricula for children concentrate on story-telling: on seeking incidents in the biblical record which are then related as excitingly and interestingly as possible. Thus the biblical facts, the historic data of the faith, are communicated. Normally following the story recital, a moral or behavioral precept is given. Thus the pattern of communication is:

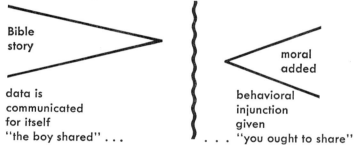

Bible
story

data is
communicated
for itself
"the boy shared" . . .

moral
added

behavioral
injunction
given
. . . "you ought to share"

Figure II-1

Pattern of communication in most contemporary
curricula for children

Aside from the much raised and all too valid criticism that the Scripture's intent is often distorted in the process, it should be clear that little is done in this pattern to relate the biblical data to the reality (biblical world- and life-view) which, in context, it reflects. The Bible is taught as stories without *meaning*.

A different pattern, with a different role for biblical data, is shown in Figure II-2. Here communication starts with a concept (a doctrine, teaching, belief) distinctive to the biblical portrayal of reality. The concept is then developed in its relationship to attitude, feelings, behaviors, and values, with biblical data introduced to (1) indicate to the learner that the concept is derived from the biblical revelation, and (2) to illustrate the concept in its impact in human experience.

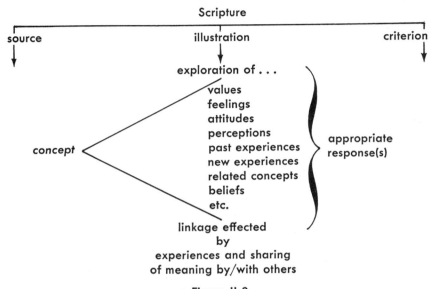

Figure II-2
Pattern of communication in proposed alternate system,
showing roles of Scripture and experiences in process

Rather than adopting the method of contemporary materials, where one moves from biblical data to a predetermined and specific moral or behavioral injunction, the approach outlined here begins with a concept which is given added meaning by exploration, not definition; by opening out, to see the implications of the concept for values, attitudes, feelings, behaviors, and one's perception of the structure of life. Rather than viewing the biblical data as information to be communicated and as a source of specific moral or behavioral "oughts," Scripture is viewed as (1) the source of the concepts to be taught, (2) a reservoir of illustration of meaning of the concepts for the human experience, and (3) a criterion against which one can test responses made in the hearing of the Word.

This does not mean that the alternate curriculum will not "teach the Bible." But it does recognize the fact that the Bible is an adult book. For children, faith's content needs to be drawn from Scripture by adults, who can then state it in ways meaningful to them. Scripture passages and stories should be used: to relate truths taught to their source, to keep the children aware of the centrality of the biblical revelation to Christian faith, and to demonstrate that the Bible is a living book, through which the vitality of faith's life is communicated. But one should not feel that "teaching the Bible" is always and only communicating biblical data.

1.3 *Faith's belief-content should be taught in experiential form.* The Bible emphasizes the experience of faith's belief-content. The sensible man is presented by Jesus as the one who "hears my words and does them" (Matt. 7). The disciple, who comes to know by experience the freedom Christ promises, is one who is "faithful to what I have said" (John 8:31, Phillips). And so James begs, "don't only hear the message, but put it into practice" (James 1:22, Phillips).

If Scripture is viewed as a portrait of reality, then only experience of that reality can be a valid terminal goal for Christian education.

But experience of reality cannot be viewed only as the goal of an educational system. It must be viewed as an essential part of the educational process. For it is just this, the sensing of beliefs *as life*, as reality, which marks off education by socialization from contemporary classroom teaching. To reach its goal, Christian education must cast the belief-content of faith within the framework of the experience of life, and give learners insight into meaning by letting them feel as well as know. The greater the variety of educational activities provided through the curriculum that encourages the learner to experience that which is taught, and the more creatively belief is linked to past and present experience, the more accurately the curriculum will communicate and present a faith which *is* a life.

1.4 *Faith's belief-content should be taught in a relational framework.* It is important to share in a warm loving relationship with a person who can serve as a model of faith's life. It is clear that materials must stimulate significant interaction between the learner and parents, and with the in-church staff.

It is also important that the content itself be cast in relational form. Christian faith invites men to a personal relationship with God through Jesus Christ, and growth in faith is intrinsically related to a deepening of relationship with God. To communicate biblical concepts apart from their relational implications and meaning would be to distort them and rob them of the dynamic role they play in the Christian faith.

1.5 *Cognitive and affective domains should be integrated in the learning activities the curriculum prescribes.* This aspect of curriculum is suggested in hypothesis 1.2 above. While great concern is currently expressed for this kind of integration in education, no clear methodology or approach has been developed. Mary B. Harbeck suggests that one reason for the failure to establish and teach for affective domain objectives is the lack of techniques to evaluate and assess much learning. It is particularly difficult to develop objectives and strategies for teaching when one cannot tell with any certainty whether the outcomes indicate achievement of the objectives. Still, attempts are being systematically made to learn how to provide what George I. Brown, of the Esalen Institute, calls "confluent education," in which the "affective or emotional aspects of learning flow together with the cognitive or intellectual functions."

The insights from experimentation, such as is being conducted at Esalen, seem to indicate that the critical element in achieving confluence is exploration of one's own inner states and exposure to the inner states of others. This approach is in full harmony with what the behavioral sciences suggest about the dynamics of identification and internalization. Thus the primary curriculum strategies one can adopt would seem to involve both leading the learner to examine and express his own feelings and attitudes about faith's content, and to be exposed to the feelings, attitudes, values, and perceptions of others.

1.6 *Faith-sharing between parent and child should be stimulated.* To communicate truth in a relational context, to encourage exploration of one's own inner states and to provide exposure to the inner states of others who can serve as models of faith's life, the curriculum should structure both interaction between parents and children, in which the experienced meanings of biblical concepts can be explored and shared.

1.7 *Faith-sharing between in-church staff and children should be stimulated.* While the curriculum approach adopted for the Pilot program did not structure in-church activities, in-church staff were able to build on the individualized and family activities suggested in the curriculum, and did plan group sharing and learning activities.

1.8 *Maximum individualization should be provided.* It was noted earlier that present church-school curricula presuppose an in-church learning group. One of the requirements of an alternative educational system as discussed in this dissertation is that it shift the context of teaching/learning from church to home, and encourage the development of the kind of relationship between parents and children in which Christian faith will increasingly be shared *as life*. A derived concern is that curriculum materials permit maximum individualization, recognizing a wide range of children's abilities and development. Moving from group setting for education clearly requires a redesign of materials that historically have been used for group-paced learning toward materials that provide for individual- and family-paced learning.

the in-church setting

2.1 *The system should provide in-church peer group experiences.* The Christian community is a community of those who share faith's life. While parents may be the primary models for their own children, additional models are important, as is the development of a community which mirrors and reflects faith's life. Thus the New Testament places great emphasis on the nature of the Church as a body, and on the significance of the relationships within this body in fulfilling God's transforming purpose.

An in-church group experience, which is supplementary to and supportive of the communication of faith that takes place in the home, thus seems indicated. Such an experience is in harmony with the broader understanding of the Church as a community of believers. Adult leaders in the church setting may provide additional adult models of faith's life. Other children in the group may facilitate an individual's learning, and also serve as models. A sense of belonging to a wider group who perceive and experience life from the vantage point of faith may provide a broader social anchor for faith's perceptions of life than is provided by anchoring only in the parent/child relationship. A final reason for an in-church session is that in both traditional and renewal churches today, adult learning and worship is not structured for the participation of children, thus parents do want an on-their-level program for children in the church, to free adults for their own church activities.

All of these considerations indicate a need for any Christian education system to provide for in-church, peer-grouped learning experiences, if there is to be hope of wide acceptance in the Church.

2.2 *The traditional student/teacher relationship should be redefined.* In the traditional educational setting the teacher is cast in the role of one who controls and paces group learning, acting as an authority who transmits the information which has been determined by others to be important for the learner. The meta-goals of the present educational system seem to operate counter to the development of those facilitating relationships which were seen to be so integral to communication of faith-as-life.

Thus a redefinition of the role of the adult leader in the alternative system is necessary. A role must be developed which permits and encourages the growth of a warm, loving relationship between the leader and individuals in the group, between the group and the leader, and between individual members and the group. The new leader role must also encourage exposure of the adult leaders' inner states, as members of the learning group relate to each other and relate faith's belief-content to affective as well as cognitive domains.

2.3 *In-church staff should relate to the children as adult friends.* The term "friend" perhaps best reflects the mutually respecting, mutually responsive relationship that permits persons to meet as persons. Mutuality in listening, expressing, caring, and sharing mark the best aspect of the "friend" relationship, and can exist across the generations as well as between two members of the same generation. For adult staff to so treat the children in their learning group does not require "coming down" to the children's level: it rather requires being an adult who can accept and value a child and respect him as a person.

The "friend" relationship, with its overtones of affection and warmth of feelings, also encourages identification by the child with the adult who can, in the friendship relationship, also serve as a model of faith's life. In cases where parents are not participants in the Christian community, in-church staff may have to serve as the primary model of faith's life.

2.4 *Faith-sharing between adults and children should be stimulated.* Curriculum materials are to involve the children in exploring a single concept, and relate that concept to their understandings, feelings, attitudes, values, etc. But the *meaning* of the concept, as it is related to faith's experience of life, can only be communicated interpersonally. Thus curriculum materials should seek both (1) to involve learners and their adult models in activities in which various meanings of the concepts can be experienced, and (2) to involve them in sharing with one another their own inner-states — the feelings and understandings gained through personal experience of faith's life.

In the in-church setting, then, communication should be open, with free flow of affective as well as cognitive data characterizing the interaction. And a variety of shared experiences which encourage exploration of feelings and meanings should be an integral part of the educational process.

2.5 *Faith-sharing between children in the in-church situation should be stimulated.* The free flow of affective and cognitive data noted above should also characterize the interaction between members of the group as well as the participation of the adult leaders. In-church activities should permit children to "feel" the meaning of concepts explored, and encourage expression and sharing of their feelings and perceptions with one another.

2.6 *Faith's belief-content should be interpreted both through appropriate experiences and through meaning-sharing.* The in-church setting, as intimated above, should not be viewed as a place for mass verbal presentation of information. Rather the in-church setting should provide a place where meaning can be added to the concepts by shared experiences that relate feelings to concepts, and aided by verbalizing of feelings and experiences.

An in-church program designed to these specifications will vary significantly from the present "Sunday school class."

the home setting

3.1 *Parents should be appropriate models of faith's life.* The educational theory outlined suggests that communication of faith, if effective, depends on the character and commitment of Christian parents. To model faith's life, the words must be "in the heart."

In a very real sense, this precondition cannot be dealt with through the educational system. However, contemporary emergence of the renewal movement, and the healthy focus that movement places on rediscovery in the church of those relationships which mark community and facilitate personal growth, suggest that the church may be ready for an educational system which helps parents communicate faith-as-life to their children.

3.2 *Parents should accept responsibility for the Christian nurture of their own children.* Success of the proposed educational system also depends on the willingness of parents to accept responsibility for the nurture of their own children. While there is no way within the system to assure this second precondition will be met, there is increasing evidence of awareness that the church is unable to effectively nurture children and youth in the faith, and that the home must accept a greater share of the responsibility. One cause of hesitancy to accept responsibility is the absence of meaningful help and support for parents. When developed, the alternate system being explored in the Pilot program may meet both a present need, by providing practical help for parents, and also increase awareness of the need for home-centered nurture.

3.3 *Parents should be helped to develop a relationship with their children which facilitates the communication of faith-as-life.* The facilitating relationship is one characterized by honesty and openness and mutual respect. Too often inner states of parents are not expressed in relationships with their children. The educational system should encourage sharing of feelings and perceptions between parents and children; a sharing which is integral to the nature of faith-as-life and principles of communication.

3.4 *Communicative encounters between parents and children should be structured.* Curriculum materials, to implement the real goals of the system [to stimulate the sharing of faith-as-life on a socialization model] must structure communicative encounters between parents and children in which parents and children will share their own inner states as they explore together the meanings of faith's content for life.

Structured encounters (activities which children and parents can do together, or experiences which they can talk over and share) should be carefully designed to involve parental *listening to* and *sharing personal perceptions and feelings with* the children, thus moving them into a "person with" rather than "judge" or "outside authority" relationship. Both encouraged relationship and the expression of inner states are significant to the communication of faith-as-life.

3.5 *Experiences of faith-as-life which parents and children can share and discuss should be suggested.* Wherever possible a variety of experiences should be structured in which children can be involved with their parents and which can then be explored and interpreted together with reference to the belief-content of faith.

experimental findings

Our two years of testing have shown that we can make definite progress toward significant change in several areas. To date the greatest improvements have involved:

(1) Teachers can develop and teach out of a "faith-sharer"

role, with greater pleasure and a greater sense of accomplishment.

(2) Groups of children can develop closer interpersonal relationships, and meaningful sharing can take place in these groups. Children can show sensitivity to others and their concerns, as revealed in spontaneous prayers, listening, etc.

(3) Biblical concepts can have greater meaning to the children as they are freed to process concepts on their own level in a divergent learning, rather than convergent learning, way.

(4) Classes taught by retrained teachers showed growth both in size and enthusiasm.

(5) Classes taught by teachers who did not grasp or did not choose to function in the faith-sharer role *did* not show the kinds of changes in behaviors or attitudes as classes in which teachers did grasp and function in the new role.

(6) Training processes have been developed which can help a significant number of teachers function in the new role.

The greatest difficulties have been experienced in the area of greatest significance. In general, parents have *not* repatterned relationships, or modified the processing of biblical (faith/life) concepts in their homes.

Several experimental designs have shown that the provision of parent guidance material, training classes, etc., have not significantly modified parental attitudes or response. As a result, the new test sequence (scheduled for Fall 1975) reflects important, theory-rooted changes in the parent-related aspects of the program. Realizing the importance of the "in your heart" dimension of the Deuteronomy 6 communication pattern, the Sunday School PLUS approach has been redesigned to involve a parents' class in which parents will explore the meaning of truths being explored by their children. This redesign focuses on

(1) helping adults grow in the areas they will be exploring with their children.

(2) helping adults set realistic expectations for themselves and their children. [The tendency was for parents to feel they must turn their children into "instant spiritual giants" — an expectation which is totally unrealistic, and highly productive of guilt!]

(3) helping adults see how to talk meaningfully and informally about truths that are meaningful to them.

(4) gradually opening up communications between parents and children to free data flow of inner states as well as ideas and demands.

At the present time, the author and his associates are working toward a test program to involve some 500-1,000 churches in a three-year test of Sunday School PLUS. That sequence will involve constant feedback from test churches, and responsive modification of both system and materials. You can get further information, and an address to which to write, from PROBE 2, page 227.

for now

Ultimately our support of family-focused ministry to children will, I believe, demand an educational system designed to support (in content *and* methods) the socialization process through which they draw the personal meaning of their faith.

Until then, there is much we can do in Christian education to support the home.

Reading. A number of Christian and secular books on the family and on children are now available. More are being produced each year. Purchasing and encouraging the reading of these books is a step we can take now. Using a special book as basis for a discussion group (or Sunday school class) is particularly helpful, as it starts parents talking with each other about their ministry to one another and to their children.

Small groups. Sometimes small groups are formed in the church, especially for parents. These groups center on ministry to each other and adult growth, but often shared concerns about child nurture are explored.

Study classes. There *is* a place for the class when concepts *as concepts* are to be explored. There's a role for exploring basic ideas about childhood and nurture too. Parents might well profit from understanding Piaget and Kohlberg . . . and their expectations for their own children might well become more realistic! Parents certainly should profit from seeing in Scripture the context for communication of Bible truths.

At the same time, these — and other — approaches beg the question.

Our whole understanding of the socialization process insists that children learn what their parents *are*. *This means that the first concern of the Christian educator who is concerned about children must be the spiritual growth and health of parents.* If Christian parents are growing, developing Christian persons, nurture *will* be taking place! We may improve effectiveness by helping parents better understand the life-meaning of biblical truths. We may improve effectiveness by opening up the relational context for communication of adults' feelings and inner experiences. *But we can in no way substitute for an adult personality that is in the process of personal transformation.* The most critical element in the whole system is the adult who will assuredly model what he *is.*

For this reason, the key to childhood Christian education is and must be understood to be *adult* education! Our greatest efforts must be to encourage the spiritual growth of adults — both parents and other members of the Christian community with whom children come in contact. The strategy which we must commit ourselves to if we are to minister meaningfully to children is a strategy which focuses our efforts and our time on ministry to their parents! What we must be ready, then, to do is to commit ourselves to developing the Church as a discipling Body. If our theological understandings are truly to guide our decisions, we must care for children — and demonstrate the depth of that care by concentrating on the nurture of adults!

PROBE
   case histories
   discussion questions
   thought-provokers
   resources

1. There are, I suppose, a number of "radical" thoughts expressed in this section of the book. Here are a number of statements which do *not* represent positions the author is taking. See if you can state what you think he is (or would) say.
   A. Sunday school for children should be abolished.
   B. There is no room in the Church's educational program for the children of non-Christians.
   C. Children from unchurched homes can't profit from Sunday school as we know it today, or from a "faith-sharing" Sunday School PLUS model.
   D. Parents must be trained how to teach.
   E. Learning biblical content is unimportant: it's the "catching" of a life style that counts.

2. It might help to understand better the "alternative." I am suggesting to see material from a pamphlet which describes Sunday School PLUS for those interested in taking part in our testing program. Here's a reproduction of that pamphlet. Look it over and see if some of your questions are answered, and concepts discussed in this

chapter put in clearer focus. By the way, if you want more details on Sunday School PLUS, or want to be added to a free newsletter, *interchange*, you can write to 2026A W. Cactus, Phoenix, AZ 85029 for a "Starter Pack" [$15.00, refundable].

Introducing

SUNDAY
SCHOOL

PLUS

AN EDUCATIONAL SYSTEM

NOT JUST A CURRICULUM . . .
AN EDUCATIONAL SYSTEM

Sunday School PLUS is designed to help local churches communicate Christian faith and life in distinctive, biblical ways.

A biblical pattern of communication is as important in Christian education as the Bible content to be communicated. Sunday School PLUS is built to biblical specifications . . . on these critical principles:

PRINCIPLE: LIFE-FOCUSED

Scripture consistently portrays God's Word as a "hear and do" revelation.

Christ seeks to touch our whole personality — our attitudes, our values, our feelings, as well as our beliefs. It is as we respond to His Word as whole persons that His Spirit reshapes our lives.

Thus (1) the teaching/learning process must be structured to encourage a whole-person response to God; (2) each Bible truth must be understood in its meaning for relationship with God, for relationships with others, for relationship with ourselves, for relationship with our world. Bible truths must not be presented as interesting but irrelevant information, or as something that can be "believed" without making an appropriate faith-response.

Sunday School PLUS is life-focused Bible teaching.

PRINCIPLE: RELATIONAL

The relational context facilitates or impedes life-focused teaching.

The biblical concept of the teacher is a model, whom the learner becomes like (cf. Luke 6:40). For this an atmosphere of warmth, love, openness and sharing is critical.

Thus (1) life-focused teaching involves sharing of what psychologists call our "inner states" to help learners see the meaning of God's Word for attitudes, values, feelings, and behavior; (2) the experience of loving and being loved are critical motivators of whole-person response to God. The Bible must not be taught in the impersonal, "let me tell you" atmosphere of the traditional classroom. Interaction and sharing are essential.

Sunday School PLUS is relational Bible teaching.

PRINCIPLE: HOME-CENTERED

The home is the God-ordained center of Christian nurture.

Parents are a child's primary adult models. Where parents are growing Christian persons, where love and communication flourish, and where God's Word is linked with life, healthy Christian personalities will develop.

Thus (1) a Christian education system must link Sunday school and home in an integrated total teaching/learning program; (2) system elements must provide help for both in-church teachers and for parents, guiding their communication of God's Word in a life-focused, relational way. A local church must not permit its educational efforts to drift from a solid home and family base into a sterile, intellectualized "classroom only" teaching of content.

Sunday School PLUS is home-centered Bible teaching.

SYSTEM ELEMENTS

Through Sunday School PLUS, guidance materials are provided for (1) the classroom teacher [*Teacher's Guide*], (2) for each learner [*Student's Discovery Packet*], and for parents [*Parent's Sharing Guide*].

Learning is initiated each week in the Sunday school, where the teacher's role and learning activities have been redesigned to harmonize with the principles of relational communication. Then, each child in grades 1-6 continues learning at home, using his own *Discovery Packet*. Truth is further related to life during the week as parents and children are involved together in activities and sharing times, guided by *Parent's Sharing Guide*.

The next pages will introduce you to the system elements, and give illustrations from a unit entitled, "God Is Forgiving."

SYSTEM ELEMENTS IN-CHURCH

Sunday morning involves adult leaders with children in four kinds of learning. A number of learning activities are suggested in the *Teacher's Guide,* with directions for use in one- or two-hour sessions. The four "times" into which Sunday school is divided are:

SHARING LOVE
Coming to know and love each other. John 13:34

Sharing comes first, to let the children know they are special. To help set the relational tone for the hour, the teacher shares too.

Two of the sharing time "talkables" for lesson one on forgiveness are:

1. Have your parents ever forgiven you for something? How did they show you forgiveness? How did you feel before and after you were forgiven?

2. Do you like the people you know to be forgiving? Why?

UNDERSTANDING GOD'S TRUTH
Creative learning activities which give meaning to the Bible study. Colossians 1:9, 10

Next come activities that help build understanding of the basic biblical concept being taught. This broadening of understanding prepares the children to see the meaning of the Bible truth — not just to hear the truth as words.

Two of the understanding-time activities for lesson one on forgiveness are:

A. PRESENTING THE TRUTH

Develop a definition of forgiveness in practical (behavioral) terms. Do this by working with the children to complete this sentence:

A FORGIVING PERSON IS . . .

Write as many finished sentences as possible. Work as a class, or divide into smaller teams.

Afterward, write on the chalkboard, GOD IS FORGIVING. Choose two class members to read Nehemiah 9:17 and Psalm 86:5a. Ask if they learn more about what a forgiving person is like from these, and add to the list of sentences.

B. EXPLORING TRUTH THROUGH ACTIVITIES

Let each child choose one of the finished sentences to show in a drawing or painting. Have each write the finished sentences at the top of the drawings. Share these and let each person explain his picture. Make a bulletin board display of these, to keep up for this entire unit.

EXPLORING GOD'S BOOK
Seeing the Bible truth in the Scriptures. 2 Timothy 3:16

The group goes into the Bible to see the truth taught and/or illustrated. Primaries are told the Bible story: Juniors read the study passage from the text itself. Questions guide a discussion of the passage and its meaning, helping the children move beyond the facts to impact on feelings, attitude, and behavior.

The Bible study for the first lesson on forgiveness explores Luke 15:11-24, the story of the prodigal son. Discussion questions which can be used are:

1. How does this story show that God is forgiving?
2. If you were the father in the story, would you have forgiven the son? Why?
3. If you were the son in the story, would you have expected your father to respond as he did? How would you think he might have responded?
4. How do you think God feels about you?
5. How does it make you feel to know that God is a forgiving person?

RESPONDING TO GOD'S TRUTH

Applying truth to our lives. Psalm 119:11

The final segment suggests activities to help the children respond to God as He has revealed Himself or His will in the Scriptures.

A sample activity from the first lesson on forgiveness designed to encourage response is:

1. As a class write a thank you prayer to God for being forgiving. Look at all the completed sentences (PRESENTING THE TRUTH) again and decide what things you could say to God to thank Him for being forgiving.

   Then give each child a sheet of paper to copy down the prayer the class has composed. Offer God this prayer together now, and encourage the children to pray this prayer to God during the coming week.

SYSTEM ELEMENTS DISCOVERY PACKET

DISCOVERY PACKET

Each child takes home his own graded *Discovery Packet*. This reflects the approach of secular education's Individualized Learning Packet (ILP), and helps the child review and go on in his learning.

Features of the *Discovery Packet* are:

Behavioral Goals

Specific objectives are stated so each child will be able to evaluate his learning. For the first Forgiveness lesson, this *Target* is set:

WHEN I FINISH THIS DISCOVERY PACKET, I WILL . . .

1. Know that God is forgiving.
2. Be able to tell others the Bible verses and story that says God is forgiving.
3. Write in my own words what it means to be a forgiving person.

Bible story

The packet restates the Bible story and key verses.

Activities

A variety of learning activities are suggested in the packet, giving options for the children to select those of interest. For example, one activity from this first Forgiveness lesson is:

WITH DAD

> Pretend you are a T.V. or radio reporter sent to interview the father in the Bible story. If you can, use a recorder to make your interview.
>
> How: Get with your dad and write down the kinds of questions a good reporter would ask the father. Then let your dad play the part of the father in the story. As the reporter, ask him each of the questions, then share your interview tape with the whole family.

A series of "how well have you learned" questions at the end, to be done with parents, and parent-involving activities, initiate sharing in the home in a natural, easy way.

SYSTEM ELEMENTS PARENT'S GUIDE

The *Parent's Sharing Guide* shows parents how to share the meaning of the week's Bible truth with their children. Each *Sharing Guide* features . . .

Biblical/theological background

The Bible's teaching about God's forgiveness is surveyed in the first Forgiveness lesson, and the context of the Prodigal Son story outlined.

Sharing helps

Each week parents and children read the key Bible passage together. Questions to stimulate meaningful discussion of the passage are included, like these from the first Forgiveness lesson.

1. How can we know this father loved his son?
2. How can you tell your father loves you? (NOTE: parent share evidence of your own parent's love.)
3. Read again what the son decided to say to his father (vv. 18, 19). Why does he say he has sinned against heaven? (Read Ps. 51:3, 4. What does David teach about sin in these verses?)
4. As a family write on separate sheets of paper the different truths you have learned from this story and want to practice. Share what you have written with each other, and then pray together.

Activities to initiate

Each week parents are given suggestions for activities that will help impress the Bible truth through the week. One Activity suggested for this first Forgiveness Lesson is:

If your child is to understand that God is forgiving you must be forgiving too. When your child commits a sin, help him ask God for forgiveness. Then read or quote 1 John 1:9, and pray with him, thanking God for His promised forgiveness. And let your child know that you forgive him, too.

The Sunday School PLUS system can be used in three ways.

1. Whole school

   The entire Sunday school, 1st-6th grade, adopts Sunday School PLUS, and provides *Discovery Packets* and *Parent's Sharing Guides* for every home.

2. Family elective

   Parents enroll their families in special Sunday School PLUS units. A Family Elective approach involves . . .

   (1) Parents meet during the Sunday school hour and study the same lesson as the children, using the *Parent's Sharing Guide* as adult curriculum.

   (2) Children meet in a Sunday School PLUS unit, led by specially trained teachers, for either the regular Sunday school hour or an extended session.

   (3) Children receive the *Discovery Packet* and the normal at-home suggestions are followed.

   Under this plan, only those parents who sign up their family and agree to take part in the adult class are permitted to have children in the SS Plus unit.

3. Partial program

   The Sunday school uses the Sunday School PLUS approach and curriculum, and sends the *Discovery Packets* home with the children. No attempt is made to involve parents or to provide the *Sharing Guide*.

Which approach should a local church choose? This depends on Church READINESS.

CHURCH READINESS

Our research indicates that few parents will use the *Sharing Guide* if it is simply "sent home" to them. This is particularly true where people have grown to expect church educational agencies to perform the tasks of Christian nurture. Many Christian parents today simply will not bother about their children's spiritual growth! So Sunday School PLUS is not a magic solution; an "easy way" to nurture. How it is used will depend on a church's state of readiness.

READINESS Level Three

Little or no responsibility is being taken by parents. Church heavily programed, with many activities and agencies, people very busy in church programs. Little awareness of "renewal" or "body life" by members.

Churches at this level might choose either the Family Elective or structure (partial program). Or set up one experimental Family Elective unit.

READINESS Level Two

A number of people express concern about their own and their children's spiritual growth. Awareness of "renewal" is present, yet significant numbers not involved as yet in "body life" type activities.

Churches at this level might choose the third approach, to enroll all interested in a one-year Family Elective program.

READINESS Level One

This is a "renewal" church. Most members are in small sharing groups, spiritual growth is evident, some "body life" elements mark congregational meetings.

Churches at this level might choose either the Family Elective or structure their whole school (children, and adult) in the Sunday School PLUS pattern.

BECOMING A S.S. PLUS CHURCH

At present Sunday School PLUS is in an experimental and foundation-laying stage. "Clusters" of five or six churches in a locality are being set up, at a rate of 5 per quarter (in January, April, September, and October). These clusters of "Pioneer" churches may serve as the base for nation-wide expansion, should Sunday School PLUS prove of significant value to the Church.

If you want to be involved as a Pioneer Church, share this brochure with other churches in your area, to see if enough are interested to form a cluster.

Possibilities

YES, we are interested in Sunday School PLUS. Please send me the Starter Pack with more details about what Sunday School PLUS means for our church.

Name_____

Church_____

Address_____

Position in church_____

DATA

Church leadership has been informed about SS PLUS and expressed interest.

( ) Yes   ( ) No

Other area churches have been contacted (please give names)

_____

_____

_____

Question list enclosed ( ) Yes   ( ) No

TO: Sunday School PLUS
2026A W. Cactus
Phoenix, AZ 85029

I understand my $15 check will remain uncashed for 40 days.

3. To close out this survey of some childhood education issues, why not write a brief statement of your own philosophy of ministry to children. It is (obviously) not necessary that you agree with me. But it is important to have a basic understanding of what you are trying to do in children's ministry, and to be able to defend it educationally and theologically. So if you do write out your own philosophy, you will need to make some statement about your understanding of children's development, children's learning, the nature of Scripture, the role of adults, the place of parents, and so on.

This isn't a particularly easy thing to do. But it is important. It's important because our *practices* ought to be *defensible*. And our defense must include not only recourse to tradition, or assumed benefits, or unstated assumptions, but to foundational understandings of just those issues we have explored. And it should include evidence that the theories and practices derived have at least some empirical, as well as theological, justification. So try it. You may not like it. But it *will* help.

adult education: the nature of ministry

There are many reasons why our educational ministry, like Jesus' own, must focus on adults. Jesus welcomed the children . . . but He chose adults to train as His disciples.

If the Church today is to have an impact like that of the early church, it will be because we have rediscovered that focus. A focus on adults. And a focus on discipleship.

* the nature of ministry
conditions facilitating ministry
educational strategies: one to one
educational strategies: small groups
educational strategies: Body Life
educational strategies: worship
educational strategies: the
    preached Word

It's amazing to me that so many books on adult education in the Church begin by defending the proposition, "adults can learn." The sketchiest knowledge of the New Testament makes this clear. From its early beginnings the Christian movement depended on reaching and discipling adults. As adults came to know Christ they were integrated into a local body of believers. There they became a part of a community which involved them, together, in a transforming process.

We have several descriptions of this educational process in Scripture. Strikingly, it bears little resemblance to what we have come to think of as "adult education." That is, it is not marked by classes, planned curriculums, or special "schools" for discipleship or skill training. Instead it truly is involvement in the life of a community: a nonformal educational process which is marked off in definite and significant ways.

Probably the earliest description, found in Acts 2, stresses both that sense of unity (identification) which is so vital in nonformal education, and also stresses specific elements of the community life, such as the focus on God seen in constant exploration of the apostles' teaching, in prayer, and in praise.

> They devoted themselves to the apostles' teaching and to the fellowship, to the breaking of bread and to prayer. Everyone was filled with awe, and many wonders and miracles were done by the apostles. All the believers were together and had everything in common. Selling their possessions and goods, they gave to anyone as he had need. Every day they continued to meet together in the temple courts. They broke bread in their homes and ate together with glad and sincere hearts, praising God and enjoying favor of all the people (Acts 2:42-47a).

Another description of times when believers came together is found in 1 Corinthians 14. There the apostle is discussing excesses in this church in regard to what we call today the charismatic gifts. Yet even his correction reveals how nonformal, how involving, assemblies of the early church were.

> When you come together, everyone has a hymn, or a word of instruction, a revelation, a tongue, or an interpretation. All of these must be done for the strengthening of the church. If anyone speaks in a tongue, two — or at the most three — should speak, one at a time, and someone must interpret. If there is no interpreter, the speaker should keep quiet in the church and speak to himself and God.
>
> Two or three prophets should speak, and the others should weigh carefully what is said. And if a revelation comes to someone who is sitting down, the first speaker should stop. For you can all prophesy in turn so that everyone may be instructed and encouraged (1 Cor. 14:26-31).

One final passage about the believers' gathering reinforces the impression of the nonformal, yet Spirit-controlled process by which adults were helped to grow in their faith.

> And let us consider how we may spur one another on toward love and good deeds. Let us not give up meeting together, as some are in the habit of doing, but let us encourage one another — and all the more as you see the Day approaching (Heb. 10:24, 25).

It was through educational processes like these — unsophisticated, unplanned, without curriculums, classrooms, trained teachers, or the other elements we associate with formal classroom training — that men and women in the early church came to know Christ and grew, rapidly, into discipleship. And how rapidly they did grow! In Antioch Gentiles soon were calling converts "Christians" — a derisive term meaning "little Christs." The likeness had begun to show through!

In an explosive spontaneous movement the good news of Jesus swept the first-century world. Little clusters of believers planted by itinerant evangelists in antagonistic pagan cultures not only retained their identity, but they also had such vital power that they jolted their society! In Ephesus the livelihood of the silversmiths who made statues of Diana was threatened (Acts 19:23-27). History records that believers in the Roman armies refused to worship the Legion Eagles ... and their generals feared that the corps' effectiveness would be lost because of their great numbers. Tertullian in a brief century or two could write from Africa, "though we be *all but a majority in every city,* we conduct ourselves with quietness."

The dynamic transforming power of the gospel demonstrated itself! Jesus' great commission to "go and make disciples" was being fulfilled.

These biblical and historical records challenge us today. They challenge us by reminding us that Christian faith is essentially a vital, reproducing *life.* They challenge us by setting goals that are not for a single church (to be "big") but for *the* Church ... to overwhelm and have a jolting impact on our whole society and culture! They challenge us to once again see the educational ministry of the church in terms of bringing *adults* to experience the transformation of discipleship.

And they challenge us to look again into Scripture to rethink our idea of what "education" involves. We need to get in focus once again the critical elements of a nonformal "transforming" educational process ... and then we need to rethink everything that we are doing in the local church, to bring the means by which we attempt to communicate and nurture Christ's life into fullest harmony with the nature of life and life's message.

the nature of ministry

When we think of educational ministry to children, it's easy to miss key concepts about the nature of ministry. Children are ministered *to.* The adult/child relationship is one in which the *flow of ministry* will be primarily (although not exclusively) one way; from adult to child.

However, as we look at the relationships between adults as portrayed in the quoted passages (and revealed consistently throughout the New Testament), we get a different picture entirely. Here, between adults and their leaders, and adults and one another, the *flow of ministry* is *two way!* Ministry is essentially a *transactional* process involving everyone with one another.

ministry. The root concept of both Hebrew (שרת) and Greek (διακονέω) terms for ministry speak of "being of service" (of any kind) to someone. In the Old Testament priests and Levites were set apart to serve God through sacrifice and worship. Often in the New Tetsament the term "minister" simply involves help or support of another person (Matt. 25:44; Luke 8:3; Rom. 15: 25; Heb. 6:10). There are a number of ways in which people are said to minister. For instance, Peter's mother-in-law after being healed by Jesus got up and ministered to them by preparing dinner (Matt. 8:15). [Angels did the same for Jesus after His temptation (Matt. 4:11).] Paul brought financial aid to Jerusalem as a ministry (Rom. 15:25). Even the function of secular government is viewed in Romans 13:4 as a ministry of service.

There are, of course, many "spiritual" ministries. Evangelism is viewed as a ministry of reconciliation (2 Cor. 5:18). Another ministry involves edification (Eph. 4:12). There are ministries of the Word and of prayers (Acts 6:4). And, of course, the early church recognized an office of ministry [deacon]: that is, individuals were set aside to serve others in specific ways and were recognized as "ministers." In fact, the office of the apostles and of prophets are seen as ministry offices (Acts 1:17; 1 Tim. 1:12).

What is significant here is, of course, that *the critical concept underlying "ministry" is one of service and support of others of any kind.*

spiritual gifts. This designation comes from two Greek terms, the first (πνευματικός) indicating "caused by the (divine) Spirit" and the second (χαρίσματος), indicating a gift graciously and freely given. Biblically the terms (together, and often separately) refer to special gifts or abilities to minister given by God to individual Christians. The key passages on spiritual gifts (Rom. 12; 1 Cor. 12; Eph. 4; 1 Peter 4) list a number of these gifts, which in context are clearly defined as related to the ministry of believers to one another.

It's important to note several things about the gifts as they relate to ministry.

(1) *they are Spirit-given.* Perhaps the best way to define a spiritual gift is simply to say that a "gift" is "that way in which the Holy Spirit ministers to others through you." Gifts do not rest on natural talents or abilities, but are instead dependent

entirely on the Spirit's sovereign placement of the individual in the Body.

(2) *they are for each person.* The Bible makes it clear that each member of the Body of Christ has at least one spiritual gift (1 Cor. 12:7) which enables him to minister and contribute to the common good. A critical passage says, "There are different kinds of spiritual gifts, but the same Spirit. There are different kinds of service (ministry), but the same Lord. There are different kinds of working, but the same God works all of them in all men" (1 Cor. 12:4-6).

(3) *each person's ministry is essential.* The concept of the Body being an interdependent unit is emphasized in the "gift" passages. The argument of Paul in 1 Corinthians stresses the fact that every member's contribution is "indispensable" (1 Cor. 12:22), and this thought is picked up in Ephesians 4 where growth is seen to come "as each part does its work" (4:16).

Thus the Bible's teaching on spiritual gifts intrinsically and explicitly emphasizes the *transactional* nature of the church's educational process. Ministry is something which . . .

* involves each believer
* supports and serves others
* is carried on in a Holy Spirit determined and empowered way
* results in spiritual growth of individuals and the local Body.

correspondence

This brief sketch of two of the New Testament's key educational concepts ("ministry" and "spiritual gifts") helps us see the appropriateness of the biblical descriptions of the Church gathered up (pp. 229-230). In those descriptions we see believers "together." We see them meeting in temple courts and homes. We see them exploring the apostles' teaching, praying, and praising. We see everyone contributing — a hymn, a word of instruction, etc. We see encouragement, exhortation, "spurring one another on" toward love and good deeds.

This picture of *assembly as transaction,* and of *a two-way flow of ministry,* is completely appropriate if ministry involves every believer using his Holy Spirit-given gift to support and serve others. The dynamic outcome — spiritually mature individuals and church bodies — is also appropriate if it is through this kind of *process* that "the whole body, joined and held together by every supporting ligament, grows and builds itself up in love."

This brief sketch of "ministry" and "spiritual gifts" does *not*, however, fit well with what normally happens in the Church today when adults assemble. It fits neither what happens during our church services, nor our "adult education" activities. What characteristically happens in the settings where adults assemble in our churches today in fact violates ministry principles.

	characteristics of normal adult education settings	characteristics appropriate to educational process implicit in "ministry" concept
Flow	one way	two way
Ministry	the pastor or teacher's role	the role of each believer
Gifts seen as operative	"teaching" or "exhortation"	*all* gifts involved
focus	cognitive learning	total person (cf. 1 Cor. 14: 26; Heb. 12:24, 25)
essential	the leader alone	each person's involvement
occasion	formal services, classes	formal and informal settings both are appropriate

It becomes very important, then, not to think of a renewed emphasis on "adult education" as just the planning of a new set or series of formal classes for adults. Instead, what must be involved *is to build into all experiences of the adult in the community of faith those elements of educational process which facilitate and are necessary for transformation to take place!*

conclusions

On the surface this chapter looks like a call for a complete rejection of everything we have been doing in the Church, and a restructuring along "New Testament church" lines.

It's important to get below that surface! Such a call, if made, would hardly be realistic. We all live in *today's* culture. The current perceptions of people in our churches have developed through the very nonformal processes which I've suggested are the key to a "life style" education. To suddenly "change everything" is not an option simply because such radical change *could not be understood or accepted* by believers who have grown to have the perception of "church" most now hold.

But at the same time, we can hardly accept the status quo. We can hardly abandon biblical guidelines and understandings simply because the prospects for change seem distant or dim. Instead what I believe we must do is to take the biblical principles giving insight into the Church's educational ministry very seriously . . . *and gradually begin to integrate these principles into the Church's life.*

Earlier I noted that nonformal education is something of which we are not normally conscious. The frame of reference for life, shaped in nonformal ways, provides the standpoint from which we evaluate, and is itself seldom evaluated. This is one reason why we are only today rediscovering lost principles about the Church. Our past assumptions about the Church and about education were part of our frame of reference. When we read Scripture we did not question the frame of reference. We simply "saw" in Scripture those aspects of its teaching which our frame of reference brought into focus.

What, then, is the best way to help the local church (and thus the Church as a whole) gradually shift its perspectives, and develop a new frame of reference? Surprisingly, the best way is not by explicit teaching about the Church! *The best way is by consciously redesigning the critical nonformal elements.* Certainly explicit teaching will be a part of any local body's discovery of its identity. But that teaching *must* be done in a context where the principles espoused are themselves being implemented. When the critical nonformal elements of our educational settings are in harmony with the concepts about the Church which we teach, *then* the concepts' meanings can be grasped, and believers will gradually develop a changed perspective.

It may well be that the church today needs a new face; a radical restructuring to fit better the biblical portrait of its nature and ministry. But that radical restructuring must await the preparation of the people of the church for change . . . and that preparation is essentially an educational process.

What we need to do in these next chapters, then, is to look at the critical nonformal elements of a meaningful adult education ministry. We need to look at the services and activities of the church which involve adults. We must see how in each setting we can gradually change those nonformal elements which constitute the hidden — but most powerful — curriculum, and thus bring the present generation to a fuller experience of transformation.

PROBE
case histories
discussion questions
thought-provokers
resources

1. In this chapter the author implies or states several critical ideas. You might find it interesting to compare the listing below with positions taken in current books on Christian education of adults. Compare particularly some of the unstated assumptions implicit in the approaches taken in the books you do read.

   Here's the list of the author's concepts as expressed in this chapter.

   (1) Adult education is the critical task of the church.

   (2) Adult education is to be viewed as the total involvement of adults in the church's life — not in a "program" or "class" framework.

   (3) Adult education is focused on transformation, and is essentially concerned with "making disciples."

   (4) Adult education is to be planned primarily as an educational process, not from the standpoint of the content to be taught.

   (5) Adult education casts each adult in the role of minister as well as in the role of one being ministered to.

   (6) Adult education takes place as believers exercise their Holy Spirit-given "gifts" to minister to one another.

   (7) Adult education is to take place in each and all gatherings of believers together as Christ's body.

   (8) Adult education effectiveness depends on designing the "hidden curriculum" (the educational setting itself) to facilitate the kind of transactional ministry described in the other items above.

2. The whole area of spiritual gifts is one which deserves extensive treatment. It certainly is one which you might wish to explore in some depth. I think there are some guidelines which help open out our understanding, and sensitize us to see things in the gift passages (1 Cor. 12-14; Rom. 13; Eph. 4; 1 Peter 4) which we might otherwise overlook. Let me suggest the guidelines, and then several avenues of research.

   Guidelines

   ● Spiritual gifts are enablements for ministry. Thus our understanding of the nature of ministry must color our understanding of the gifts and their exercise.

   ● Spiritual gifts listed in Scripture are not inclusive but illustrative. *All* ministries are dependent on the Holy Spirit's endowment.

   ● Spiritual gifts are not *institutional* but *interpersonal*. It is a mistake to equate a gift with an office (as, for instance, that of "teacher" with "Sunday school class teacher"). There is *no institutional setting* in view in the New Testament, but rather an interpersonal setting. The gifts are exercised as adults share with one another in the transactional setting described in this chapter.

- Spiritual gifts require an interpersonal setting for their exercise. The two-way ministry flow is critical for a free functioning of the gifts.

Research

- Read Old and New Testaments to make an exhaustive list of ways in which believers minister to (support or serve) one another. Do these deserve place with Paul's listing of gifts in the New Testament?

- Read carefully the New Testament gift passages, and do an analysis of the relational context in which they are to be exercised. What do you believe might be defined as *necessary* conditions for the full exercise of spiritual gifts?

- Read several books on spiritual gifts. Note particularly the ways the authors seem to see the context in which gifts are exercised, and the function the gifts have. From your study, how do you believe each writer views the church? How does each view ministry? How does each view education? *Does a person's perspective (frame of reference) really make a significant difference about the way he understands Scripture?*

3. I suggested in this chapter that our understanding of ministry and the process of adult education (e.g., transformation) leads us to the necessity of rethinking and redesigning critical elements in the settings in which adults meet to worship and to learn.

   One church, noted earlier in this book, has attempted something like this. You might want to review their approach, found on pages 88-105.

4. Paul Bergevin and John McKinley (in *Design for Adult Education in the Church*, pp. 65, 66) give the following description of formal and nonformal approaches to education. Their book, explaining the Indiana Plan, proposes a highly structured group training process. Review the contrasted characteristics, and jot down your thoughts on the relational implications.

   What difficulties do you see in attempting to implement an informal learning style in the typical church? How is what the present author suggests different?

FORMAL AND INFORMAL METHODS DISTINGUISHED

Attempts to distinguish between formal and informal education by careful definition for our use is difficult. It should be recognized that a distinction should be made between formal and informal education, and formal and informal methods of education, or ways of making education possible. Formal education according to Dictionary of Education is "(1) any training or education that is conventional, given in an orderly, logical, planned, and systematic manner; thus formal education is said to end with school attendance; (2) in a derogatory sense, any educational program that is confined to the experiences of the students within the classroom itself, failing to make use of the student's incidental and varied experiences outside the classroom."

Informal methods include those which allow the learner in varying degrees to participate to the extent that he can clarify, assimilate and make meaningful, on the spot, the information and ideas being treated. Group discussions, seminars, and various kinds of forums are often referred to as informal methods. Because the Indiana Plan is based on situations and needs at a particular time with a unique group of persons, it endorses and uses the educational methods which seem best to help participants to reach the educational goals of a given meeting.

This program of adult religious education recognizes the need for maintaining the interest of learners over a long period of time in order to maintain attendance and thereby assist learning. Using a variety of methods is therefore desirable. No particular method is used all the time. Changes in physical arrangements, leaders, speakers, resource persons, books — all help enrich the program and maintain an interest level.

D. Formal and Informal Characteristics

These lists are not exhaustive since the purpose here is to present a few characteristics often associated with the words formal and informal education in order to become better acquainted with those terms. No attempt is made here to judge any of these characteristics as "good" or "bad."

1. Characteristics of formal adult educational procedures.

   a. The students are usually thought of as an audience and they listen. Their task is to learn what is presented. They are not often called upon to speak. The lecture or sermon often is a predominant feature.

   b. Programs are usually prepared for the learners by others.

   c. In religious and secular education the word "class" is associated with formal activities — a teacher and a group of pupils, both of which are to be regularly present at a particular time and place.

   d. The word "school" is frequently used in formal educational activities (e.g., church school, Sunday school, high school).

   e. Credit or some sort of tangible reward is closely allied with formal educational activities in secular education. So many points or hours of credit are given for the satisfactory completion of an area of study. Credit also means the certification of the completion of a course of study.

      f. "Course" is a vital word in formal education. The educational program is usually arranged around courses or established limited subject areas in which instruction is given.

      g. "Subject" as used in formal education means a particular field of organized knowledge — like mathematics or English.

      h. The teacher is the "boss."

      i. The program in formal education is often highly organized and conducted over a specific period of time.

      j. "Examinations," or tests, are usually given periodically to determine whether the student can satisfactorily recall and organize, usually in written form, the information that has been transmitted to him in a course.

      k. The teacher's evaluation of the student is of great importance.

      l. The students usually compete.

2. Characteristics of informal adult educational procedures.

      a. Great flexibility and variety in methods, techniques and resources are used.

      b. In organized informal education the teacher or leader acts as a catalyst, a stimulator, a helper, a guide, a coordinator. He is not the "boss."

      c. Each individual is a teacher-learner.

      d. Direct participation by all, or as many persons as possible, is vital.

      e. Sharing ideas, experiences, and information by all persons involved is necessary.

      f. The work or study is based on problems and needs expressed by those who are involved.

      g. Subject materials are a means, not the end.

      h. Some informal education might be called incidental education.

      i. We become involved because there is a demand or need put upon us by ourselves. Our goal is to satisfy that demand or need, not to get a grade.

      j. To an increasing degree the participants determine what is to be studied; when, where, how, and how long it is to be studied; and who is to help them. Participants to a large extent determine both process and content.

      k. The participants' evaluation is of great importance.

5. In this book I am suggesting that we look at adult education as involving *every* experience of adults in the church. I am also suggesting that critical to this concept is the redesign of the nonformal elements of each occasion for gathering to appropriately support and communicate concepts about the nature of the Church, the person and role of the believer, and the whole pattern of life-to-life learning in the socialization pattern.

    You might at this point wish to read several other books on adult education, to get their perspectives and for comparison. Why not choose two books from the following list (or of your own choice) and write a brief report on the underlying principles expressed in each.

Paul Bergevin and John McKinley, *Design for Adult Education in the Church.*

Robert S. Clemmons, *Adult Education in the Methodist Church.*

John Fry, *A Hard Look at Adult Christian Education.*

Lawrence C. Little, *Wider Horizons in Christian Adult Education.*

Martha M. Leypoldt, *Learning Is Change: Adult Education in the Church.*

Roger Shinn, *Tangled World.*

adult education: conditions facilitating ministry

We see "ministry" as involving each believer in serving and supporting one another, using Holy Spirit-given gifts to stimulate personal and corporate growth in the Body. This understanding immediately directs our attention to the interpersonal relationships existing within the Body. Ministry is transactional. It takes place as believers interact with each other. It is an interpersonal kind of thing.

We need then to ask, What kinds of relationship are necessary, if we are to facilitate ministry?

the nature of ministry
* conditions facilitating ministry
educational strategies: one to one
educational strategies: small groups
educational strategies: Body Life
educational strategies: worship
educational strategies: the preached Word

Recently I received a letter from a sister in Canada responding to a book I've written about Christian interpersonal relationships, *Becoming One in the Spirit* (Scripture Press). In the letter she shared a poem she wrote about a year ago; a poem expressing some of her frustration in a strong Christian community where unity is viewed as conformity, and differences dare not be shared. Her words reflect the kind of situation in which ministry will *not* take place; the antithesis of what Scripture reveals of the Body relationship in which God's ministering children find their unity in Christ. What she writes portrays the experience of all too many believers today.

> Abba, Father, deeply grieving
> To behold His children thus —
> Smiling face and friendly greeting
> Hidden inner walls secreting —

Surface only — inward lonely
All withdrawn — but courteous.

Walls of wounds in memory dim,
Walls of fear that dread to share,
Deep mistrust of one another —
Guarded, cautious with a brother;
Solitudes politely merging,
Underlying feelings surging,
Straining, striving to appear
In joyful fellowship sincere.

Trying hard to make it seem
What the heart so deeply craves
Is NOT illusion, NOT a dream —

Contrast this poem with the remarks of Carolyn, a new Christian at Mariner's Church in Newport Beach, California. "The warmth of this church is incredible among the Body. I go to the Tuesday women's prayer group, and that has meant more to me than anything. The women's prayer group gives you the feeling of being part of the Body. You know, I don't have any problem sharing at all. There's just a tremendous amount of love, really. If anybody would have told me about it a year ago, I wouldn't have believed it."

The difference between these two women's experience is the critical difference. The hidden inner walls, the mistrust, the caution with a brother, effectively isolate believers from that ministry to one another on which growth depends. The sharing, the sense of being a part, the freedom to love and be loved, all mark the relational context in which ministry *will* take place, and transformation will be in process.

biblical descriptions

The kinds of relationship marking the Body, which define the context of ministry, are described in several ways in the New Testament.

love. This is one of the key terms. Jesus' "new commandment" of John 13 sets the standard for the Christian community. Believers are to "love one another, just as I have loved you." No longer is the standard of loving others "as ourselves" sufficient. In the Body, Jesus' own love is to be expressed through those sharing His life.

Love can be understood in an operational or behavioral way by looking at the key word "one another" as it appears in the New Testament. In the "one another" relationship we see exactly what Jesus means by the commandment of a loving life style.

Believers are to bear one another's burdens (Gal. 6:1), to admonish one another (Rom. 15:14), to make allowances for one another (Eph. 4:2), to forgive one another (Eph. 4:32), to show hospitality to one another (1 Peter 4:9), to submit to one another (Eph. 5:21; 1 Peter 5:5), to encourage and motivate one another (Heb. 10:24), and so on. These, as well as the great love passage (1 Cor. 13), describe the climate of the Body: a climate in which persons are so close to one another and so confident of acceptance that sharing burdens, forgiving, even taking one another to task, is no threat to the relationship.

acceptance. Another critical element in the relational context is acceptance, or, put another way, the freedom to be oneself. Human organizations seek to find unity through demanding conformity (a process described in *Becoming One in the Spirit*). In Christ, differences of culture, background, race, social status, educational background, age, opinion — even doctrine — are swallowed up in a unity based squarely on relationship with Jesus Christ and mutual sharing in His life.

Thus Romans insists we welcome (accept) one another and refrain from judging one another (Rom. 14:15). Thus too Paul insists that the vast cultural differences between Jew and Greek have been made irrelevant in Christ, as in the cross the differences that stood as barriers between them were broken down (Eph. 2). The church is *open* . . . in the sense that all who know Christ are welcomed as brothers . . . accepted *as they are* and their differences affirmed as important to the life and functioning of the Body.

There are, of course, objections to this point of view when doctrinal concerns are at issue. These objections have a certain validity, and yet are essentially invalid. The validity rests on the insistence of the objectors that there is Truth, and that Truth can be known and is to be accepted. This is, of course, right. Doctrine is important. But the conclusion of the objectors (who want to reject or to insist on a change to the "true" point of view as the price of acceptance) misses the fact that growth is a process. That learning takes place over time. That misunderstandings are best cleared up by freeing a person to grow, rather than forcing a confrontation in which we insist he change whether his understanding has changed or not.

Paul deals with this issue in 1 Corinthians 8, where he discusses a doctrinal dispute over meat sacrificed to idols. This issue had been dealt with in the church on a "truth" basis, with the result that two opposing sides had formed. Each claimed to "know," and justified its nonacceptance of the other on the basis of being "right" and the other "wrong." How does Paul respond? Here are the first thoughts he shares: "We know that we all possess knowledge. Knowledge puffs up, but love builds up. The man who thinks he knows something does not yet know as he ought to know. But the man who loves God is known by God" (1 Cor. 8:1-3). Phillips paraphrases this well: " 'knowing' may make a man look big, it is only love that can make him grow to his full stature."

The argument here is clear. We all have a lot to learn. So we're foolish to take pride in our "knowledge," and attempt to impose our understandings on others. This approach will only puff us up. But if we relate to others on the basis of *love,* we will help that person (and ourselves) grow to our full stature! And as we grow, we and the other person will mature not only in our character but also in our understanding! So it is *vital* to accept others *as they are* and to love and affirm them as they are. Only love will open up their lives and ours to growth.

How foolish then we seem when we attack a new brother who may have a warped understanding of even so central a doctrine as that of the virgin birth. Surely we can share our understanding, and the Scriptures on which it is based. But surely too we can give him time to grow — time to learn. Surely we can give him love, encouraging him to open up his life to God by accepting and loving him. *This is not a retreat from Truth.* It is instead realization that coming to understand Truth involves a growing process. It is instead concern that we create the conditions for growth rather than insist on apparent acceptance of a truth we ourselves have *grown* to understand. We must give other persons the freedom to be themselves, and accept them and love them as themselves, without insisting on any "price" for our love.

But what if they're not yet brothers, but only think they're believers because they misunderstand the gospel itself? Then nothing is lost. For love and acceptance are themselves perhaps the clearest invitation we can give to anyone to come to Christ. A person whom *we* reject is unlikely to be convinced that Jesus is eager to welcome him!

honesty. With awareness that we are accepted comes the freedom to be honest. New Testament injunctions to "speak the truth one to another" imply far more than an absence of lies. It implies that kind of honesty which lets others know us as we are, secure in our acceptance by God and by them, and based on the affirming experience of love.

243

Even when under attack, the apostle Paul opened his heart to others, to share with them his inner feelings and experiences (2 Cor. 1:3-9; 2:1-4; etc.). He could claim without hesitation that those who met him came to understand his motives fully (cf. 1 Thess. 2).

This trait of honesty in our relationships with others and with ourselves has a countermodel in the Pharisees. These men were labeled hypocrites, because they were always play acting. It is probable that their life styles finally meant that they were deceiving themselves as well as attempting to deceive others. How striking that this is the one group of people whom Jesus was unable to touch. They had lost contact with reality, and lived in their own world of pretense, cut off from all that could save them.

John deals with this same issue in his first epistle, and in insisting that we "walk in the light" he first of all points us to the necessity of being honest with ourselves (and others) about our sins and failings (1 John 1:1-9). Freedom to know God's progressive cleansing comes only with honesty about our need, and confession of it.

These, and other lines of biblical argument, stress the necessity in the fellowship of believers for a relational context in which believers can be real with one another, and thus actually *know* and then *take on* one another's burdens, where forgiveness can be asked as its need is confessed, and where it can be freely given.

Body passages. Another approach to discovering the relational context which facilitates ministry involves looking carefully at the gift passages. Strikingly, in each biblical setting where gifts are explored *careful attention is paid to relationships!* In Romans the reference to spiritual gifts in chapter 12 leads immediately into an extended discussion of believers' lives together, beginning in verse 9 with the statement, "Love must be sincere." In fact, all of Romans 12–15:13 moves into an analysis of interpersonal relationships to exist in the Body, and contains such statements and exhortations as:

> "Be devoted to one another in brotherly love" (12:10)
> "Share with God's people who are in need. Practice hospitality" (12:13)
> "Live in harmony with one another" (12:16)
> "Accept him whose faith is weak, without passing judgment on disputable matters" (14:1)
> "Stop passing judgment on one another" (14:13)
> "Let us therefore make every effort to do what leads to peace and to mutual edification" (14:19)

"Each of us should please his neighbor for his good, to
build him up" (15:2)

"May . . . God . . . give you a spirit of unity among yourselves
as you follow Christ Jesus, so that with one heart and
mouth you may glorify . . . God" (15:5).

And these are just a few of the phrases that reflect a concern
seen over and over again in the whole argument. Where the
gifts are exercised, and ministry takes place, love, sharing, harmony, acceptance, unity, concern for others, all are facilitating
and *essential* conditions.

These same elements can be seen by studying the other gift
and ministry passages! Where ministry is in view, the relational
context is of critical importance.

implications

These considerations help us see even more clearly that if we
are to build into the life of the Church the educational processes
explored in this book we must give initial attention to the nature
and quality of interpersonal relationships existing within the
Church. Too often those concerned about renewal attempt
changes in program and activity without attending to the gradual development of a relational context which is required if the
"programs" are to be effective!

If we are starting from a "typical" church situation in which
relationships are superficial, and little interaction takes place in
"church" settings, we might sketch the needs of church this way.

First concerns: preparing the ground

needs
opportunity for personal contact and interaction.
encouragement for believers to come to know one another
as persons.
development of an attitude of acceptance and a valuing
of others as brothers and sisters in Christ.

outcome
a growing trust relationship and person orientation.

Central concerns: deepening fellowship when ground prepared.

needs
increasing experience in sharing inner states (feelings,
experiences, values, etc.).

245

increasing interaction focus on Christ in our lives.

outcome
a growing ministry and exercise of gifts in the Body.

It is important not to attempt to force believers into relationships characterizing the central concerns before they have grown in areas expressed in the first concerns. An attempt to force too quickly "depth" relationships is frightening to persons, and counterproductive. Instead we need to be willing to invest the time, using appropriate strategies, to help people grow gradually toward readiness for full involvement in ministry.

How do we prepare the ground? How do we promote a gradual growth? What are some of the strategies we can use in the different settings in which believers meet together to develop a relational context facilitating ministry? These questions are explored in the next chapters as we look, not at the nature of ministry, or at the conditions that facilitate ministry, but at the nonformal educational elements in all our meetings which will lead us to *experience* ministry.

PROBE
    case histories
    discussion questions
    thought-provokers
    resources

1. Evaluate each of the following "plans" to improve a particular dimension of church experience in view of the requisite relational context for ministry. Which are likely to be successful? Why? Which are likely to be unsuccessful? Why? What might you do to make the unsuccessful strategies more likely to succeed?

    A. You've noticed that there is little participation in the adult Sunday school classes in your church. So you plan a series of teachers' meetings for the adult staff. In the three sessions you intend to train them in specific skills: asking effective questions; guiding discussion; developing a participation-centered lesson plan.

    B. You have noticed a gap between teens and adults in your church, and particularly conflict in several Christian homes. You plan to meet that need with a parent/teen retreat, to which teens can come only if they bring one or both of their parents (or an adult parent-substitute from the church). Because time is short, you plan an intensive study approach, with four forty-five minute lectures followed by forty-five minute "action groups," in which five teens and five adults will work together to list "ways we can apply these truths this coming month." The four lectures you've chosen to give are: God's purpose in parents; Obedience isn't just optional; Let's listen to each other; Love is an action word.

C. You've read Ray Stedman's book, *Body Life,* and are convinced that this experience is just what your people need. You ask the board members to read the book, and then propose that every fourth Sunday evening in your church be given to a Body Life meeting. The first Sunday it's due, you announce it in the morning service, and have the local electrician (a member of the church) fix up a long roving microphone.

2. It is sometimes hard to grasp that the *simplest* approaches to building toward interaction are the best and most effective . . . particularly as they apply the "model" or "example" concept stressed in our educational theory.

For example, in a church board meeting yesterday we discussed the fact that many young teens in our church come to our morning services (which are open, participating services), but do not feel a part. The question was raised, how do we help young teens feel that this is their service, and that they are a part of the Body? The answer? Not to *tell* them they are participants, but to *show* them.

In the next weeks we'll be asking three members of the body to lead us in prayer in one service: a young teen, a mid-range adult, and an older adult. We'll have some sharing from young teens returned from Junior High camp. As Ron hears of God working in some of the young teens, he will encourage them to share in the morning service (and help them plan if they need encouragement). By taking time and making the effort to involve young teens in the sharing, we'll let them know nonverbally that they are participants. Over a period of time, we'll expect to see the young teens participating more fully and spontaneously — something I have seen in other churches of which I've been a member.

The basic idea here is to in a simple, nonthreatening way make *small* changes that speak loudly.

In another church I served as D.C.E. a sense of progress was lost when the pastor left. We wanted to shift the focus of the membership from program to *people,* and help them sense God's working in individuals. This led to a short "God at work" segment in our regular church services, in which a member of the congregation was asked to dialogue with me about what God had been doing in his life that week. This short five-minute segment in a traditional service nonverbally communicated to the congregation the importance of God to people, and helped them look within themselves and each other for evidence of God's blessing. It was a powerful tool for change — until some six months later an interim pastor felt it robbed him of five minutes of preaching time and it was eliminated!

What we do can have a dramatic impact on people's perceptions. *To give principles concrete but simple expression can have a vital effect on the life and the relational context of a local church.*

With this said, try your hand at thinking of *five ways* that the persons below might act to present a simple model of a desired change in a typical church. Remember that at this point we are not dealing on the "critical change" level, but thinking of the average local church as you know it. The changes you think of should be something which can be done without great threat to the people, yet *within the present framework* provide the kind of example which has an impact on people's perception of what is appropriate behavior in that setting.

A. As a pastor, you want to help people in your Sunday morning service begin to perceive themselves as ministers. What can you do without totally and radically changing the service format?

B. As a pastor, you want to help your people see that what is important to God is what is happening in persons — not just that which can be measured by "nickels and noses." What can you do within the framework of the total church program to help them shift perceptions?

C. As a Sunday school superintendent, you want your teachers to perceive themselves as persons who share their faith in Christ, rather than simply as transmitters of true information. What can you do to help that perception develop?

D. As a church board member, you want to help members in your church see the need for and possibility of a deeper fellowship relationship with one another. What can you do to communicate that concern and help others see that deeper relationships are desirable?

E. As a pastor, you want to help your people realize that they can be and are accepted, and at the same time that it is valid to share more of themselves with each other. What ways are open to you to "signal" to them that such openness and acceptance are valid and valuable behaviors?

In working out strategies for each of these situations, remember that we are concentrating on *modeling* actions which nonverbally communicate and validate a concept. These *modeling actions* may be taken by an individual, or in the context of institutional action. For example, a pastor who preaches that "all are ministers" but who retains all the significant functions of the morning service and performs them himself is nonverbally telling the congregation that *he alone* is the minister. If on the other hand he increasingly involves board members and other members of the church in those functions thought to be "pastoral" (such as the Sunday morning pastoral prayer), he is communicating to the congregation that he truly does perceive them as ministers along with him.

It is the combination of the verbal teaching and the nonverbal "signaling" that over time changes perceptions in a gradual, growing, and relatively painless way.

adult education: educational strategies: one to one

Once we have defined our concept of teaching/learning Christian faith, and developed an understanding of "ministry" and its relational settings, we're able to explore the various situations in which adults come together as the Church. And there we are ready to define some of the elements in each situation that we want to pay particular attention to in designing the hidden curriculum to support transformation.

the nature of ministry
conditions facilitating ministry
* educational strategies: one to one
educational strategies: small groups
educational strategies: Body Life
educational strategies: worship
educational strategies: the
   preached Word

It's important to affirm that our theology of Christian education remains constant across the age groups.

It is relatively easy to see that a socialization process takes place in the case of children, and that they grow as linked beliefs, attitudes, values, and behaviors are communicated through shared experiences with adults with whom they identify. It is also, perhaps, relatively easy to see that the church body may learn the same way from the local leadership team. But we often lose sight of the fact that adults who come into the Christian community through conversion — and even adults who have been Christians for years — also are discipled in the same kind of process. For *all* ages the model is essential; a relationship with the model in which identification is encouraged and significant sharing of the inner life of teacher and learner takes place is critical; a "real life" rather than formal setting for shared experience is vital.

Please note that in defining these three dimensions of the teaching/learning process I am *not* "leaving out" the Word. The process defines *how* Scripture's "meaning for life" is shared: the fact that the Christian faith and life are essentially biblical is implicit. The correspondence between Scripture's portrait of the believer's faith and life, and the model's actual character and life style, is, of course, a keystone in true Christian education.

This socialization model of teaching/learning helps us pinpoint requisites for adult Christian education in the church. These requisites cannot be stated in terms of "what is to be known" but rather in terms of what transactions need to take place in meetings between adults if "what is to be known" is to be known in a life-transforming way! In a real sense, the Christian educator's task in adult C.E. is to so design the "hidden curriculum" that when adults do meet — in whatever setting — one or more of the following requisites is being met, or movement toward it is being encouraged.

The five requisites which are immediately suggested by the socialization model are:

1. Adults model for one another the realities Scripture portrays.
2. Adults talk about the Bible terms portraying the reality they live.
3. Adults come to see and know one another as persons "like them" (which is critical for identification).
4. Adults come to care for one another deeply (which is critical for motivating desire to be like the model).
5. Adults come to share in one another's lives (so that the "real life" setting of faith's meaning is perceived).

It is important for us then to encourage an interaction that moves toward realization of one or more of the five requisites in every setting where adults come together. This means first of all that we need to see *every* meeting of adults as an educational opportunity, and second, that we analyze the meeting situation to see how we can better design the hidden curriculum to support and encourage the kinds of transactions implied by the five requisites above.

educational strategies

The concept of education we've been exploring in this book

is essentially an interpersonal and transactive one. Thus in looking at the various educational strategies we might adopt in adult education, it's helpful to define the different settings on the basis of the number of persons involved, and the kinds of interactions that take place. In *each setting* we should be able to work with the "hidden curriculum" to facilitate progress toward encouragement of behaviors appropriate to one or more of the five requisites.

It also is important to realize that each of the settings (or, as we're calling them here, the strategies) has a place in a well-designed adult education ministry. In a real way each strategy has something special and unique to offer that is important in encouraging growth toward transformation.

The settings, and their unique advantages, can be defined as follows:

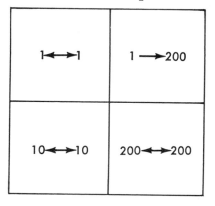

Four Educational Strategies

The one to one. This strategy involves encouraging interaction between two persons concerning the faith. Examples include the traditional "discipling" approach of groups like the Navigators, helping a young husband and wife launch their life together as a spiritual unit, two neighbors meeting together for talk and prayer over mid-morning coffee, friends who talk regularly on the telephone, and so on.

The one-to-one strategy has advantages in encouraging development of close relationships, and also advantages concerning accountability. A person can be lost in a group: but when a person is one of two, his or her functioning is critical. This is one of the reasons why evangelistic organizations increasingly try to tie new converts not only to local churches and small fellowship groups, but also to "buddies" with whom they will meet for weekly sessions.

One to two hundred. In the diagram the arrow for this setting points only one way. Often in the larger meetings of the church communication will involve only, or primarily, a one-way flow from the pastor or pastor-substitute to the gathered people.

We see this primarily, of course, in the "church service" held on Sundays and other occasions. While there are ways in this setting to help believers see themselves as participants, the sermon itself is usually central, and during it the one-way flow is maintained.

There are advantages that this educational strategy enjoys. It is well designed to communicating information and concepts. This is, of course, an important element in Christian education. Cognitive structures, concepts, an intellectual understanding of the faith and faith's life *is* valid and important for Christian growth. But this educational setting and strategy has been overused in the church. While it can contribute toward encouraging movement toward the second requisite (page 251), it makes no provision at all for realization of requisites three through five.

We do not want to eliminate the use of this strategy in our Christian education of adults. In fact, we want to enhance it and make it more effective by clearly defining its purposes, values, and how to maximize them. But we want to *resist permitting this one-way flow pattern to characterize all (or even most) of our times together in the church!* Surely there is little or no excuse for adopting this pattern in the smaller groupings of the "class," and even less excuse for adopting the "designated teacher" approach in the home Bible study.

Ten to ten. This setting is the "small group" setting, in which few enough persons are involved to permit each of them to participate fully. This setting has many advantages. Its size encourages coming to know others and caring for them. Its potential for intimacy makes it more likely that "real life" sharing will take place. Its informality also encourages individuals to share their perceptions of Scripture and its meaning to them.

The small group setting is probably the most powerful setting and strategy for mutual ministry to take place, for modeling and identification to be experienced. It also is one of the most powerful sources of motivation for growth, as growth is seen in others, and caring supports the individual in his own struggle to trust God and open up life to Him.

Two hundred to two hundred. This strategy is the one popularized under the "Body Life" title, in which larger congregations of believers share with and minister to one another. There are a number of advantages to this strategy as well. It permits those who still feel strange in the "ministry" role to participate vicariously. It helps build identity with a larger body as well as with a few known individuals. It expands the vision of body beyond the few we may come to know well. It provides multiple models of different dimensions of the Spirit's working in people.

While Body Life experiences cannot replace other strategies, there certainly is a significant place for them in the total operation of the Church.

In summary, then, we need to realize in thinking of adult education that *each of the strategy settings* charted has a value and a place in the total experience of adults. Traditionally the church has relied on the 1-200, one-way flow setting to transmit the faith and to nurture in it. This reliance has been a tragic mistake. For the reasons developed in the first ten chapters of this book, the product of this "single strategy" approach to ministry has necessarily been an intellectualized faith, which has come to be experienced more as a "belief" than as a "life." But this does not mean we should repudiate this strategy entirely, or reject the sermon's role in church life. Instead it means we need to carefully define the function of the one-way strategy, develop it carefully to fulfill this function, and at the same time provide a balanced experience of learning by developing the other three strategy approaches as well.

Just how these strategies might be effected in a local church is, of course, the focus of these next chapters.

one to one

The pastor of an Indiana church shared with me how one-to-one ministry developed in his church. One of his board members approached him one day, bursting with enthusiasm. He had been reading about Christ the Shepherd in John 10, and it struck him that every believer was also either a sheep or a shepherd. "Pastor," he announced, "I think we ought to get our shepherds together with our sheep!"

Together they developed a simple plan. The board member explained his idea to the congregation, and asked all who wanted to take part to put their names on slips of paper and designate themselves either "sheep" (someone who needed help) or "shepherd" (someone who felt able to give help). Of the fifty-seven who responded, nearly all claimed sheephood. After a number of phone calls and conversations, enough sheep were willing to view themselves as shepherds to permit pairing.

From here on the plan was simple. Each person was given a short, basic Bible study guide. Each was to complete the "fill in" study, and then get together for one hour each week with his or her partner. They were to talk over their answers, and pray together about each other's needs. They also were to pray daily for each other during the eight weeks of the study.

When the pastor shared this with me, the "sheep and shepherd" ministry had been underway for over a year. Over one hundred and fifty members were involved. In most cases the "one hour" meetings has expanded naturally into several-hour times of sharing and prayer. The partners had become increasingly close to one another, and the warmth of their relationship had spilled over into other relationships as well. Learning to talk with one person about his faith and his life had also affected what was being said and shared in classes, prayer meeting, and other gatherings of the church. To the pastor this one, simple, spontaneous "program" had done more to revitalize the church and its ministry than anything he had seen in more than seventeen years in the pastorate.

This is one of the few examples of "programed" one-to-one ministry I've run into. Normally the one-to-one relationship is something that develops as persons have the opportunity to come to know one another. Thus all activities that bring people together and encourage the development of relationships has potential to contributing to one-to-one contacts. At the same time, elements in the context of church life which encourage personalness and validate the desirability of coming to know others as friends stimulates the one-to-one potential. In a young adult Sunday school class I taught in Wheaton one or more couples held "open house" each Sunday afternoon for visitors to the class and one or two other regular couples. For one quarter each year we had studies led by two different couples each week. The studies were parts of series; each "teaching" couple met two or three times to study the topic together and to plan how to help the other class members discover what they discovered when their week to lead the class came. Several close one-to-one and couple-to-couple relationships grew out of these preparatory meetings. In the same class, a weekly newsletter was sent, reviewing what had been covered in class, what different individuals had contributed, giving suggestions for preparation for next week to the young husbands and wives in the class, and chatting about class members. While the letter did not directly promote one-to-one relationships, it still helped to create a climate in which one-to-one and other personal relationships were encouraged.

It is, of course, still basic to see the need for leadership modeling the one-to-one relationship. This often is discouraged in seminary training, as likely to lead to charges of favoritism on the part of the pastor and thus to create schism in the church. What apparently is not realized is that leadership sets the tone of church: an *impersonal* leadership style will tend to stimulate an impersonal church and be terribly destructive to ministry.

Probably from a leadership standpoint a critical question is *with whom* should one-to-one relationships be cultivated? For a pastor in Elmhurst, Illinois, the answer was the church board. Using one-to-one skills developed through years in the Navy as a navigator, the pastor developed mature men through constant one-to-one involvement. Later when he left the church, it not only survived a three-year period without a pastor — it grew during that interim.

The one-to-one relationship is a relationship with an exciting building and nurturing potential, whether it involves a planned thrust for developing others by church leaders, or simply involves two believers who are both in early stages of growth meeting to share with and encourage each other. Not everyone in a local body will, or should, be involved in the more intensive one-to-one relationships. But there's no doubt that this is just the relationship that many need to stimulate and maintain spiritual growth.

PROBE
    case histories
    discussion questions
    thought-provokers
    resources

1. Insight into the function of the one-to-one relationship in the life of the early church is given both on the leader-to-special-individual level and the nurturing level. For the first case, Paul's relationship with Timothy is the classic example. For the second, the apostle's style in establishing a new church is striking: he can remind the Thessalonians "you know that we dealt with each of you . . ." (1 Thess. 2:11).

Looking through the New Testament . . .
   A. Find out all you can about the relationship between Paul and Timothy, and write a paper exploring implications for church leadership today.
   B. Find out how many "pairs" Scripture reports. For example, Paul and Barnabas were for years together in a one-to-one relationship unlike the "training" relationship Paul had with Timothy, and Barnabas had with Mark.

2. In this chapter I suggested four *strategy settings* for ministry with adults, represented on the chart to the right. I also gave a list of five *requisites* for facilitating the kind of learning we're concerned with in Christian education: life-to-life learning that moves the individual toward transformation.

1←→1	1 →200
10←→10	200←→200

Look over the five requisites again, and rate the potential of each setting for each being met effectively. That is, what are the percentage chances that each setting will provide opportunity for modeling, for talk about Bible terms, etc.

The requisites, to test against each of the strategy settings, are:
 (1) Adults model for one another the realities Scripture portrays.
 (2) Adults talk about the Bible terms portraying the reality they live.
 (3) Adults come to see and know one another as persons like themselves.
 (4) Adults come to care for one another deeply.
 (5) Adults come to share in one· another's lives.

3. On the basis of your analysis above, what kind of balance between the various strategy settings would you think might be "ideal" in a church's life? That is, it should be clear that while the 1-200 setting can meet requisite 2 above, and even permit the pastor to function as a model as he shares from his own life and experience in his preaching, little opportunity is provided in this setting for, for instance, requisite 3 to be met. This means that either the traditional preaching service needs to be restructured to involve additional elements of interaction, or that other gatherings of the body need to be designed especially to facilitate relationship development, sharing, modeling, etc. Both of the smaller settings (the one to one and the ten to ten) have great potential here. The question that arises, then, is, what balance between large and small group activities, between "audience" and one-to-one, is likely to best facilitate spiritual growth? Should ten percent of our time together be in the 1 to 200, or eighty percent?

For now, why not simply give your own best estimate — give your reasons — and check out the ideas of others as well.

Desirable percent of one to 200: _____
Desirable percent of ten to ten: _____
Desirable percent of 200 to 200: _____
Desirable percent of one to one: _____

4. Theory testing always is important in Christian education, as is establishing a *base line*. By establishing a *base line* I mean getting accurate information on the present pattern of behavior, the present situation, before thinking about change or taking action. The theory testing dimension comes in when we check the existing situation and its impact against what theory suggests the impact of a particular pattern ought to be.

For instance, let's say we establish the following baseline information about a particular local church:

baseline information

Ninety percent of the membership are in a "church" meeting only when more than 150 others are also present. All "meetings of the church" other than prayer meeting take place in the auditorium. Prayer meeting in fellowship hall is also a large group activity, and chairs are set in the same order as pews. There are three adult Sunday school classes, attended by approximately seventeen percent of the adult members of the church. In each a one-way pattern of communication is dominant. No laymen take part in the Sunday services, except for the lay song leaders, and the pastor's preaching is doctrinal. (Analysis of the past six months of sermons according to the bulletin shows eighty-five percent "expository" sermons, with topical sermons related to Easter season dealing with authentication of the resurrection.) Analysis of the past four weeks of preaching shows only nine personal references, none of which share a weakness or need, or demonstrate vulnerability. The only "small group" activities of the church (e.g., 10-10) take place when boards and committees meet to transact business. In these meetings *Robert's Rules of Order* is used, personal sharing does not take place. The focus is on organizational problems and how to solve them. During the past three years there have been fourteen people added to the membership: three by conversion (a Billy Graham crusade), eight by transfer of letter, and the others members of church families who reach church membership age. Sunday school numerical level has been steady during the three-year period. Visitation to classes, and testing of teachers for their perception of their ministry, both indicate that a belief-transmission, "school" pattern dominates.

theoretical evaluation

Given this and other baseline information, our theory would suggest that we would find people in this church unaware of models of process. Others might most likely be perceived as "more perfect" than they, and thus relational pressure against self-revelation and interpersonal closeness would be heavy. We would also expect little interpersonal closeness, little sense of love and being loved, very little sharing in one another's lives. We would also expect that

Scripture would be talked about by these people only on "religious" occasions, and that a cognitive orientation would be maintained in contrast to a talking of how Scripture speaks to individuals personally.

hypothesis testing

With the baseline established, and a portrait drawn from our theory of the expected patterns of relationship and growth, we might then move on to test the theory and our perception. For instance, we might hypothesize that the expected condition would be revealed in:

(1) Church members listing more ways that they perceive themselves as *unlike* the pastor than *like* him.

(2) Church members failing to list other members when asked to name "one person who really knows me as I really am" (the expected answer . . . God!).

(3) Church members listing other members as "one person outside of my family whom I often speak with" — but when asked to report the topic of conversations during the past week failing to mention personal spiritual life or growth issues.

(4) Church members on a personal inventory scale tending to reveal low self-image and failure to perceive themselves as "warm" persons *if* they are perceived by other church members as "committed" Christians.

(5) Church members heavily involved in church work and activities perceiving the church as lacking warmth and friendliness to a greater extent than those who are "Sunday" members.

And, of course, we could go on, and suggest many, many more possible indicators, including things like "conversations overheard after services *not* involving mention of God or the topic of the service," and so on.

result analysis

After testing our perception of the church against various hypotheses, we might find one of two things. Our theory is borne out and the indicators reveal significant breakdowns in each of the five requisite areas for effective adult education. Or the indicators contradict our expectations! In this later case we have to go back and attempt to discover why. There are several possibilities. First, our theory may be wrong. If in analyzing a number of churches our indicators constantly contradict our expectations, we will want to question our theory. But this is not the only possible reason. Second, we may have missed something significant in our baseline analysis. For instance, let's say that our indicators do show the expected results for men in the church, but are contradictory for women. Talking with the women we discover a "hidden church" operating beyond the formal organization. The men essentially run the organization, but the pastor's wife has worked over a ten-year period informally in a one-to-one way. There is constant telephoning, going from home to home to visit, informal "women's club" meetings in which the Bible is central and deep sharing takes place. In this situation an "underground" educational ministry — neither recognized nor named! — has been taking place; the results are demonstrated in transformation, and in the operation of the five requisites. *It is probable that in many local churches one or more such "hidden churches" do exist unrecognized either by the organizational leadership or the hidden church's own membership!* Third, it is possible that our indicators themselves are inappropriate. Fourth, it is possible that the kinds of tests we selected rely too much on the members' *perceptions*. For instance, take the fifth item on page 259. Often a church is perceived as "friendly" and "warm"' by individuals who have no standard against which to measure! Or, as to item 4, it may be that church is so insignificant in the life of all the members that their sense of identity and self-image are tied to some other group in which they *are* perceived as successful and warm.

The point of all this, of course, is twofold. First, evaluation and testing are important in validating our perceptions and ideas. And second, evaluation and the interpretation of test results is not a simple process.

Still, with this said, I'd like to suggest that you take time at this point to do some testing of your own theory! In PROBE item 3 (page 257) you gave "ideal" percentages for the mix of strategy settings in adult ministry. Why not take time now to gather *baseline* information on your own or a nearby church? Then, on the basis of that information and on the basis of the balance or imbalance it shows with your "ideal" situation, see if you can determine testable indicators of the functioning or nonfunctioning of the *requisites*. If your hypotheses are disproven, see if you can discover why. If they are proven, think a bit about what this means for the life and future of the church involved!

Personally I am convinced that we *must* work carefully and consciously with the development of strategies and settings which will result in a natural, spontaneous, and almost "unplanned" Christian nurture of adults. We *dare not* see adult education as simply a challenge to invent a few more classes and create a few more curriculums.

5. Back now to the one-to-one strategy setting. Here are a variety of ways to explore and deepen your understanding of this approach.

    A. List all the "natural pairs" you can think of for a possible one-to-one relationship. For example, include husband/wife, pastor/board member, neighbors, etc.

B. For each "natural pair," think of at least five ways to encourage development of a nurturing relationship.

C. Think of at least five ways to help people sense the value of one-to-one relationships.

D. Get literature from the Navigators, and find out all you can about them and other groups stressing one-to-one discipling.

E. Review study guides available that might be used in a sheep/shepherd program like that described in this chapter. What criteria would you use to evaluate such a guide? What materials, by your criteria, seem most appropriate?

261

adult education:
educational strategies: the small group

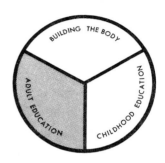

Today many are looking to the small group as "the answer" for the Church. Certainly the small group movement in Christianity is significant. Providing opportunity for growing and sharing in smaller, more intimate groupings, is an essential part of the strategy we need to adopt in structuring the Church's life for ministry to and by adults.

But "small groups" are not the answer. At times they can be counterproductive!

The term "small group" is a problem term. It has so many different connotations for Christians, ranging from the negative "cell" and "sensitivity group" notions to the highly positive "cottage prayer meeting." So it is helpful to point out immediately that one and only one factor defines a group as a "small" group: size.

Even size is not a constant factor. Much secular literature points to a small group size of five as optimum. Most Christian writers with ministry groups in view talk of ten or twelve persons. I've been involved in a group in a home which started small, but which retained the relational climate associated with the small group through growth into the high thirties. What seems important about the size of the group is its potential for more intimate relationships than in a larger grouping where the individual is lost in the mass. Rather than being a means of reducing the individual to one of a "group," as some have charged, the small group setting has great potential for using and enhancing the strengths of the individual: far greater potential than the accepted congregational meeting where the individual is lost.

For our purposes here, then, we will think of any group as a small group where the number of persons involved permits and encourages the fullest participation of each individual. If you wish to pick a median number as representative, probably the most accepted number is ten or twelve.

However, now that we've said that size alone is going to be the criteria by which we label a group of Christians a "small group," we have to go on to note that *the purpose for which the group is assembled* will have the utmost impact on the way it will function, and whether in that grouping those requisites of adult Christian education which can best be met in a small group will in fact be met.

For example, here are some of the kinds of small groups which we might find functioning in a single local church.

Work groups. The C.E. committee meets to plan the camp program, set up scholarship programs for those who can't afford to go, determine what to do about children's church where staffing is an increasing problem, and listen to Mrs. Jenson's complaints about the third-grade Sunday school material and her insistence that a different curriculum be used.

Or the deacons meet to discuss current finances, evaluate a report of the building maintenance committee on the heating system, and explore the need for three buses now that the gas shortage has curtailed their use.

Prayer groups. Half a dozen "regulars" come to church Saturday mornings at 7:45 for a season of prayer with the pastor.

Or cottage prayer meetings are held at each of the deacons' homes for six weeks before the local evangelistic campaign.

Study groups. The adult Sunday school classes are set up on an elective basis, with an average of fifteen students each. Topics studied are Events of the Second Coming, How We Got Our Bible, Christology, and The Christian and Politics.

The pastor teaches a New Convert class for those applying for membership. He covers basic doctrines of salvation and the Christian life, church organization and polity, etc.

The Bronsons are excited about Hal Lindsey's latest book,

and get five other couples together to read and talk about it for twelve Thursday evenings at their home.

Lou and Ellen are tape freaks: they have a regular group who spend an hour and a half Sunday afternoons at their home listening to the best excerpts Lou has selected from the sermons, teaching segments, and music he's listened to during the week.

Therapy groups. Each Saturday from seven in the evening until midnight the young associate pastor gets together with the nine divorced young people in the church for a therapy session. They each talk about their feelings and needs, and support each other with sympathy and advice.

Nurture groups. Three small groups of people meet in homes during the week. These groups are concerned most of all with growing as Christians. Each week they spend about three hours together, with considerable sharing mixed in with Bible study and prayer.

Action groups. The college age young adults plan and carry out evangelistic projects, including beach trips for witnessing, two or three "lectureships" given at the local junior college, etc.

Each week the three commanders of the Christian Service Brigade meet to plan meetings and activities for the boys involved in this ministry.

Five of the ladies of the church have become concerned about several families in the local "ghetto" area. They meet not only to plan practical help for the families, but also to write letters to politicians, develop petitions, check out governmental programs that might be available, and in general do what they can to stir the conscience of the community.

Several of the other men have worked up a band that plays regularly now during evening services. They practice in the church basement every Tuesday night . . . often staying much too late to suit their wives!

Mrs. Evans has worked hard to develop a small core of women who will serve as nurses' aids at the local hospital. She gets them together frequently, often getting one of the local doctors or nurses to give lectures and demonstrations.

Evangelistic Bible studies. Carla and Ken have asked their Sunday school teacher to lead evangelistic Bible studies in their home every week to reach some of the friends they made before their conversion. The teacher prepares a weekly lesson on the Gospel of John, gives those who come an underlined Gospel booklet, and teaches them for about forty minutes before they have refreshments.

T-Group experiences. Young professor Jenkins at the Junior College is turned on by the NTL approach to group training, and he has started a T-group (with mostly young couples involved) that uses the strategy of the Indiana Plan. The group works with here-and-now feelings, talks about their feelings about themselves and others, and is supposed to be developing a sensitivity to persons which will carry over into the other life-situations they find themselves in.

Small groups? Yes . . . there are *many* small groups that already function in the local church. But different purposes for which they gather have a dramatic impact on the relationships that develop within the groups — and on their educational impact in terms of the growing transformation of their members.

potential values

The significance of the small grouping in the Church is simply this: it provides the optimum setting for meeting all or most of the five requisites for effective "socialization" education!

It's easier to come to know people personally in smaller groupings. Each person can come to be known: none is lost in the mass. Most people find it easier to share and take part in smaller groups than in large ones: self-revelation and sharing are encouraged. In a smaller grouping too it is easier to see both individual strengths and weaknesses, and thus identification of others as "like me" is encouraged. Coming to know others is a process: that process is faster in a small than in a large group, as trust between the members develops more rapidly.

It is easier to come to care for others in the small group. Practical love is a function of knowing others. Often small group experiences encourage individuals to meet or talk outside the group situation, and relationships deepen.

It is easier to share in one another's lives in a small group. This sharing may be in actual shared experiences as members of the group step into daily life to act together. Or it may be vicarious: it may involve simply sharing about the real experiences of one's life, and so gradually seeing one another as full sharers in it.

These same factors make members of a small group much more ready models for one another. Knowing and caring about each other, with identification established, modeling has its impact.

Finally, talking about Scripture and its reality in one's life depends in large part on establishing those relationships where trust permits honesty in sharing and interaction.

While the smaller groupings of believers in the church have the *potential* of providing a context for transforming ministry, smaller groups will not necessarily have this impact. Size is no guarantee of intimacy or warmth. In fact, it is possible (and probable) that membership of most persons in a local church in one or more smaller groups will *cut down* the potential for transformation *if those smaller groups maintain a formal, impersonal atmosphere!*

It is particularly important, then, that time be taken and effort made to develop a warm and sharing climate in all of the smaller group meetings of the church.

Helpful and harmful practices. There are a number of practices which, in general, increase the formality and decrease the personalness of smaller group gatherings. Let's take, for example, a meeting of the church board, contrasting two actual situations.

* The meeting is called to order, and the secretary reads the notes of last month's meeting, which are approved by the group. The chairman passes out agendas to each member, and opens the meeting in prayer. Agenda items include OKing new purchases for "learning center" equipment for the Primary Sunday school department, discussion of the pastor's suggestion that the membership be divided geographically and board members accept "pastoral" responsibilities for them, discussion of the D.C.E.'s revision of his job description to limit and focus his areas of responsibility, and the hearing of reports from the long-range planning and building committees. In addition several proposals are made on which the board debates, then moves to a vote. *Robert's Rules of Order* is used by the chairman to run the meeting. At the end of the meeting, several of the men are asked to pray. Through the whole session, no mention was made of personal items, but data flow focused on a logical and orderly discussion of issues and ideas.

* This board meets regularly each Saturday morning from 7 to 10 A.M. The time together begins with donuts, and each member shares his experiences during the week, and any needs he feels. Conversation during the time shifts focus, from Scripture (which is sometimes read and studied for the men's personal enrichment, and sometimes explored for insight on a problem the church faces or needs to face) to individual needs of members to evaluation of aspects of the church's life to community needs. The time together also

regularly includes about a half hour of conversational prayer. While no voting or business is conducted as such, decisions facing the board are discussed and prayed over during these weekly meetings. When (often after weeks or even months of discussion and prayer) decisions are made, they are made unanimously, with full consideration of feelings and attitudes and values as well as the logic of the issues.

In describing these two patterns of interaction between members of two different church boards, it is apparent that in the second there is constant maintenance of a personal climate, and that *decisions are made in the context of ministry by the board members to one another.*

This is not to suggest that the decisions of one board will be always right and the decisions of the other always wrong. But it is to suggest that the personal and ministry climate of the second board *facilitates ministry and thus transformation.* In the long run the impact of this board on the life of the church as a whole will be far greater, for these men are growing into better models of faith's life, and, as a team, are growing together into better models of the Body!

Educationally speaking — and it is the growth toward transformation that Christian education, and the Church itself, is primarily concerned with — the first board is ineffective and will have a *negative* impact on the life of the church. The second board is effective, and will have a growing, positive impact on the life of the church.

What are some of the specific practices that make the first board ineffective and inhibit rather than facilitate ministry? (1) Formality. *Robert's Rules of Order* and similar plans for ordering meetings to accomplish business are designated to validate the processing of certain kinds of "issue data" and invalidate the processing of personal "feeling" or "inner state" data. In a formal situation people do not perceive sharing, speaking about their personal relationship with God, etc., as valid behaviors. (2) Voting. This approach to decision-making tends to polarize. Presenting an issue, arguing for one's point of view, and working to gain a winning vote for one's own side, are not cooperative behaviors or behaviors which place high value on others, their feelings, and their opinions. Over time in most "vote" situations two or more parties will form, and rather than identification with one another being enhanced, a sense of "difference" from one another will grow. (3) Designated leadership. Normally the formal location of "leadship" in an office or individual will inhibit free development of the group's relational style. A chairman who orders the meeting and controls its process gives a group a structure and a sense of safety, and is effective when a businesslike approach to decision-making is at issue. This kind of leadership, and the location of leadership in an office, is not however beneficial when educational (ministry) functions are concerned. Letting leadership roles shift and be filled by different members of the group as each is gifted and as the occasion warrants is far better. Thus, for instance, on the church board on which I serve Rod "leads" us to share and to keep the personal in view, while I tend to "lead" when it comes to analyzing problems or possible courses of action.

Each of these factors has an impact on the kind of topic which will be talked about (personal/impersonal) in a board setting. To the extent that patterns of behavior in a smaller group's meeting tend to reinforce formal, impersonal behavior these patterns are harmful, and should be modified. As a matter of fact there *are* practical alternative procedures to accomplish the purpose of each formal pattern of behavior in a group's time together. Normally these alternative procedures will be more time consuming. But they will at the same time help the small group grow as a center of ministry, and thus will make direct and critical contribution to the quality of the total life of the whole church.

PROBE
    case histories
    discussion questions
    thought-provokers
    resources

1. *Resources.* The whole area of "small group" experience has been much explored by behavioral scientists and by many clergy. There is a vast amount of experimental and reportorial literature easily available, going into far greater detail than could possibly be attempted in this book.

   Much of the material deals with the encounter group, or therapy group. Two recent books from Jossey-Bass, Inc., Publishers, San Francisco, survey the field well and include helpful bibliography:

   Arthur Burton (Ed.), *Encounter*, 1970.
   Lawrence N. Solomon and Betty Berzon (Eds), *New Perspectives on Encounter Groups*, 1972.

   Typical of the Christian works in this general classification is an excellent work by Cecil Osborne, *The Art of Understanding Yourself* (Zondervan, 1967).

Another tradition is that of the T-Group, which attempts by intensive small group experience to develop in participants sensitivity to others and produce freer flow of feelings as well as ideas. An older book by Leland Bradford, Jack R. Gibb, and Kenneth D. Benne (John Wiley & Sons, New York, 1964) remains an excellent orientation here. Bergevin and McKinley *(Design for Adult Education in the Church)* reflect this tradition in Christian or religious education.

As noted in the first ten chapters, there is an educational tradition as well that believes improving "group dynamics" in educational settings will have a positive impact on learning. This is reflected in many Christian education books. Martha Leyboldt's *"Learning is Change* (Judson Press, Valley Forge, 1971) gives many practical "how to" suggestions in this area.

In addition there are a number of books which focus on sharing groups as a nurturing strategy to produce individual and community growth in Christ. Three books that ought to be read in this area are:

Robert C. Leslie, *Sharing Groups in the Church* (Abingdon Press, Nashville, 1971).

Robert Arthur Dow, *Learning Through Encounter* (Judson Press, Valley Forge, 1971).

Larry Richards, *69 Ways to Start a Study Group* (Zondervan, Grand Rapids, 1972).

As this brief review indicates, there are many resources in this field available, and many different points of view represented. In most seminaries and ministry training schools, group dynamics courses or group experiences are significant parts of the training. Familiarity with the whole field, however, will not in fact find sufficient attention paid to the issue raised in this chapter. That is, that *in every meeting in smaller groups* in the church, it is not only appropriate but also *necessary to design that group's life and functioning to facilitate ministry within the group itself!*

There is a danger in *institutionalizing ministry processes,* and thus effectively isolating them from the real life of the Christian community. The educational leader who realizes the need for improving the relational climate of the church, and immediately falls on the *starting* of "small groups" (thus institutionalizing and isolating "sharing" by giving it a special validity in the "small group" setting it has not been given in the already existing smaller groupings of the church) has failed to understand the pervasive power of the hidden curriculum, and probably has *reinforced* impersonal patterns of behavior in other than "sharing group" settings!

2. *Strategy.* As the last paragraph above suggests, it is vital to take steps to bring the five requisites for socialization into play in the already existing groups of the church. It is *not* sufficient to "begin

small groups," although this may be a part of the overall strategy for affecting both existing small groupings and the church as a whole.

We need to begin then with the conviction that *intergroup ministry* does not harm but rather helps *any kind* of small group perform its function! Task groups, prayer groups, boards, and so on will be more effective rather than less effective if ministry takes place between their members.

For instance, the small groupings in Trinity Church in Seattle, Washington, are organized around action or ministry modules. There members focus beyond themselves on serving others. But this does not mean that ministry within the groups is ruled out as they meet to plan. In fact, ministry comes first!

Mary, who heads a ministry group to women through a Bible class, tells about what happens at a board meeting when the women meet to plan for the coming month. "Well, there are about seven of us, and we meet at my house usually. We have coffee — except once I forgot. We usually visit a bit, just about things that are happening in the families of the people on the board, and we have quite a good time of prayer for one another, and for people having trouble in the church. And then we go through the practical details of planning showers and meetings, and you know."

This same thought is picked up by Gary, a pilot who developed a Sky Club ministry for boys that now extends far beyond the local area. "I look at board meetings as something more than just discussing business. It's a time for fellowship together, to learn a bit about each of us, and what God is doing in our lives, and any problems. It's as much a time of fellowship as it is of business."

It is this climate, and the development of it in all the small groupings in the church, which is of primary concern to the Christian educator seeking to design the hidden curriculum to promote ministry and produce transformation.

3. *Implementation.* How do we help members of the smaller groupings in our church learn to function in an interpersonal and ministry way? From each of the following trials select the one approach you believe would be most helpful or productive, and the one which you feel would be least helpful or productive in working toward this goal.

A. Plan a retreat at which you . . .

(1) Define the responsibilities of each small grouping.

(2) Plan "headstart" meetings of each grouping and give each ten hours of time together.

(3) Involve members of each group in relationship building activities with other members they will be working with.

B. Help members of all task groups to redefine their function to validate ministry relationships and behaviors by . . .
   (1) Giving each group member a book on ministry to read.
   (2) Meet with the group for their first six meetings to get them on the right track.
   (3) Meet regularly with the chairmen of all groups in the church to train them how to lead a group into ministry.

C. Encourage informal relationships within groups by . . .
   (1) Promoting regular get-togethers of families involved in the various groupings for fellowship times.
   (2) Helping leaders learn informal methods to accomplish functions currently performed by formal (such as vote, agenda, etc.) means.
   (3) Starting a regular "premeeting" time during which sharing and Bible study will be expected before going into the "regular meeting" activities.

D. Concentrate on long-range change strategies by:
   (1) Encouraging nurturing relationships on the church board, expecting that members (who are involved in other small groupings as well) will infect those other groupings.
   (2) Planning a limited enrollment, repeated "fellowship training" class to continue for eight weeks. Train as many members of regular smaller groupings as possible in relational skills, and show specifically implications for other small group settings.
   (3) For three months have a policy of conducting a regular "Serendipity" relational Bible study to precede all committee and other meetings. (See the Lyman Coleman material, published by Word Publishers, Waco, Texas.)

E. List additional ways you might help groups move toward the desired goals.

4. *Analysis.* In one sense, the five requisites discussed in chapter 21 are relatively clear. Participating in a smaller group meeting we soon sense their presence or absence.

There are other indicators which tend to define situations in which ministering relationships have developed or have not. Here are some of the parameters involved, and a continuum chart along which we can see behaviors which are less or more likely to facilitate development of ministering relationships.

Factor	Less likely	More likely
Time	1 hour .... 3 hours	
Frequency	monthly .... weekly	

| Leadership | formal, ... informal, |
| | designated | shared by all |

| Decisional process | vote .... consensus |

Procedure	formal agenda .... open agenda,
	formal rules	no formal rules
	(Such as *Robert's Rules of Order*)

| Non-meeting contacts between members | seldom .... frequent |

Stability of group	rotating .... non-rotating
	membership	membership, three or
	one-two year average	more year average

| Openness of group | new members .... new members |
| | seldom added | often added |

| Function of group | organizational .... personal or |
| | task | "ministry" focus |

5. My personal bias is toward the establishment of many groups in the church that have a direct ministry or nurture purpose. This kind of group is described at some length in my book, *69 Ways to Start a Study Group* (Zondervan), and one I participate in is referred to often in this text as illustrations are drawn from it.

Often I'm asked about the *leadership* dimension of this group. "Who teaches it? Who's the leader?" In one sense I have a leadership role in the group. But many others also function as leaders. Most critical for the success of the group however has been removing the "teacher" rule from the group and involving each member as teacher of and learner from one another. This has been done by simply making *preparation* the role of each person in the group. Rather than a "teacher" preparing a "lesson," each member of the group studies a Scripture passage and works toward personal application before our meeting. Then during the group's meeting time on Thursday nights, all are ready to minister and share what God has said to them through the Word.

These three-hour sessions involve sharing, exploring what we've discovered in Bible study, and prayer for one another. Here are two of the Study guides which we are using in the group as I write these chapters.

Colossians No. 3
"On Being a Real Christian"

Before you read

One really wild Bible teaching is that we're all "ministers." Each believer has a contribution to make to the growth of others. Think a minute about members of our group . . . how does each "minister" to you and the rest?

Jot down several names . . . and contributions . . . here.

1. Colossians 1:1-2:5

   If we're ministers, it's good to have a minister's heart and vision. Look over what Paul says about himself in this passage. What do you learn about *ministry* here?

2. From the above passage, what applications do you see . . . to yourself as an individual and/or to our group?

Colossians No. 4
"On Being a Real Christian"

"Freedom" is one of the big themes of the New Testament. Colossians lets us look at it. We might look at it in this pattern.

Freedom in Christ
from human regulations (Col. 2:6-23)
from sin's domination (Col. 3:1-17)
from lawless rebellion (Col. 3:18-4:6)

For now, let's look at the first of these sections on freedom and its meaning.

Colossians 2:6-23

1. What does each of the following sections say about our freedom in Christ?
   A. Colossians 2:6, 7.
   B. Colossians 2:8.
   C. Colossians 2:9-12. NOTE. The theme here is "identification," the teaching of the Bible that when we trusted Jesus He took our sins (and paid for them in His death) and we took *His* experiences and character. We were *united with Him,* so what is His became ours. For the baptism referred to here, see 1 Corinthians 12:13 . . . and for fun, Matthew 3:11.
   D. Colossians 2:13-15.
   E. Colossians 2:16-19.
   F. Colossians 2:20-23.

2. Here are two types of people who need to find freedom. From what we've seen in this passage, how would you advise them?

    A. Johnny was brought up in a church where everything was marked off as either "right" or "wrong." Everything from the kinds of clothes to wear, food to eat, what services to be at in church, what people to spend time with as friends, what to do when, etc. How would you help him?

    B. Cathy feels very inadequate and unable to live as she thinks God wants her to. She's also uncertain about just what God does want! Her friends seem to have such conflicting ideas. What is there in this passage that Cathy needs to understand?

adult education: educational strategies: body life

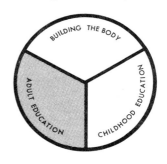

The term "Body Life" has been popularized among evangelicals by the little book of that name by Ray Stedman. In it he tells about the evening service at Palo Alto's Peninsula Bible Church, where about a thousand people gather every Sunday evening to be taught — and then to teach, exhort, share with, pray for, and encourage one another.

The concept of Body Life has spoken hope to many concerned about depersonalization in the church. And the concept ought also to speak to us!

Just the name "Body Life" has a ring to it — and seems to echo the kind of church service we earlier saw described in 1 Corinthians: "When you come together, everyone has a hymn, or a word of instruction, a revelation, a tongue, or an interpretation. All of these must be done for the strengthening of the church. ... Two or three prophets should speak, and the others should weigh carefully what is said. And if a revelation comes to someone who is sitting down, the first speaker should stop. For you can all prophesy in turn so that everyone may be instructed and encouraged" (14:26-31). This freedom in the Body for a ministry of believers to one another is of course in fullest harmony with what the Bible says about who each believer is . . . a priest, a minister, gifted to build up others and called by God to exercise that ministry. What Body Life has done is to make us aware that this need not happen only in the small group (the original location for ministry suggested by small group proponents), but is appropriate also when the larger congregation has gathered.

Body Life, a term that captures the dimension of ministry by Body members to Body members, can and should have a place in the *congregational* meetings of the local church. Thus the 200-200, and the 1-200, are settings we need to consider carefully in designing the meetings of the local church to facilitate the spiritual and personal growth of adults.

why the large group setting?

In a nearby church the pastor and minister of Christian education are concerned about the pattern of involvement of their people in their church's life. Of those who faithfully come to the Sunday morning service, hardly fifteen percent of the adults attend Sunday school. The Sunday evening elective study program initiated with enthusiasm a couple of years ago has dropped to about thirty-five attending, with the evening service in the forties. Very few of the church members are involved in the growth kind of small group that encourages mutual ministry, and while the Sunday school staff is generally enthusiastic and leadership there is good, the other small groupings in the church are poorly attended and have no solid "ministry" dimension.

To most of the adults in this church, "church" is what happens on Sunday morning! This is the one function they participate in regularly, and this is the one function that through its hidden curriculum (that pattern of *how* things are done) "teaches" adults who they are as believers and what is expected of them.

This is perhaps the central reason why the 1-200 and 200-200 strategy settings are so important. It is the large group meeting that adults identify as "church," and it is particularly the Sunday morning meeting through which each is most likely to see himself as involved in church.

If then the large group meetings fail to communicate the believer's identity and role as a "minister among ministers," and if the large group meeting fails to support and enhance the importance of the five requisites, there is little chance that the church as a whole will significantly accept a ministering identity no matter what is verbalized from the pulpit!

If we review our five requisites here for the ministering (or "socialization learning") context, we see immediately why it seems difficult to build them into congregational settings. In some instances the group simply seems too large for the personalness implied: in others a level of participation required seems impractical. The five were:

1. Adults model for one another the realities Scripture portrays.
2. Adults talk about the Bible terms portraying the reality they live.
3. Adults come to see and know one another as persons "like them."
4. Adults come to care for one another deeply.
5. Adults come to share one another's lives.

While these requisites seem difficult to meet, they can and must become part of larger congregational experience as well as part of the smaller group experiences of the body.

the Body Life strategy

The Body Life strategy meets the issues here head on, and says, "we will structure a larger congregational meeting *just for* operation of these requisites." Thus a special time (such as Peninsula's Sunday evening) is set aside for sharing. One of the church staff normally teaches from a passage of Scripture, and then the meeting is thrown open. Microphones are passed, adults and young people stand to share problems ... others respond with encouragement and suggestions drawn from their personal experience of similar problems ... questions can be raised, exhortation given, some truth God has impressed that week expounded to the Body, testimony and praise be offered. Because the meeting is understood by all to be set aside for this kind of mutual ministry, and because of the example of those who do share, more and more involvement is encouraged.

This direct "have a Body Life meeting for the congregation" approach has been picked up and tried in churches across the country. In Mesa, Arizona's, Church of the Redeemer, bringing a Body Life dimension into the evening service seemed natural and exciting. The pastor of some ten years was a warm, personable, and person-sensitive man: most of the members seemed ready. The Body Life meeting did flourish, spilling over into the fellowship hall after the service as families and collegians continued to talk and share for more than an hour after the service was over.

But in other churches, the attempt at this direct approach has failed. Awkward silences have made Body Life times uncomfortable. Sharing has fallen into superficial patterns: "pray for

Aunt Jane who's going into the hospital" has proven the water-mark of personalness. Simply setting aside a meeting time for sharing and ministry has failed to produce either sharing or ministry. And gradually the frequency of the Body Life meetings has lessened until this too has been discarded as simply another "method" that worked for some — but not here.

The problem, of course, is in seeing the Body Life meeting as a method. It isn't a method. It's a strategy — an approach to encouraging and giving opportunity for sharing and mutual ministry. But its effectiveness depends on other factors than itself.

weekday life. In point of fact, "body life" is what is happening in members of Christ's Body during the week. It is their growing experience of and with Him; the working out of the realities that Scripture describes as God's enablements of believers to live the Christ life.

The Body Life meeting, then, must be seen as providing a time when Christians can share with one another what Christ is doing in their lives, and encourage and motivate one another to deeper commitment and faith. In a very real sense, the quality of any Body Life meeting will depend on the quality of daily life of the Body!

This means first of all that we cannot depend on a Body Life meaning to *create* reality in our relationships with God. Instead, the Body Life strategy is ideally designed to *reflect an existing reality*. Where there are growing disciples, disciples who are experiencing the touch of God's Spirit, their modeling and sharing will encourage others to step out in greater faith. But where a growth vacuum exists, it is a tragic mistake to start a Body Life meeting or movement. There are better, more significant, and far more effective means of building a congregation to greater awareness of the importance of persons and an experience of God's presence.

large, small group interactions. There is also a direct relationship between involvement of body members in smaller transforming groupings and the effectiveness of Body Life approaches. In general, we can learn to relate to one another in ways indicated by the five requisites far better in small groups. It is there we can best learn to talk meaningfully about our faith and experience with God. It is there we can come to have appropriate attitudes toward others — attitudes of caring, concern, interest, respect, identity, etc.

As values and perceptions shift through small group experience, the new attitudes carry over easily into the larger congregation experience *if they are viewed as appropriate there.* This is one great advantage of the Body Life strategy. It is perceived by participants as being "just like" their smaller group experiences . . . only involving more people.

The primary *feeder flow* into the Body Life setting then comes from the small group. In the church of which I'm a member seventy percent of our people are in small, house "little churches" that meet weekly for ministry, prayer, and Bible study. In our sharing times it is clear that those who do share are those who are involved in our little churches. And it is through the little churches that we see most spiritual growth taking place.

At the same time there is a secondary feeder flow from the congregational sharing into the smaller groups. Those who share reveal God as a real Person, at work in His people now. This living evidence of God at work is a highly motivating, deeply exciting thing. It not only stimulates worship; it reveals in living examples what God seeks to do in each of us. Thus through the large group sharing a sense of need for greater involvement in Christ and the Christian community often comes, and with it greater involvement in the smaller groupings best designed to support ministry and transformation.

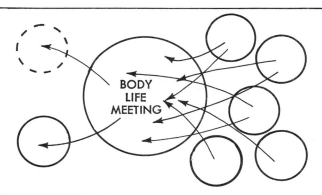

New Individuals for Smaller Groups	Congregational "Body Life" Experiences	Smaller Ministering Groups

In general, the quality of what is shared in a Body Life meeting depends on involvement of members in smaller ministering groups. The greatest impetus to growth takes place there, is reflected in the members' daily life, and is shared in the larger Body Life setting. This in turn stimulates others to seek involvement in ministering groups which will support their transformation.

validating a minister identity

Setting aside a congregational meeting for Body Life is one way that some churches validate the taught concept that each believer is a minister. By setting aside a "regular meeting" of the church for such ministry, the leadership is saying in a dramatic and clear way "we view you not as 'laymen' but as ministers."

As such a validation, as an element in the hidden curriculum of adult education, times of Body Life ministry are important. It is vital that in meetings of the whole congregation as well as in smaller groupings we design the setting to encourage realization of the five requisites. But a jolting introduction of Body Life to a people who are not yet ready is counterproductive. Our form affirms that the role of each believer is a ministering one: the failure of significant ministry to happen will *deny* that affirmation, and set back our educational efforts!

preparation. This consideration encourages us to look at opportunities to begin to build into the more traditional services of the church experiences which will gradually, without jolt, help communicate the same ministering and relational ideas as those affirmed in the Body Life meeting. It also encourages us to look to the Body Life meeting as a *later* rather than earlier element in a local church's progress toward changed image and life style. In the next two chapters we'll look at these traditional services, and explore the less obtrusive means we can use in our design of the hidden curriculum.

options. It's important to realize that we can have Body Life experiences without committing ourselves to regular, weekly Body Life services. What are some of the options?

(1) special occasions. The Easter morning service in one California church is given regularly to the people, and members are urged to come with something to share about the meaning of Christ's resurrection for them and their families. Another church sets aside the Sunday evening after family camp for sharing by those who attended. Another church follows up special meetings in the area, like a Bill Gothard seminar, with opportunities for participants to share what they learned and what it has meant in their lives. Infrequent and special occasions are more easily accepted by all as appropriate times for sharing, and as meaningful experiences become part of each member's frame of reference, the way is prepared for more and more Body Life emphasis.

(2) focused occasions. At times the pulpit ministry can focus on a time of response which involves Body Life experience. This is most effective when designed as part of a series, using some of the *response* aids we'll look at in chapter 25. That is, say the messages for three weeks have focused on Christ's preeminence and the believer's response of thankfulness for knowing Him. Each week response suggestions have been given: encouragement to express thankfulness for knowing Christ in practical ways at home, on the job, in personal life, etc. The culmination comes when the third Sunday evening is set aside for the congregation to share both what the fresh realization of knowing Jesus means to them, and how during the last weeks they have responded to Him to express thankfulness for the privilege.

The *building toward* a Body Life experience in this kind of plan is of course the key. It helps each person build into his life that which can be shared; it motivates response; it provides a common framework in which all will be expressing themselves and learning. It also helps express Bible truths which have been taught verbally in life style terms, and motivates not only personal learning but identification with others in the Body who are responding to the same truths. Focusing traditional service of the church on a culminating Body Life expression is a meaningful and significant approach.

(3) integrated occasions. The notion that it is necessary to set apart a congregational service as a designated Body Life service to involve the congregation in Body Life experience is a wrong one. Many churches make Body Life experience a regular part of the normal service. At Our Heritage Church in Scottsdale, Arizona, the members are given opportunity each Sunday to share, question, exhort, give prayer requests, etc., after the preaching. The service at Our Heritage is a long one, extending from 10:00 until approximately 12:00. It involves congregational singing and worship activities, followed by preaching and teaching, and culminating in the time for congregational sharing. This weekly expression not only lets the people hear God as He speaks through the Word, but also to see Him as His working among them is reported.

In this approach Body Life is not seen as a "special" occasion, but as a natural and integral part of the Body's gathering.

Whatever options we work toward, it is important that we realize the significance of the Sunday service(s) of the church in adult education. Whatever concepts and principles our ministry is constructed on, those concepts and principles must be

282

exemplified in the pattern of the regular services. And certainly Body Life is a significant and meaningful strategy which, in some form or another, should become part of the life of all.

PROBE
case histories
discussion questions
thought-provokers
resources

1. If you haven't, you'll want to read Ray Stedman's *Body Life,* a paperback published by Regal.

2. List the advantages and disadvantages of each of the following choices made by church leadership. Explore carefully the educational significance of each choice (that is, what does each choice imply about the nature of the church, its ministry, and the role of each believer). Finally, define as carefully as possible conditions under which you believe each strategy would be successful or unsuccessful.

   A. Sunday evening service becomes a Body Life meeting each week.

   B. A Body Life dimension is integrated into the Sunday morning meeting of the congregation, which is expanded to fill a two-hour time block.

   C. The preaching/teaching ministry is organized in units of three weeks or a month in length, and culminate in Body Life experiences, designed either for a Sunday evening or for a portion of the morning service the last week of the unit.

3. It's important to begin thinking about the congregational meeting of the church on Sunday as a (or perhaps *the*) critical teaching time for a local body. Why not take a short time and develop a list of some dozen or twenty topics (or emphases) which might lend themselves to practical application and response. For a starter, here are several areas in which teaching might be given and response shared by the congregation.

A. Topical	B. Doctrinal	C. Contextual
1. Enriching your prayer life	1. You in God's image	1. Understanding redemption (survey of Exod.-Deut.)
2. Family first?	2. The Holy Spirit *is* with you.	2. Full salvation (the Book of Hebrews)
3.	3.	3.
etc.		

adult education: educational strategies: worship

Up to this point we've focused our attention on relationships within the body that
facilitate its transforming
function. But we need to remember constantly that the
Church is a Body with a
Head! And the life of this
Body and each individual
member is found in the person of Jesus Christ.

Jesus Christ is central in all
of our educational ministry:
in the life of the individual,
in the conversation within the
Body, and in the attention of
the gathered community.

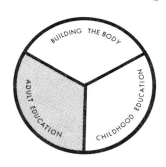

the nature of ministry
conditions facilitating ministry
educational strategies: one to one
educational strategies: small groups
educational strategies: Body Life
* educational strategies: worship
educational strategies: the
    preached Word

Nowhere is the centrality of Jesus seen more clearly than in
the assembly of the congregation as a whole. In fact this assembly, normally on Sunday mornings, should have as its basic
purpose to focus the attention of the Body on Christ and the
shared commitment to Him. In many ways the gathered Body
will affirm the identity of each member as a minister, and express
its experience of transformation. But each affirmation should also
support and encourage the focus of individuals and the community on the person of Jesus Christ.

The focus on Christ is seen in two ways in the assembled
Body. It is seen first in worship (the toward God dimension of
the service), and second in the ministry of the Word (the from
God dimension of the service). It is important that both these
dimensions of the community's shared life involve us as individuals who have an identity as members of the Body: it is as a

people of God that we worship, and as a people of God that we covenant together to respond to God in loving obedience.

This is part of the reason why it is so important to pay close attention to interpersonal relationships. Christians need to see their fellow believers as like them, to come to know and love them, and to become more deeply involved in one another's lives so that when we do come together as a Body we can sense and affirm our unity. The deeper a sense of unity we have as brothers and sisters, the more meaningful and compelling our community experience of worship will be, and the greater will be our commitment to do, rather than simply listen to, the Word.

The focus on Christ as our Head, which is a particular and special function of the community's gathering as a Body, helps us add two more *requisites* to the five already suggested as critical for the education (discipling) of adults.

The first five requisites deal with the relationships of the believers within the body with each other.

These two additional requisites deal with the relationships of all members of the community with Jesus.

Thus we can call the first five interpersonal relationship requisites, and the last two inter-Personal relationship requisites.

interpersonal requisites

1. Adults model for one another the realities Scripture portrays.
2. Adults talk about the Bible terms portraying the reality they live.
3. Adults come to see and know one another as persons "like them."
4. Adults come to care for one another deeply.
5. Adults come to share in one another's lives.

inter-Personal requisites

6. Adults participate with the Body to attribute worth to God for who He by nature is (worship).
7. Adults participate with the Body in hearing the Word of God in expectation, and in responding to the Word of God in loving obedience (the preached Word).

When a sense of unity and identification has been established within a local Body, participation in worship and responding to the Word becomes a powerful means of transformation of the individual. As community worship trains the individual to recognize just who God is and to priase Him for Himself, great freedom is found to trust God and praise Him in the private situations of life. As community response models for the individual how he is to hear and do this Word of God, a daily pattern of obedience, which is critical for spiritual growth, is also encouraged.

What we need to do, then, in our exploration of adult Christian education, is to turn to an examination of the community gathered (the 1-200 setting), and to see how this critical experience can be one of real worship and one of hearing (to do) the Word of God.

worship

Worship is something of a lost art in many of our churches. To rediscover it, we need to begin with a definition of what we mean by *worship*. Both Old and New Testament primary terms flow from roots meaning to "bow down" in homage. Interestingly, both give images of bowing down *toward*... of looking toward the object of our worship and, overcome by wonder at His Person and attributes, expressing our awe and praise in our posture.

A study of references to worship in Old and New Testaments shows that a wide range of human responses to God can be viewed as expressing worship. Each daily task can be done "to the praise of His glory." Acts of obedience, such as Jacob's prophetic blessing of his sons (Gen. 49), are identified as worship. Yet the *primary focus* seen in worship as this term comes to us through Scripture involves the response of God's people attributing worth to God for who He by nature is.

This last phrase, "attributing worth to God for who He by nature is," is one I've gained from association with David Mains, pastor of Chicago's Circle Church, and creator of some very practical and exciting helps for pastors interested in working with their people toward a gradual introduction into their church's life of those dimensions of ministry this book is concerned with. Most of what I'll have to suggest about worship in this chapter has been stimulated by David's creative ministry at this Chicago inner-city church.

Accepting as central in our understanding of worship the attribution of the worshiping community of worth to God for who He by nature is, let's see how a Sunday service can be designed to involve the Body.

coordination. Getting coordinated in the focus of our worship service is particularly significant. If our focus is to be on God, all elements of the service need to be designed to direct our thoughts and praise to Him.

Services at Circle Church, and in a growing number of churches, are coordinated by building the worship elements around an attribute of God appropriate to the main Bible truth to be communicated in the preaching/teaching (see possible attribute listing below, taken from the Step 2 *Fingertip Consultant* program written by David Mains). Take for example, a message on Jonah, organized around this key truth: "God invites us, as Jonah, to share His own great compassion for those who do not yet know Him." Worship might well be designed to praise God for His character as compassionate, or His attributes of mercy or patience or love. If all that is done by the gathered Body focuses in a coordinated way on the Person of God, praising Him and lifting up His Person, an exciting new awareness of each individual's identity as part of His people is fostered. And the *vertical* as well as *horizontal* dimension of the Christian's relationships is affirmed.

Possible attributes:

omnipresent	spirit	love	light
sovereign	trustworthy	creative	holy
interesting	absolute	jealous	communicative
infinite	life	unique	purposeful
unity/trinity	good	merciful	truth
well-balanced	personal	immutable	patient
just	eternal	omnipotent	wise/omniscient

God is characterized:

as a guide	as a disciplinarian
as master of His stewards	as a wise counselor
as a refiner	as a confronter of people
as a protector	as a great memory bank
as a covenant maker	as a good listener
as a perfect bridegroom	as Head of His body, the Church
as a master tactician	by a keen sense of humor
as a great physician	by emotion
as a close friend	etc.

**Sample attributes around which to focus a
coordinated worship service.**

the vertical. This affirmation of the vertical is a vital aspect of true Christian education. Our educational theory grows from a theological position: a theological position that (1) sees *life* as

287

the heart and secret of Christian faith, (2) sees the process of transformation toward Christ's likeness an ongoing discipleship process, and (3) sees social modeling (the disciple becoming like his teacher) as the critical mechanism in the operation of that process. Thus interpersonal relationships within the Body are tremendously significant. Thus too the surprisingly strong emphasis in the New Testament on relationships between believers is explained. Love, identification with one another, example leadership, openness and honesty within the fellowship, sharing of one another's lives, all these biblically defined and exhorted dimensions of Christians' interpersonal relationships . . . are vital in the socialization (social modeling) process.

But it also is important to remember that what binds believers together in a vital and meaningful horizontal relationship is the vertical relationship each shares with the others in Jesus Christ! Only because we know Him do we have His life in common with others. Only when our sense of identity with others as brothers and sisters is rooted in our growing awareness that we are together in a family of which Jesus is the Head, a family which constantly reaffirms Him as the center of our faith and of our life, do we have a basis for the horizontal.

This affirmation is never to be absent from the life of believers: the smaller groupings' sharing will refer constantly to Him as His Word gives structure and meaning to individual experience. But to learn how to make Him central, and to affirm His centrality, the Body needs to gather together as a local community to praise, worship, and listen to Him.

We can never afford to lose sight of the significance of the Sunday congregational service. We can never afford to see the "church" as entirely a household kind of thing, existing solely as small groups meeting in homes.

It is important, then, in our gatherings as congregations, *to assert the vertical relationship which we maintain as individuals as a Body.* This assertion and affirmation of the vertical is important not only because God Himself is pleased with our worship. It is important not only because it is right. It is important *educationally.* It is important to develop disciples who will individually and in every Body relationship have a deep sense of God's presence and power, and who will build their lives on the Person of Jesus Christ.

All this leads up a practical suggestion: a simple yet important aspect of the design of our worship to actually affirm the vertical relationship. David Mains expresses it clearly in the Step 2 Handbook, *Experiencing God's Plan for Your Church.*

Worship means attributing worth to deity. This is best accomplished when we talk *to* God rather than *about* God. By definition sermons, announcements or any part of a service addressed to the congregation belong in another category. The church is at worship when the assembly speaks directly to God in praise or thanksgiving regarding His matchless qualities.

structure. Seeing worship as addressing ourselves directly to God helps us see a need seldom met in many of our churches. The need is to design the congregational experience so that the total time together is coordinated, and so that a significant part of it leads the congregation to speak together *to* God in worship.

A possible structure that enables this to happen, and also encourages response to the Word (something to be discussed in the next chapter), is this format taken from Circle Church.

October 1, 1972

Introduction to Sermon Series
Learning a Song
Prelude

Approach to God in Worship (God is Light)
Choral Call to Worship
Invocation
Musical Selection
Congregation led in praise
Hymn 4 "My God How Wonderful Thou Art"

God Speaking through His Written Word
Sermon — Pastor David R. Mains
Choral Selection

The Response of Obedience
Suggestions for Life Response
Congregational Hymn
Offering and Offertory
Benediction

A glance over this order of service shows a structure which permits retention of most traditional aspects of a Sunday service, yet organizes those elements to focus the service and the attention on the congregation.

involvement. Worship is not something to be planned for the Body by church leadership alone. The "professional touch" is far less important than the need to live together always as a ministering people. Thus it's important to <u>involve the congregation in both planning and leading worship.</u>

In Circle Church, the pastors meet with rotating groups of members of the church. These members not only share in exploring the possibilities for worship, they also have a share in shaping the teaching and the response elements of the service. During the services these lay members of the congregation also are given leadership roles . . . in music, prayer, special readings, etc. Thus continually — even in a service in which the focus is on the vertical relationship — the importance of the horizontal and the character of the Body as brotherhood of ministers is affirmed.

In every sense, then, the Sunday services which bring the congregation together as a whole are vital parts of the educational ministry to adults. It is here that the primary focus of the Body on God is sensed and communicated. It is here too that many members of the Body can be involved, learning together and modeling for each other the meaning of worshiping God.

PROBE
   case histories
   discussion questions
   thought-provokers
   resources

1. Several criteria for the Sunday services of the church are suggested in this chapter. These criteria are developed from principles of nurturing of believers' lives with each other and with God. It is helpful in exploring their significance to try to apply them to our own recent Sunday experiences.

    We simply can think back over our last Sunday's experience. But it's probably better to attend church this coming Sunday and to *look for* the presence or absence of criterion elements. So why not, when you attend church Sunday, approach it with a sensitivity to each of these criteria.

FOR MAXIMUM EDUCATIONAL IMPACT, THE SUNDAY SERVICE
(1) should focus attention on God and who He by nature is.
(2) should be coordinated to direct praise and thoughts to Him.
(3) should lead worshipers to talk *to* God rather than simply *about* Him.
(4) should be structured to clearly guide the community into worship, hearing of the Word, and response.

(5) should involve members of the Body other than the pastor alone in modeling and leading in worship.

To these criteria we can add one which cannot by nature be observed on Sunday.

(6) should involve lay members of the Body in planning and preparation.

2. After the service you analyzed (in PROBE 1, above), why not take time to *redesign* it following the structure reported in this chapter. What attribute of God seems appropriate to the passage and the message? In what ways might the congregation be led to address praise to God? What different kinds of experiences might have prepared them for such worship?

3. Two books you may wish to read will help in exploring and deepening your appreciation for worship. The first is J. I. Packer's *Knowing God,* which concentrates on understanding and appreciating Him for who He is. The second is a revision and re-release by Marshall, Morgan and Scott (London) of Ralph P. Martin's *Worship in the Early Church.*

4. In most of the areas covered by this book there are few resources defining clearly just *how* to implement the principles in a gradual non-threatening way. This past year has however seen the appearance of an *excellent* resource designed to guide introduction of critical elements in the Sunday morning service and at the same time increase involvement of the church members in planning and presentation.

These materials are produced by Step 2, Incorporated, 1925 N. Harlem Avenue, Chicago, Illinois 60635. Included in the *Finger Tip Consultant* produced by this group (with which the author has recently became affiliated) is a ninety-minute a week step-by-step "how to" program for pastors and other church leaders, utilizing audio and visual materials as well as a written manual.

I highly recommend you look into this resource, which is introduced briefly in the following excerpts from Step 2 materials.

OBJECTIVES OF STEP 2, INC.

The objective of Step 2, Inc., is to serve Church leaders, clergy and lay, as follows:

To highlight for them the basic SCRIPTURAL PRINCIPLES that govern how the local church is to function.

To suggest to them PROGRAM GUIDELINES that will help their churches to function by the SCRIPTURAL PRINCIPLES.

To expose them to PATTERNS emerging in churches across

America which show how the SCRIPTURAL PRINCIPLES and PROGRAM GUIDELINES look in actual church life.

To encourage them and help them to develop PATTERNS unique to their congregation which more effectively cause their local church to function according to the SCRIPTURAL PRINCIPLES.

More simply stated, the objective of Step 2, Inc., is to help local churches more fully experience God's plan for each body of Christians.

STEP 2 FINGERTIP CONSULTANT

Planning Creative Sunday Morning Services

First Quarter	Let's Get Coordinated
Second Quarter	Let's Get the Right Response
Third Quarter	Let's Really Worship
Fourth Quarter	Let's Do It Together

Release one quarter at a time

adult education:
educational strategies: the preached Word

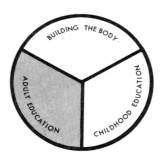

Our relationship with God is inter-Personal. We not only approach Him in worship; He approaches us and speaks to us in His Word.

It is critical then that in the assembly of the congregation the interpersonal nature of our relationship be expressed. Worship by the Body is vital. And so is a hearing of the Word of God.

the nature of ministry
conditions facilitating ministry
educational strategies: one to one
educational strategies: small groups
educational strategies: Body Life
educational strategies: worship
* educational strategies: the
    preached Word

The central role given to biblical preaching in the conservative churches is educationally as well as theologically appropriate. Not only is Bible content important in itself as Truth; it is appropriate also when God's people gather. *Listening to Him* together helps to point each individual's attention to this dimension of the vertical relationship believers enjoy with Him. Thus even when we stress the importance of sharing, as illustrated in the Body Life movement, we do not want to eliminate or reduce the attention the community focuses on the Word. Hearing together the Word proclaimed does, if you will, "act out" in a graphic and meaningful way our commitment to God as Lord of our lives and director of our ways.

However, to suggest that the proclamation of the Word in

the "sermon" has educational importance and validity *is not* a blanket endorsement of preaching as we know it in many churches! As I've said often, what we do and the way we do it communicates a vivid message . . . a message that in the pattern of its communication *must* agree with the content communicated. We say, for instance, that the Word of God is reliable and relevant. But how does our preaching affirm its relevance? In point of fact most of our preaching is focused primarily on understanding what a particular passage of the Word means . . . and for this purpose the "lecture" approach of the sermon is appropriate. But it is not particularly appropriate to "lecture" about application! And if the relevance of the Word is truly critical, *we need in our proclamation and in our preaching services to design as carefully as we do the message the ways in which we encourage people to respond!*

The fact that we need to design our communication setting and process to harmonize with the nature and purpose of the message leads us first to examine those truths which must be affirmed, and then to see how our practices can bring media and message into harmony.

theological commitments

As we explore this area it's clear that our theological commitments will be of critical importance. So without arguing for them, it remains necessary to state them:

Revealed truth. Scripture stands not only as a work of men conditioned by their time and culture, but also and essentially a work of the Holy Spirit who spoke God's words through them. Scripture then cannot be adequately understood as the searching of religious men for God and for understanding of the ultimate: it must be understood as the revelation of God to men of truth which they could not otherwise have come to know.

Revelation so understood has a dual dimension. It is on the one hand revelation of a Person. God makes *Himself* known in the Word. At the same time it is a revelation of propositional truth about God and from God. (The relationship between these two dimensions of revelation is something I've discussed at length in an earlier book, *Creative Bible Teaching*, published by Moody Press.) As Scripture puts it, "no one knows the thoughts of God except the Spirit of God," and goes on to affirm that the Spirit is the One who reveals exactly this to us in words (1 Cor. 2:6-15).

Purposive truth. God has chosen to communicate with us for a purpose. That purpose can never be summed up in "knowledge." Certainly truth which God has revealed is to be understood and believed. But we can ill afford a conservative provincialism that takes pride in knowledge of truth and belief in truth *for its own sake.*

It is clear from Scripture itself that the Word is designed to be lived rather than simply known. Biblical Christianity is no esoteric system of abstract and theoretical truth. Instead, it is a vital approach to daily and to eternal life, based on the conviction that in Scripture God has revealed experienceable reality, and that as our perceptions and personalities are shaped by the biblical world-view, our lives will bring glory to God and meaning and joy to ourselves.

Thus Scripture maintains a clear focus on the believers' *response* to the Word, and the use of Scripture in giving daily guidance to life. The mark of the foolish man in Jesus' famous parable is that he hears the Word of God . . . but does not do it. The mark of the wise man, who builds his life on a solid foundation, is that he hears the Word of God and does it. *We need to make it clear at all times and in every way that there is no great merit in hearing the Word of God if that hearing is not accompanied by response.* A form of communication which magnifies hearing at the expense of responding — and preaching services so often do — works against the ends for which the Word is to be presented!

Relational truth. Scripture affirms that "all Scripture is God-breathed and is useful for teaching, rebuking, correcting and training in righteousness, so that the man of God may be thoroughly equipped for every good work" (2 Tim. 3:16). This expression helps us see the Word of God not only as reliable and relevant, but also as *for* the "man of God." Truth has a direct, personal relationship to the individual in the totality of his life and personality.

Often today the concept of a "relational" truth is limited to the emphasis on horizontal, or interpersonal, relationships. This is a true but limited expression of the relational implications of revelation. In fact all revealed truth is relational, in the sense that it serves to guide believers in appropriate and varied interrelationships: in relationships with God, with self, with other believers, with family, with society, with non-Christians, with material possessions, etc. The "relational" emphasis that is appropriate and must always be stressed is simply this: every Word of God to us invites us to examine our lives and bring our personalities (our understanding, attitudes, values, affections, behaviors, habits, etc.) into fuller harmony with God's total creation and all that He intends it to be.

I might note here that the interpersonal relational aspects of revelation do have a certain primacy. Scripture consistently teaches us to value persons, and to use things. But we need always to keep in mind that truth God has revealed never stands off from us in some kind of splendid isolation. Rather truth God reveals comes to us, and invites us to examine all the transactions that take place between us and our material and social environment. Truth is relational in the sense that every truth of Scripture enlightens and guides us in some facet of our lives.

experienceable truth. It is important that we maintain this perspective as well as the others in our approach to Scripture. Too often preaching holds up as ideal states which no one has attained . . . and then loads guilt upon the back of failure. This negativistic and legalistic approach to Scripture is totally out of harmony with its spirit.

While the Word of God is blunt and honest about man's inadequacy and his willful choice of evil (both outcomes of sin and evidences of our lost condition), Scripture also trumpets hope. The message of the Scripture to inadequate men is that through the work of Jesus Christ and in relationship with Him believers can be transformed! All that God intends for us to be is now possible for us. In Christ we are invited to experience as reality that which the greatest philosophers have held as distant ideal.

It is a fact of life and part of God's plan that such an experience of truth as reality in our own lives is a progressive thing. *Growth* is part of the process, and is at its heart. Transformation is not worked in a single miraculous act (either at conversion, or in some special work of the Holy Spirit subsequent to salvation). Instead transformation is a progressive reshaping of the believer toward Christlikeness. Transformation is a progressive reshaping of the believer toward that pattern of life revealed in Scripture as God's ideal for man, His special creation.

For this reason we need to approach and proclaim the Word of God with hope and expectation. We need to proclaim the Word of God as His invitation to us to become what we are: to experience more and more of the enablement He promises us as we trust in Christ and step out in faith to obey.

In most conservative churches today Scripture is accepted, and presented, as a revealed and reliable truth. The very preaching of it week by week affirms its importance as God's Word to us. *But we need to take great care that other dimensions of our understanding of Scripture and its nature is communicated in our services as well.* And communicated not only in words, but also in those actions which symbolize and express to every member of the community the importance of these commitments.

Our communication setting itself needs to proclaim that the Word we hear is purposive and that we are committed to respond. Our communication setting itself needs to affirm the relational nature of revealed truth, and to affirm with joyful expectation our confidence that what God has revealed, He *will do* . . . in us.

proclamation and its setting

Probably one of the greatest needs today is for the development of a theology of preaching; a theology that goes beyond the methodological track of most homiletics books and courses, with their attention to introductions and illustrations and persuasive techniques and gestures, to the root questions of how can preaching communicate what the Word *is* as well as what it says.

In the first section of this chapter I sketched some of my own ideas about the nature of the Word which must be expressed in preaching. Here are a few suggestions concerning implications and methodology.

single concept focus. The Bible itself must be understood as God's revelation, of truth as well as of Himself. In most types of biblical literature, and particularly in the New Testament, Scripture is organized in clear sequences of developed thought. That is, the Bible is not made up of a series of random thoughts, dropped unorganized from this pen or that. Like a story or an essay of today, sentences, paragraphs, chapters, and whole books are *organized.* There is a discernable structure of developing and developed concepts which are being communicated.

It is important when we study the Bible to realize that our first concern is not to search for a proof text for a pet doctrine of our own, nor to read until some thought suddenly illumines us with a "blessing." Instead when we study the Word of God our first concern is to follow the thoughts of God. We need to come to know His mind, and to understand reality as He perceives it.

It is more than just interesting that the "renewing of our mind" is mentioned more than once as a touchstone to transformation (as in Rom. 12:1, 2). The Greek word translated "mind"

297

here does not refer to the computerlike processes we normally associate with mind. It indicates "perception." When we begin to perceive life from God's perspective, and when His perceptions become ours, it is then we have "the mind of Christ," and then that all else in our experience can fall into place.

For instance, in Colossians Paul begins by expressing thanks to God for all that He has worked in the lives of the Colossians, and he reminds these people of their rescue from darkness and established position in Christ and His kingdom. In his prayer Paul asks that they might be filled with such wisdom and spiritual insight . . . such an understanding of God's purpose . . . such a knowledge of and trust in God . . . "that you may be able to pass through any experience and endure it with joy" (1:11, Phillips). Even the tragic and the difficult experiences we "endure" can be transformed *if we see them from the divine perspective*. If our understanding and our perception of experiences includes awareness of God's active involvement in our lives, commitment to His transforming purpose for us, realization that in His will the difficult and the tragic are designed to work together "for good," we will have the renewed mind.

This divine perspective is not one which we, rooted in our single egocentric viewpoint, know by nature or by choice. God instead must lift us out of ourselves (as He *has* in Christ) and bring us to stand where Jesus takes His present stand in the heavenlies. God must reshape our understanding, and give us a new perspective.

When we have that new perspective all things do become new. From the divine perspective, new attitudes and values and feelings and behaviors are discovered to be appropriate. And when we have the divine perspective, *as it is related to the whole person*, the patterns of our life and character do change . . . a change worked gradually in a growth process by the Spirit of God.

It is, then, vitally important in preaching that we concentrate on communicating the developed thought of Scripture. That we probe to discover, and then to proclaim, the divine perspective revealed. To do this we need to discipline ourselves to make a single, clear, written purpose sentence — which expresses the divine perspective conceptually and which also expresses its meaning — the core of every message. Whether we preach from a passage, a paragraph, a verse, a psalm, a narrative incident, or a prophecy or teaching section, we need to give our message a single focus.

298

That focus should involve a single concept.

That focus should express something of the meaning of the concept for those who, hearing and believing it, make it a part of their own personal perspective on life. *remember*

In the last chapter, when I suggested that worship might be organized to praise God for an attribute which is related to the key truth of the sermon, I suggested a sample purpose sentence which might be written out to guide development of a message on Jonah — because it accurately reflects the emphasis *of* Jonah. "God invites us, as Jonah, to share His own great love for those who do not yet know Him." To bring the concept aspect of that purpose sentence into clearer focus we can now revise it: "God's own great compassion for those who do not know Him challenges us to reach out in love to those around us." Now the single concept, which expresses one facet of God's revealed perspective, "God's own great compassion for those who do not yet know Him," is highlighted. And the relational impact of that understanding . . . the fact that we (as His children) are to share that compassion and reach out to (rather than piously cut ourselves off from) the lost around us . . . is also included.

Perhaps one of the most practical — and one of the first — steps in bringing the preaching ministry into harmony with what the Word itself is, then, is to concern ourselves in preaching with what is God's concern in revealing! Like God, we must focus sharply on presenting the divine perspective, and showing the impact of this perspective on our experience as whole persons living lives in this present world.

emphasis on response. The purpose sentence to which we've come in studying the Word not only gives focus to the concept we want to communicate, it also gives focus to response. It is critically important to make sure that we see the relational and response implications of truths we preach. All Scripture *is* profitable and equipping in nature. We need to explore its meaning, and to respond appropriately.

However, if response is to have an adequate expression and symbolization in the service of preaching and worship, more than simply a closing illustration or two, or an exhortation at the end of the message is required. *We need to give the same kind of specialness to response that we give to worship in our Sunday services.*

How might we give specialness, validity, and educational significance to response to God's Word in our preaching services? There are many possibilities. In our own church, opportunity is given in the sharing following the morning message. At times we've also included "assignment" sheets in the bulletin for families to work on when they return home. It's possible to simply invite two or three members of the congregation to share after the message how they see themselves responding during the coming week. This is particularly helpful if these members were involved in the kind of sermon and service development team I mentioned earlier as an appropriate way to involve members of the Body in the morning service ministry.

One Circle Church service illustrates several possibilities. The key biblical truth of the morning was expressed in this sentence: "To understand Christ's position of preeminence is to be filled with gratitude for the privilege of knowing Him personally." Following the message, two members of the congregation were asked to share how they intended to express their gratitude for the privilege of knowing Christ personally. Following this the congregation was told of postcards in the bulletin, addressed to the church. Each person was asked to take one home, write on it his way of showing gratitude, and mail it in sometime during the week. In addition, the congregation was told they would be given fifteen minutes before the start of worship the next Sunday to come and share their response or response plans, and that responses would be published in the bulletin as well (some of the responses that were made are included in PROBE 3).

Remember that in the last chapter we saw an outline of the Circle Church service. It included three distinct elements:

> Approach to God in Worship
> God Speaking through His Written Word
> The Response of Obedience

By providing a distinctive and visible place in the service for response to the Word, and by involving members of the congregation significantly, the whole Body in its gathering together affirms the importance of response and affirms a shared commitment *to* respond in obedience to God as He speaks.

In the same way, the relational dimension — its meaning to me — is affirmed and taught.

expectancy. One last element simply must be mentioned, because of its educational significance. Put simply, the *tone* of the preaching will communicate and set a tone for the Body and the believers in it. Too often in the preaching I have heard the dominant tones range from discouragement to condemnation. Too often ministers seem to hold up the Word of God as a standard which we need to be ashamed of *not* meeting. A negative, a *failure*, attitude is conveyed.

It is of course understandable that pastors and others become discouraged. But it is tragic that the *spirit of the Word* is so often distorted and disguised. Scripture speaks out vibrantly with hope: not the kind of "hope" that expresses uncertainty, but the kind of hope that exists as a settled confidence that God is in control and that God will work out His will in us.

The truths, the standards, the exhortations of Scripture are not cast in the tone of a desperate nagging parent, frustrated by the perverseness of his children. The truths, standards, and exhortations of Scripture express the joyful invitation of God the Father to His children to *experience* every reality portrayed! What God shows us in the Word *we can expect Him to do in us.* Yes, our experience often lags behind our desires. No, taking time to grow isn't fun . . . and it may be discouraging to see the slowness (in our eyes) of the progress. But the constant presence of the Holy Spirit and the constant purpose of the God who has called us to Him in Christ is a solid foundation for hope! He who has begun a good work in us *will perform it* (Phil. 1:6). So the tone of shame, the tone of guilt, the tone of frustration, the tone of failure, *do not reflect the Truth as God has revealed it!* Instead, the Bible speaks in vibrant tones of victory won. And so must we! The Bible speaks in tones of hope and expectation. And so must we.

The proclamation of the Word of God *is* a vital element in the Christian education of adults. If in the proclamation we are successful in teaching and preaching in harmony with what Scripture is, we shall significantly help all members of the Body to . . .

* discover the divine viewpoint and make God's perspective their own.
* relate God's Word to their own life and respond appropriately to Him.
* maintain that joyful attitude of hope and expectation which is to characterize a people who know God, and who are known by Him.

PROBE
case histories
discussion questions
thought-provokers
resources

1. I feel badly that I must speak so briefly to such an important issue

as the congregational service of worship and preaching. I'm glad, however, that an excellent resource is available to show how each of the concepts expressed here can be practically implemented in church life. I'm referring, of course, to the FingerTip Consultant developed by David Mains and published by Step 2, 1925 N. Harlem, Chicago, Illinois 60635.

2. Much of what is said in this chapter grows out of and expresses certain convictions about Scripture. If you want to explore more in this area, I've tried in two earlier books to express what seem to me to be the truly basic issues.

   The first of these, *Creative Bible Teaching* (Moody Press, 1970), explores the interrelationship between propositional and personal revelation, and also examines structuring teaching of the Scripture to focus on both concept and response.

   The second, *Creative Bible Study* (Zondervan Corporation, 1971) examines in some detail the question of Scripture's "tone of voice" and the expectancy with which we can approach it.

3. The invitation to respond to the sermon at Circle Church by sharing how congregation members expressed thankfulness led to the return of cards with these reports.

TO EXPRESS MY DEEP GRATITUDE TO CHRIST FOR THE OVERWHELMING PRIVILEGE OF KNOWING HIM PERSONALLY I HAVE:

—*Decided to become the kind of mature Christian person that Christ wants. This involves a tremendous upheaval in my current way of living.*

—*Presented the years of my life and energies to His service, in my vocation and home/church activities.*

—*Reminded myself that I am crucified with Christ and that love is my aim, have cut back on a number of projects I would personally like to accomplish and have recommitted myself to carry out well a smaller number of things I believe God wants me to do.*

—*Pledged to work with the poor in any racial group through living, teaching, reaching and learning with them. If necessary, I will go back to school for more education or else learn by doing. I also pledge to regard others as more important than myself; look out for the interest of others; and to become more like Christ by working as a bond-servant and becoming obedient to God's will.*

—*Decided to try to get in touch with an old friend who has deeply disappointed me and to renew contact.*

—*Promised to be more in touch with older people, beginning with a monthly activity with each of my grandmothers.*

—*Decided to spend more time with God in prayer about my friends, and more time getting to know God.*

—*Arranged to have the series of tapes on Colossians sent to Circle's missionaries so they might sense Christ's position of preeminence in a new way.*

—*Shared a personal knowledge of Jesus Christ with a few students at E.I.U. Told them what I believed and asked them for their opinions, questions. Offered to give them names of some full-time E.I.U. students who are Christians and who would be glad to talk with them further.*

—*Determined to walk obediently in an area where His Spirit is convicting me.*

—*Joined a prayer group to pray for others and to testify to my belief in prayer.*

—*Specific prayer requests for two church missionary families and will pray more specifically and earnestly for them.*

—*Committed myself to taking more time to enrich this relationship with Christ. Very much lacking self-discipline, I commit myself to a more regular time of fellowship and communion with God through the study of His Word and through prayer. I also pray that this will result in a more vital faith which can then be more effectively communicated to those who don't know Christ personally.*

4. I noted that sending home discussion or application guidance materials is another way to encourage response to a sermon or message. Here is a guide sheet used at Our Heritage Church in February of 1974, following up a sermon on the honesty and sharing appropriate in God's family.

OUR HERITAGE CHURCH
FEBRUARY 2 and 3, 1974

"HONESTY"
No. 1 PERSONAL STUDY

1. There are many motives for dishonesty (shading the truth in our favor, keeping some things back, our outright lies). How many can you think of that might motivate people in a close, personal relationship (such as marriage, the Church family, parent/child relationships, etc.). List at *least* 5 possible motives.
2. Which of these motives do you feel is most likely to affect *your* relationship within your home? Why?
3. Looking over the story of Ananias and Sapphira (Acts 5:1-11), what do you think motivated them?

No. 2 TALKABLE
(between husband and wife)

1. Share your answers to the first series of questions, and share also at least one incident in which you were not completely honest with

303

your spouse. Why did you act as you did? Is there any way your spouse could help you avoid similar incidents? How do you avoid such temptations — is there anything you have found that helps you remain open and honest with him/her?

2. Think about each of your children as an individual. Do you feel he or she is quite honest with you? (What makes you think so?) Are there any behavior traits that you've been troubled about recently? (Try to pinpoint specific incidents.) Think together about this: Are there ways you respond to your child that make it difficult for him/her to be honest with you? (Sometimes overdisciplining, suspicion and doubt of expressed motives, etc. actually encourage your children to shade the truth!) See if you can help each other see any ways of responding you have developed that may not be helpful and talk over how to correct them.

No. 3 DO-ABLE
(with the family together)

1. Read Acts 5:1-11 together, and talk about the following questions. (Parents, make this a time to *listen* to your children's opinions and to *share* your own ideas and experiences. DON'T JUST TELL THEM what they are to think and do.

   * Why do you think these people planned to tell a lie?

   * What was so bad about this particular lie?

   * Would this kind of dishonesty with other members of God's family bring people closer together? Why, or why not?

   * What helps our family (parents and children) feel close together?

   * Do you ever feel "far away" from other people in our family? Who? What makes you feel this way?

   * Do you feel it is important for us to be honest with each other all the time? What will help us be really truthful?

   * God punished Ananias and Sapphira very severely, because what they did hurt the church family. This helped others learn not to do what they had done.

     What will help us stop when we are being dishonest?
     What will help us be really truthful with each other?

2. Make a "family fellowship flower" with one petal for each member of the family. When any member of the family feels "far away" from the others because of something he needs to tell to be really honest, he can take his petal and move it away from the "flower."

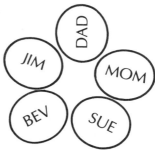

Sometimes it is hard to start sharing something that makes us uncomfortable. So when we notice a petal that's been moved "far away" we can sit down and talk with that person and help him tell us what's wrong.

Thumbtack petals on poster, or tape them to a kitchen cupboard. Move your own petal when you have something you need to tell the others.

Let's see if we can't keep our family fellowship flower close together all week! And let's help each other be honest with us by listening and caring.

5. Finally, try to integrate all we've been saying about adult education by attempting this rather tough assignment.
   A. Use the baseline information given for the hypothetical church situation described on page 258. Now project ahead *ten years* and describe the same church *as it might be* if there were an "ideal" adult education situation existing.
   B. Then attempt to reconstruct possible *steps* marking the transition from "real" to "ideal." Which strategies might be introduced first? How might the principles explored in the first chapters of this book be applied as various adult education strategies are employed? At least twenty-five pages of "process" discussion would be appropriate here.
   C. Then discuss with others their reconstruction. What problems do they foresee? How might they be overcome? What principles guide each step?

   While this is admittedly a very abstract exercise, its primary benefit is in seeing some of the complexity involved. And also growing sensitivity to and familiarity with the principles which must guide our ministries in the Body.

PART III

RESTATEMENT: A SUMMARY

restatement: critical issues in Christian education

In this section of the book I want to briefly summarize and integrate some of the things that have been the burden of this exploration of the theology of Christian education.

To an extent it is repetitive. But it may be helpful repetition. Particularly as we turn first to the most critical elements in Christian education: the role of Scripture, of the teacher, and of interpersonal relationships.

the role of Scripture

If I were asked to express what seems to me to be the core of Christian faith, I suppose I might say something like this: "The core of Christian faith is the confidence that our Creator God is, that He has acted in Christ Jesus to redeem, and that He has revealed both Himself and Truth to us in the written Word." I would include the last phrase because I am convinced that Christianity is a revealed religion, and that as such our doctrine of Scripture does lie at the core of faith.

Thus, without in any sense accepting a "bibliolator" label, I would insist that serious and reverent attention to Scripture is critical for spiritual growth and health, and critical in any attempt at Christian education. At the same time, it should be clear that our understanding of Scripture and its purpose will determine how it fits into the educational process. So we can perhaps best define that role by restating some assumptions about Scripture that already have been expressed.

a revelation of reality. Sometimes we approach life unrealistically; idealistically. The utopian dream, the "possible worlds" of science fiction, the daydreams we imagine for ourselves, all are rooted in the notion that this is a universe of *infinite possibilities*. Relativism accepts this view, and speaks of decisions being "right" for one person and "wrong" for another depending on the individual's persuasions and convictions. Social scientists explore how perceptions of reality are developed, and write fascinating books on "reality's" social sources. Piaget and others mentioned in this text postulate a structure of the human personality, but deny the possibility of a structure for the universe within which man finds himself.

The Bible makes an entirely different assumption. Scripture assumes a world of *limited possibilities*. Even as gravity limits the possibility of you and I flying without artificial supports, so the structure of the moral universe, the order and laws of the spiritual universe, the nature of man as fallen (and redeemed), the character and purposes of God . . . all these limit and impose a structure on human experience. It is this structure, the divine perception of total creation, that is reality, no matter how human beings may perceive the world they live in.

When the Scripture makes the claim for itself that it is Truth (as it does in many places), this claim involves the affirmation that what Scripture reveals is *in fullest harmony with reality.* Scripture is true not simply because God spoke it and He is trustworthy. Scripture is true because it accurately represents the way things are.

In essence, Scripture is the sharing with us of God's own understanding of life and meaning. This claim does not, of course, imply that through Scripture we will come to know *all* truth, or to know it fully. Instead, it is a claim that what we can understand through Scripture, what God has revealed, is both reliable and relevant. Scripture provides the only accurate perspective on life and its meaning that man can gain. In fact, we are warned to avoid "high sounding nonsense" that "is at best founded on men's ideas of the nature of the world" and by faith adopt as our own the perspective shared with us in Christ (cf. Col. 2).

The nature of Scripture as a portrait of reality provides a vital clue to its role in Christian life and education. God has revealed reality that we might share His mind, and that our perspective might become more and more like His. As we come to evaluate life through the perceptual grid Scripture provides, our perspectives (and increasingly all aspects of our personality) will be reshaped as well.

a reality to be lived. Not *all* of reality has been revealed to us. But what we have is sufficient to guide our choices and our values. What we have is to be *lived*.

Thus Scripture has a consistent, challenging *invitation to respond* inherent in its very nature. A child who discovers the meaning of "hot" through a painful experience is likely to be guided by that perception for some time! God, in desiring the best for us, comes to us with specific guidance for living and warns us against the "hot" within and around us. Where Scripture speaks to us, we are expected to respond in loving obedience, and thus to experience reality.

This is, of course, the emphasis of Jesus' words recorded in John. "Continue in my words . . . and you shall know [by experience!] the truth, and the truth shall set you free." Freedom for the believer is found in accepting Scripture's revelation of life as reliable, and in faith responding appropriately to that revelation.

a reality to be seen. Strikingly, because Scripture does portray an experienceable reality, the truth of Scripture can be validated by our own and by others' experience! This is the significance in part of the model concept. In other persons we actually see incarnated what we read of in the written Word.

The idea that Scripture is to be authenticated or validated by others' experience should not be misunderstood. To say this is *not* to say that the "truth" of the Bible "depends" on our experience of it. It is simply to say that because the Bible is true, and speaks out about reality, we would expect a correspondence between the experience of believers who live by it and what it promises their experience will be.

But the importance of authentication educationally goes far beyond this. In the "example" of the one who demonstrates in his own life the nature of Scripture as experienceable reality we have the vital link between "concept" and "perception." While a "concept" may be grasped as something abstract from and irrelevant to one's life, a "perception" is something through which one evaluates life. Discovering truth in and through an individual's life testifies that Scripture does not serve to present abstract concepts, but rather as a lens through which all of life must be perceived.

It becomes vital, then, in communicating Scripture that the educational approach be designed to process Scripture *as reality to be lived* and *reality to be seen.* Educational settings which are designed to process Scripture primarily as *concepts (or information) to be believed* are not only inadequate, but they also are almost certain to distort the "reality" character of the Word.

Where then is the place of Scripture in the Christian education ministry as outlined in this book? Simply put, Scripture is central in every setting!

Recently in our church board meetings we have been concerned about our budget: not so much that it be met, but that our use of money reflect the divine priorities and values. So we've explored Scripture, trying to get the biblical history and guidelines in perspective, and seeking ways that we can bring our church finances into greater harmony with God's concern for the poor and the needs of human beings.

In our Thursday night "little church" we've been studying Colossians, and particularly have been seeking to relate Paul's portrait of the Christian life to our own experiences.

In church services we hear regular messages from the Word, and in addition much of the sharing expresses believers' experiences shaped and colored by Scripture.

In each of these settings, and in our personal lives, Scripture serves as a guide by which individuals, small groups, and the entire Body live. Scripture guides, not as "law" rigorously and rigidly applied, but as a living voice from the living God, interpreted and applied by His Spirit.

In a very real sense, the place of Scripture in the daily, ongoing experiences of members of the Body as they live their separate lives and as they come together, is far more significant than the formal classes where we have "taught" the Bible.

As the Word is integrated more and more into the life of the community, in just the ways explored in earlier chapters, so the Word comes to have its rightful place in believers' lives.

In looking at teaching materials designed to communicate the Word, we can find those designed to transmit its information, those designed to use the Bible as a jumping off point to stimulate development of interpersonal relationships, those designed to encourage and motivate response, and those designed to shape our perceptions by showing the impact of God's truth on human experience. Each of these approaches can find a place in the experience of the Church . . . some will have more important places than others.

But the critical factor remains one.

Is the Word being lived and being used to guide the life of individuals and of the Body? Only if Scripture finds a central place in every activity of believers, and is searched as a reliable and relevant guide, will growth in Christlikeness come.

the role of the teacher

In secular education many tensions exist as the role of "teacher" is examined and defined. So many possibilities exist. The teacher may be anyone from Carl Rogers' facilitator, on to a classroom manager who guides children to choose and use the right resources, on to the behavior modifier who by contingency management "shapes" the individual and the group.

In Christian education, however, there should be no confusion. Certainly the old role of the authority who transmits truth is ruled out. And the new role is sharply expressed. The teacher of spiritual truth is the person who through personal experience of truth has moved on in transformation process! The teacher is the example who can disciple others toward his own likeness.

This image of the teacher harmonizes completely with the Bible's teaching about the servant nature of spiritual leadership, and with the concept of "example" developed in the New Testament. The new image also helps us define several aspects of the teaching/learning situation which now are seen as of dramatic importance.

First, the teacher as a model does not present himself as one who is an authority but one who is subject, with the learner, to the authority of God through Scripture. The teacher is one who learns with the student, and who essentially is concerned with showing the learner how to understand the Word as livable truth.

Second, to serve as an example of Scripture's life meaning, there must be a relationship between the teacher and the learner which is close and personal, and which lets the learner come to know the teacher as a person. Exposure to the teacher's inner states is of vital importance if learning is to be a life-sharing (rather than concept-sharing) kind of thing.

Third, a love relationship between teacher and learner is important as well. The process of identification, implicit in the "example" teaching of Scripture, is enhanced as a deep caring for one another develops. This relationship of love is also important because of the stress in Scripture on love as a touchstone of Christlikeness: love will be one of the truths the teacher is expected to model.

313

Fourth, <u>interaction in settings</u> where the learner can <u>see the truth</u> lived by the teacher has priority over other settings. The traditional classroom approach to teaching/learning tends to limit the kinds of data that are processed, and gives little or no opportunity for the learner to see the teacher functioning as a whole person.

These considerations help us to see that the role of teacher is not something that should be framed in the traditional classroom image, but expanded to all settings and occasions when believers come together to interact. To limit our idea of teaching to that which secular culture has defined is to emasculate the concept as it is biblically portrayed, and to shut our eyes to the significance of life itself as the principal occasion for a teacher's ministry.

In short, then, our understanding of "teacher" has shifted from an organizational role to that of an interpersonal function: from a "job" to a quality of maturity and gift that functions in all of the teacher's interactions with other believers. For this reason and others we've stressed the nonformal aspects of Christian education, convinced that the nonformal rather than the formal setting is the one in which the most significant teaching takes place.

the role of relationships

One of the most vital perceptions of Christian education must be that it involves the Christian community as a Body. The Body nature of the Church must be experienced and affirmed in a unity that is found only in a deepening and fervent love of members for one another. The relational context of and for spiritual growth and ministry has been stated often in this book: it can never be lost sight of.

In the context of love, trust, openness, honesty, acceptance, caring, support, forgiveness, correction, and affirmation, growth in Christian faith as life can take place. Without that context, growth must be stunted and delayed.

We can easily see why. Such relationships bring us closer to one another, and facilitate identification. Such relationships permit the knowing of one another well, and thus provide multiple models of faith's life. Living close to one another, we see the truth of God being lived out, and find the claims of Scripture fully authenticated. God and His Word become reality to us, not just "beliefs." In the context of such relationships we discover ourselves as well. We discover ourselves as loved and valued, and God's attitude toward us is made real by the attitude toward us of others who share His perspectives and values. Living close to one another, we are free to minister to each other, using the gifts that God has given us. The context of relationships makes possible a two-way flow of ministry, freeing us from the limitations of a one-way flow. Living close to one another also provides us with a sense of belonging that motivates us to share the commitment of the community.

We cannot have an adequate Christian education without attending to and fostering the development of the kind of relationships which Scripture describes as appropriate within Christ's Body.

Thus the issue of interpersonal relationships takes on a far greater importance than we have tended to give it! No longer can we pretend to train Christians in the faith through classes and services that are essentially impersonal. We must develop the relational context in which life style learning is to take place as a major part of our educational task.

Each of these considerations once again leads us to focus our attention on the nonformal rather than the formal educational setting. *We can no longer limit our educational thinking to how we process Scripture in the classroom, to how the teacher communicates, and what methods are most appropriate, and to how to help learners in that classroom setting express personal applications.* We must pay attention instead to the total life of believers as they function within the Body. We must explore ways that Scripture infuses every interaction. We must recognize the teacher as a leader especially equipped by God to take the lead in bringing others to Christ's likeness — not as the classroom expert. And we must consider every interaction — the boards and committees, the growth and action groups, the congregational services, the phone calls and the fishing trips — settings in which to facilitate the development of ministering relationships that affirm the unity and love of the Body.

Christian education has broken out of the classroom. Now we need to explore how its principles can infuse the Church's life.

restatement:
design elements in Christian education

The isolation of the critical elements in Christian education and the description of their interrelationships leads us to a position drastically different from that taken by most Christian educators. Rather than focusing the educational ministry of the church through school-like agencies designed for that task, our discussion has led us to emphasize the nonformal rather than formal educational processes. The transmission of faith-as-life and the nurturing of faith through discipleship into likeness is more akin to what we've come to call socialization than what we've named education.

Thus the Christian educator's task is significantly different from that most often described. Thus too design elements ... the role of learning settings, the role of curriculums, the role of the hidden curriculum ... are seen in new and challenging ways.

The task of the traditional Christian educator, cast as administrator of the Church's educational agencies and the trainer of workers within them, must be redefined if we take seriously the socialization model of Christian education. As soon as the transmission and nurture of Christ's life is accepted as the task of Christian education, and discipleship toward His likeness the goal, older methods which focused on belief transmission are seen to be inadequate. The Christian educator now becomes a designer of the life of the Church, for it is in the total life of the Church and in all its interactions that the believers' life style is shaped.

What's more, Christian education as a theological discipline is no longer the providence of the "minister of education." If everything in the life of the Church teaches, then every church leader must become an educator. Every church leader must understand the principles of life and growth within the Body, and must develop a capacity to design the gatherings of the church for the transforming task. As we have seen, this design extends beyond the traditional "teaching" meetings of the church (Sunday school, and the morning service) to every interaction of the Body, from meetings in committees and homes to action groups and times of Body Life.

So it's helpful to review briefly design elements we have seen in operation in other chapters, and to reaffirm priorities which have been stated or implied.

the role of learning settings

I've suggested that every occasion of interaction between believers is, and must be perceived as, a learning setting. I've also suggested that those settings which are not labeled "educational" have, in fact, the greatest impact on a person's growth and discipling. The primary distinction here is between formal learning settings and nonformal learning settings.

formal settings. The formal settings are those of the school and the church "service." In these settings, culturally defined processes take place, with persons acting in appropriate roles ("teacher," "superintendent," etc.) and Bible content processed in appropriate (cognitive) ways:

I've attempted to marshal considerable evidence to show that the formal setting is not particularly appropriate for communicating faith as life, and is not very effective in bringing the learner beyond understanding to action. This means that we cannot rely on formal education settings for our nurture or transformation functions. *It does not mean that we should abandon the formal setting entirely.* In fact, the formal setting is appropriate when our goal is to encourage cognitive mastery. And we should never lose sight of the fact that a framework understanding — of theology, of Bible history, of the sequence of progressive revelation, of the setting and culture of various books, etc. — is important equipment for the believer. A framework knowledge makes it possible for a person to *apply Scripture more accurately* ...not falling into the trap of applying to himself truth or injunctions specific to a certain person or certain time.

In fact, one of the educational concerns of the local church and of church leaders in general ought to be this: What framework knowledge is needed, at what ages, to maximize application and personal growth through the study of Scripture?

In general, I believe that the principle which ought to govern our educational strategy is this: let the formal setting be used to do what it does best, but never rely on the formal setting to contribute directly to the discipling and transforming mission of the Church.

nonformal settings. Nonformal settings, which have been discussed extensively before, are marked off from the formal in many ways. They are not viewed as "school." They do not have the clearly defined roles of "teacher" and "learner," of "subject matter" and "achievement." Instead nonformal settings are viewed by participants as part of life itself, not as a set apart time for learning.

There are elements of the nonformal which we can, and should attempt to integrate into the traditional formal setting. For instance, we can use the "Sunday school hour" of tradition for an educational experience that is not "school." In one section of this book I suggested that for the Christian education of children we need to change what happens during the Sunday school hour, first by changing the teachers' image of himself, then the role of telling to that of sharing, then the relational context and perception from "student" to "friend," and so on. Over time this formal setting may well take on more characteristics of the nonformal than the formal!

But even at best, such redesign of elements is not sufficient. For effective Christian education of children we *must* focus on the home, where parents serve as the primary models for the young child and thus must become the primary models of faith's life. *Christian education cannot afford to rely on what happens in the formal educational setting ... even when that happening harmonizes with nonformal principles.* Instead, Christian education must stretch its perspective to explore those settings in which the Church's life is in fact lived. It is these settings, and the design of these settings for transformation, that must become the focus of our educational concern.

In this book, then, I have been arguing for two vital things. First, that we recognize the inadequacy of what we have been thinking of as education. And second, that we see the total life of the Church and its every interaction as the *real* educational experience of the believer.

Only when we design the nonformal settings for interaction to facilitate the requisites for socialization into faith's life will we rediscover the dynamic and transforming power evidenced in the early church.

the role of curriculums

The role of curriculums is established and easily justified if we retain a notion of education that is essentially formal. Beginning with the assumption that there is a body of truth to be learned, curriculums are designed to transmit that truth in a logical and organized way. Hopefully, following the transmission, time will be taken for exploration of meaning and for personal application. But the subject matter itself imposes order and structure on the learning experience.

Socialization, on the other hand, assumes a set of perceptions and understandings which have been integrated into a society or culture's life style, and which the individual confronts as he lives in that society or culture. What is learned when is determined, not by the logical organization of context, but by the ongoing experience of the individual within the culture. Thus in socialization life itself structures the learning experience. That aspect of content (e.g., the perspective on reality maintained as beliefs and expressed in life style) which an individual confronts is determined not from without, but from within the situational context.

For example, I recently wrote a book for both new and older Christians, titled *Born to Grow* (Scripture Press). In this book I suggest perspectives the believer needs to develop to be in harmony with God, patterns of life that will play a role in growth, and understandings of God that are critical for a solid anchor in life. One of those "behavior" chapters deals with "little daily steps" of obedience to God's Word.

Now, a person reading this book, or a class based on it, will necessarily come to this chapter in its sequence: it will come to his attention the seventh week into the course, no matter when he may need it. But a person living in the Christian community (should that community build into its time together a focus on "the response of obedience," as suggested in chap. 25), will confront the need for obedience in a different way. As he grows into the community, he'll see in the life style of others a commitment to God and to the doing of His Word that will, at some point, challenge him to evaluate his life. He may interact on this issue in a small group if he's part of one. Or with a Christian friend. But the issue of commitment to obey God will be raised in a natural way, a way in which the issue is correctly viewed as a question of life style, and supported by the observed life style of the Body, rather than simply as a "belief decision" to be made.

This does not, of course, mean that "curriculum is bad," or that some truths might not need to be learned in logical and interconnected sequence. It merely points out that no curriculum for any age can be designed to perform well the task that the Church must perform ... the discipling of believers young and old into Jesus Christ. And we should therefore not depend on curriculums to do what the nonformal process can do better!

What role then do curriculums have? I see two primary roles. The first is to structure those things which can best be learned in the formal educational setting. I am personally critical of my own and of others' seminary training. I was not equipped to minister or lead the church. Nor are others. Yet I am constantly thankful for my seminary training and its emphasis on mastery of the Word of God. I feel sure that often the categories used in theology are artificial and even harmful ones. But I nevertheless needed to learn to think in these categories, to master the content and historical settings of books of the Bible, to use Greek and Hebrew and come to see something of the patterns of thought these languages reveal. But this role of curriculums, while important, is still limited and of less importance than the process of nonformal education in the local church!

The second role of curriculums is seldom recognized, but is of vital significance. *Curriculums can be designed more for structuring of roles and relationships than for the communication content.* By this I mean that in the long run *how the curriculum structures the teaching/learning situation* may have more impact on the learners than the specific content it deals with. I also mean that a vitally important criterion by which we evaluate curriculums ought to be the process they encourage as well as the truths they deal with!

For instance, a curriculum for young teens ought not only to introduce young teens to appropriate Bible truths and concepts, but also be designed to involve them in discovery of those truths and their meaning. A curriculum designed to encourage personal Bible study, critical examination of discoveries, and group exploration of the meaning of truths for teen life, does far more for the young people than simply introduce Bible truths. Such a curriculum, if well designed, can unobtrusively train the young people in how to approach and search Scripture for truth that has life impact.

In the same way the Sunday School PLUS curriculum, which I referred to in chapter 18, is designed specifically to pattern the interactions between parents and children with a view to developing an open, sharing, mutual expression of and listening to revelation of inner feelings and experiences as matters of faith and value are explored. In this approach, curriculum is being used to shape the critical elements of the nonformal educational setting, and to bring media and the message into harmony.

This design function of curriculum is particularly valuable, and ought to be evaluated carefully whenever curriculums are used. This, then, gives us two occasions on which curriculums might well be chosen:

(1) when the setting is a formal one, and the goal a logical organization of framework content to be mastered.

(2) when the curriculum is designed to train in skills and attitudes which will have significant positive impact on the nonformal settings in which faith's life is communicated.

the role of the hidden curriculum

As we've worked through this book, it has, I hope, become clear that the "hidden curriculum" is the most powerful educational force with which Christian education deals. By "hidden curriculum" I mean all those elements of every setting in which believers interact which support or inhibit the transformation process.

If we really believe that ministry is the responsibility of all, in every gathering of believers we will demonstrate that conviction so that mutual ministry will be the lived experience of believers, not just a theory propounded from the pulpit. If we really take seriously the relational context which Scripture portrays as appropriate within the Body, and important for the exercise of spiritual gifts, then in every gathering of the church (whether in official boards or as believers gathered to pray and share) we will work to express and to experience oneness and love.

It is in the design of the hidden curriculum that the heart of the educational ministry actually lies. And the primary emphasis of training in Christian education (in fact, in training for any ministry), ought to be the sensitizing of the educator to hidden curriculum issues and elements, and to principles for their design. Theological considerations . . . the nature of Christian faith, the nature of the Church, the process of growth toward transformation which discipleship involves . . . all these give us guidance enough to provide just this kind of training for the future leadership of the Church, and enough practical hints for significant change in our practices today.

restatement:
the supernatural in Christian education

There is an element of abandonment in Christian education that simply does not exist in any other educational endeavor. We are called to minister intelligently; to shape our design for Christian education by principles revealed in the Word of God. But we are never called to rely on our understanding or our designs.
We rely only on God.

There are two ways we can distort God's role in the ministry of Christian education. The first is to discount it, and to see Christian growth as simply a natural process. The second is to make it a magical thing, demanding that God work against all natural processes and intervene in spectacular ways.

It is far better, and far more biblical, to realize that God works *through natural means in a supernatural way.*

When God's revelation was to be enscripturated, He did not blank out the human personality and dictate His words through them as puppets. Instead He worked with and through the individuals He chose; He worked with and through them in such a way that the books they wrote reflect their personalities and experiences and culture, and yet at the same time express perfectly in words the Spirit chose, the thoughts and words of God.

When God chose to communicate the gospel to a lost world He sent no angels to announce the way of salvation, but instead gave men like Peter . . . and like you and me . . . the commission to serve as His ambassadors. Through the natural means of conversation, speech, and writings, God's supernatural work is done.

Yes, we can point to the spectacular interventions of God in history. But the overwhelming experience of men from the foundation of the world has been that of coming to know and trust God through the unspectacular: through the natural means which God has built into the human personality to transmit any belief or culture.

To pay attention to these natural means is in no way to fail to attribute to God His direct, supernatural intervention in conversion or in growth. Jesus' words stand as a warning to any who would raise the means God uses to the place of cause. "Without me," Jesus explained, "you can do nothing." And these words remain not only true but the keystone of the confidence the Christian knows as he goes about the prosaic work of planning, preparing, and designing in the life of the church. Apart from Jesus and the work of the Holy Spirit no life would infuse the believing heart. Without Jesus and the work of the Holy Spirit no ministry could be given or received, and no transformation would take place. Without Jesus and the work of the Holy Spirit modeled faith would never stimulate the disciples' determination to follow.

The effectiveness of any and all ministry ultimately rests on sovereign grace: the determination of God to touch us, to bring us to Himself as His children, and, as children, to superintend our growth.

With this affirmation, however, we still find ourselves bound to bend our every effort to shape those means God's power infuses with effectiveness. As those committed to a belief that God is and that God has spoken, we also are committed to respond to His written revelation. Those processes which Scripture describes as critical in the Church's life and mission *must* be processes we are committed to encourage in our local situations.

Why has God chosen these means? It's not for us to ask. Why has God chosen to work within the framework of the nature of the men He created? It's not for us to question. But that He has chosen these means, and that He has chosen to work within rather than outside the natural processes of growth and transformation we can affirm. And because God has chosen, our task is clear. We must perform the ministries we've been given ... in His way.

To me this means that we must be ready *now* to rethink the assumptions we've had concerning Christian education. And, with trust in God, step out to rebuild on principles found plainly in His Word.

Indexes

Cognitive structures, 180, 193
Commitment: And youth, 57
Communication: of the Bible. *See* Word, the: communication of; biblical teaching, 34-35; channels of, 52; of faith-as-life, 41, 80, 196, 198-99, 207, 216; faith's belief-content. *See* Faith's belief-content: communicating of; organizational structure, 155-57; parents and, 36; as preaching. *See* Preaching
Crosscultural training, 110
Culture: influence on learning, 194; perception of, 192
Curriculum: alternative system, 209, 210-11; for children, 207-12; church centered, 208; for the classroom, 195-97; communicating faith, 214; hidden, 159, 251-52, 281, 321-22; for the home, 195; in-church, 212-13; role of, 319-20; as story-telling, 209

Deacons, 151, 152, 154
Death: adversary of life, 13; biblical teaching, 13; relation to sin, 13; spiritual. *See* Spiritual death
Destiny of believers, 21
Determinism, 73
Development: process of, 77
Discipling: biblical teaching, 30-31, 55; the Church and, 219; and evangelism, 119-21; as modeling, 81, 84-85; and nurturing, 120; by pastors, 143
Dissonance, 62, 63

Edification: and spiritual gifts, 23, 42
Education: formal, 64, 236-38, 317-18; group process and, 108-10, 113; meta-goals of, 110-11; nonformal, 64, 65, 144, 228-29, 236-38, 318-19; student-centered methods, 107-8, 111; value-rooted, 112
Elders: role of, 137, 149-50; and visitation, 152
Environment: and learning, 74-75, 192; supernatural, 75
Eternal life, *See* Life: eternal
Evangelism: community, 52-53; and discipleship, 56; individual, 53; relational, 52; versus discipling, 119-21; *See also* Witnessing
Experienceable truth: *See* Truth: experiencing

Faith: distorted, 71; life style of, 80; object of, 65-66; sharing, 212, 214-15; teaching, 80, 208-10
Faith's belief-content: communicating of, 208-10; experiential, 211; in relational form, 211
Fall of man, 14-15
Freedom: and growth, 46

Gospel message, 15
Group, large. *See* Large group
Group, small. *See* Small group
Group process, 108-10, 113

Holy Spirit: key to leadership, 128
Honesty, 243-44
House "little churches," 280

Identification and modeling. *See* Modeling: and identification
Image of God, 14, 15
Indoctrination, 77
Integration of truths, 171
Interns, 163-64
Interpersonal relationships: biblical teaching, 41-43; within the church, 245-46; communicative, 52; early studies in, 106-7; experienced in youth, 82; and group functions, 109-10; requisites, 285; research on outcomes, 107-9; role of, 314-15; and the teacher, 314-15; and worship, 285
Isolated learning, myth of, 17, 19

Jesus Christ: and leadership, 131-33; and modeling, 84, 132; training of adults, 228; and training of His disciples, 31-32

Kohlberg, Lawrence J., 169, 170, 177-78, 180, 182, 183-84, 185, 186, 187, 191

Laity: role of, 130-31, 151
Large group, 277-78
Leadership: biblical teaching, 132; commitment of, 152; models, 132, 150-5; multiple, 150; organizational structure, 154-56; principles, 134; role of, 130-31; as a team, 152, 153
Learning: biblical concept of, 32-34; process, 186; social dimensions of, 77; theories, 71-76; understanding of, 192

scripture index

336